Finding Shakespeare's New Place

Manchester University Press

Finding Shakespeare's New Place

An archaeological biography

PAUL EDMONDSON, KEVIN COLLS AND WILLIAM MITCHELL

Manchester University Press

The right of Paul Edmondson, Kevin Colls and William Mitchell to be identified as the authors of this work has been asserted by them in accordance with the Copyright, Designs and Patents Act 1988.

Published by Manchester University Press
Altrincham Street, Manchester M1 7JA
www.manchesteruniversitypress.co.uk

British Library Cataloguing-in-Publication Data
A catalogue record for this book is available from the British Library

Library of Congress Cataloguing-in-Publication Data applied for

ISBN 978 1 5261 0649 0 paperback

First published 2016

Typeset by Out of House Publishing
Printed in Great Britain
by Bell & Bain Ltd, Glasgow

CONTENTS

FIGURES

PLATES

The plates are situated between pages 108 and 109.

FOREWORD

It is a scarcely believable chance that so many buildings connected with Shakespeare's life survive in and around Stratford-upon-Avon: Henley Street, the Hathaway cottage in Shottery, Hall's Croft, and Nash's House. Robert Arden's homestead is almost intact in Wilmcote; there is even what looks like part of grandfather Richard's farm on the corner of Bell Lane in Snitterfield. To have all this is astonishingly good fortune.

Of all the houses he lived in, the one we would most like to know today is New Place. Bought by Shakespeare in 1597 after the death of his only son, this was his home till his own death in 1616. Although the house was rebuilt by 1702, it was demolished in 1759. For the last 250 years its presence has been marked only by a gap in the street frontage at the junction of Church Street and Chapel Lane.

That gap has almost seemed a metaphor for the man: so famous as an artist yet seemingly unknowable as a person. Yet now, unbelievably, that unpromising space has revealed more about the man than we could ever have thought possible.

The circumstances of Shakespeare's purchase have long been known, but what has remained uncertain is whether he actually lived in it until his supposed retirement in around 1611. But this chronology, though still widely accepted, is based on flawed assumptions. In this book a compelling case is made that from Shakespeare's mid-thirties New Place was always his primary residence – that this is where he lived with his family, and where he did much of his writing: a well-off, middle-class landowner who never lost touch with his roots.

But now the excavations have revealed something altogether more fascinating. The house had been built by the Clopton family at the end of the Wars of the Roses: a late medieval town house, the largest in Stratford-upon-Avon. As we know from an eighteenth-century sketch it was a five-gabled house, with a courtyard, hall, barns and garden. But it had fallen into disrepair when William bought it. In his 1733 edition of the plays, Lewis Theobald reported a family tradition from John Clopton (who had rebuilt New Place in 1702) that Shakespeare had 'repair'd and modell'd it *to his own mind*. This fascinating hint suggests that the house was not just renovated but rebuilt as a personal project. Coming on the heels of the fires and famines of the 1590s, with anti-theatre puritans in ascendency on the borough council, it is hard not to see that restoration in brick and timber as something more, as in some sense a psychological project, to put the world together again. Now the archaeology tantalisingly suggests this was so. Indeed, it may not be going too far to say that here for first time we have evidence of a project, beyond his work as a poet and dramatist, on which Shakespeare focused his creative imagination.

The remaking of the front block of the house created a first-floor gallery, 15 m in length, facing Church Street. As fashionable in interior design in the late Elizabethan period, the gallery, it is conjectured, would have been for the display of statuary, paintings and emblems (over the front door he was also entitled to display the coat of arms he had bought in 1596). Then, across a small green courtyard – the heart of the house – was a hall that the archaeologists think Shakespeare retained as a status symbol in the medieval fashion of the late Tudor world, as backward-looking as an accession-day tilt. Any reader of Shakespeare can see his nostalgia for the lost world of his grandparents' time, his parents' childhood: his obsession with history; the old kings and good friars; even his interest in shields, coats of arms, emblems and impresas. May we perhaps link this to his own ancestors, and to the 'antecessor' who, he claimed to the Heralds in 1596, had done Henry VII 'valiant service' (at Bosworth?)? Perhaps this was Thomas Shakespeare of Balsall, who was admitted to the Guild Book of Knowle with his wife, Alicia, the year after Bosworth in 1486. To this the authors add further fascinating speculations. Whether, as they suggest, the gallery had a row of portraits of kings is of course beyond proof, though Henry VII would be particularly apposite, as he was claimed as a patron by both the Shakespeares and the Ardens.

Through all this we sense the working of family memory: the poet's inheritance from the older world that made him. New Place, as we imagine it now, thanks to the archaeologists, becomes a kind of memory room for the heirless branch of the Shakespeare clan.

The archaeologists have given us is a rich harvest, and many connections to the sources of the poet's life. The house stood as a riposte to the sneers of Francis Beaumont, who, in his 1606 play *The Woman Hater*, referred to a glover's son who hoped 'shortly to be honourable' – that is, to become a knight. If the Jungians are right that the house one dreams embodies oneself, then the archaeology of New Place may have uncovered an important clue to William. 'Modelled to his own mind', this, in a sense, *is* him.

Michael Wood

ACKNOWLEDGEMENTS

The authors would like especially to thank Nat Alcock, David Fallow, Andrew Gurr, Mark James and Nick Molyneux for their expert help and advice; Tara Hamling for permission to quote from her unpublished research; Robert Bearman for the use of the reports he produced during Dig for Shakespeare, his prompt answering of questions, for reading and commenting on the whole book, and his checking of the Shakespearian map of Stratford-upon-Avon; Mairi Macdonald for reading and commenting on Chapters 3 and 4; Stanley Wells for reading and commenting on the whole book, and Nick de Somogyi for his index. Paul Taylor and his team at the Shakespeare Centre Library and Archive have been a mainstay of support, and special thanks are due to Helen Hargest, Jennifer Reid, Rosalyn Sklar and Andrew Thomas for their help with many of the images. A debt of gratitude is owed to Phillip Watson, who has much enhanced the volume with his expert reconstruction drawings of New Place, his captions for them and his Shakespearian map of Stratford-upon-Avon.

We would also like to express our special thanks to the following who helped to make Dig for Shakespeare the huge success it was: Elisabeth Charles, Mark Charles, Eilidh Duff, John Richards, Adrian Spaak, the house team at Nash's House, the Dig for Shakespeare Academic Advisory Board (which met regularly from March 2010 through to February 2015), and all of our many volunteers who made the Dig possible. In addition, we wouldn't know as much as we do now about New Place were it not for our team of finds specialists who assisted with artefact identification and reporting, with special thanks going to Stephanie Rátkai.

NOTE ON THE TEXT

Where more than one author has contributed to a single chapter the lead author is made clear through the ordering of names in the table of contents, and, in the case of Chapter 5, within the chapter itself.

In quotations from, or based on, manuscript sources, the original spelling has been preserved. Unless otherwise stated, all Shakespearian quotations are cited from *The Oxford Shakespeare: The Complete Works*, ed. Stanley Wells and Gary Taylor, with John Jowett and William Montgomery, 2nd edn (Oxford: Clarendon Press, 2005).

Introduction: finding Shakespeare's New Place

Paul Edmondson, Kevin Colls and William Mitchell

In March 2010, the Shakespeare Birthplace Trust started to lift the turf on the site of Shakespeare's family home. New Place had been a present-absence on the corner of Chapel Street and Chapel Lane, Stratford-upon-Avon, for 250 years: one reason why it has played too scant a role in Shakespearian biography. Over the next five years, a team of archaeologists (now based at the Centre for Archaeology, Staffordshire University), augmented by around 120 volunteers, would be in quest of Shakespeare's lost house.

The archaeology was complex because of the layers of renovations and remodelling that New Place had undergone, and because of a previous excavation in the 1860s, led and supervised by James Halliwell (who later became known as the great Shakespeare scholar James Halliwell-Phillipps). Archaeology then was still in its infancy. There were two main iterations of the house. The first was the original New Place built by Hugh Clopton (sometimes wrongly referred to as 'Sir Hugh') in the 1480s, which was later renovated and partly remodelled by Shakespeare from 1597. Towards the turn of the eighteenth century, the New Place that Shakespeare had owned (which still included significant parts of Clopton's fifteenth-century house) was demolished and an entirely new house (the second iteration of New Place) was built on the site (by direct descendants of Hugh Clopton). That house was itself demolished in 1759. Halliwell's excavations discovered walls from Shakespeare's time and earlier, and he also uncovered the remains of the later Clopton house.

Our task was made even more fascinating in its revealing of the evidence of Halliwell's earlier excavation. His backfill – a rich melange of what he considered detritus – contained within it a treasure-trove to the modern archaeological eye, and there was part of the site he had left unexcavated (where there stood a mulberry tree). But in applying for planning permission to re-present the site in time for the

Shakespeare quatercentenary in 2016, the Shakespeare Birthplace Trust was able to remove the tree (which had been planted in 1946, and was in a poor state), in order to reveal crucial evidence that has led to the fullest – albeit fragmentary – picture of what Shakespeare's New Place was like.

Shakespeare knew he was buying the largest house in the borough. He had just turned thirty-three and he wanted to live there with his family. His work commitments called him to London, but probably never for very long: New Place was too large and socially significant a house, and his entire family was based there. At least, that is the picture that our archaeological investigations have led us to consider. That is why we have subtitled this book 'An archaeological biography': our excavations have had a palpable impact on how we have come to understand Shakespeare's life, and to retell his story. Shakespeare did not 'retire back' to Stratford-upon-Avon after years of absence; he never really left, because New Place, and all it represented, was too significant a home for him.

He was a writer first and foremost, and New Place was his writer's base, as well as his gentleman's family home. The assumption that the leading playwright of one of the most successful theatre companies of the day was away on tour whenever the theatres were closed is too exhausting a thought to be likely. It is worth noting that the Lord Chamberlain's Men and, later, the King's Men seem not to have toured at all from the latter part of 1597 through to 1602–03 (Gurr, 1996: 303–4). Shakespeare would almost certainly have been present, though, for the Christmas seasons at Court; performing before the Queen, as the Lord Chamberlain's Men, and before the King, as the King's Men, was the primary function of both companies in which Shakespeare owned shares and for which he wrote. Shakespeare needed time and focused energy to write. He was only ever a lodger in London. Life at New Place was also the way Shakespeare positioned himself in relation to the Stratford-upon-Avon community in which he had grown up, and from where he spent conspicuously large amounts of money on major investments in the town and surrounding area.

Ever since Hugh Clopton had acquired the burgage plot in the 1480s and built the first New Place, the house had played a significant part in the economy and culture of the town. The site was chosen with care: close to the White Cross where a regular market met; opposite the Guild Chapel; and close to the schoolroom, the Guildhall and the almshouses. The archaeology suggests that, in its first fifteenth-century construction, New Place probably had a row of shops along its Chapel Street frontage. It was the first and only courtyard-fronted house in Stratford-upon-Avon, and looked therefore dramatically different from every other home, with its main family dwelling set back from the bustle of the main street. It was Hugh Clopton's original house that Shakespeare bought in 1597, by which time it was in need of repair and improvement. Shakespeare himself remodelled the front range and added a long gallery. After his granddaughter, his last direct descendant, had died in 1670, New Place returned to the Clopton family, who demolished the house Shakespeare had known and rebuilt a new one more in keeping with the architectural taste of their own period. As a result, we know more about the Cloptons' eighteenth-century house than we do about the building Shakespeare himself knew.

This account of Shakespeare's New Place is a hybrid of genres – part biography, part archaeological report – and offers a wider historical perspective on the site than ever before (with an intense focus on the years 1564–1616). In uncovering the past, we found it stretching back a long way. Shakespeare's ancestral inhabiters first started to live on the site 6,000 years ago. Their soil and what it tells us lays the foundation for Shakespearian explorations, all too appropriate for the home of a poet who wrote about the past and the ghosts that haunt our present. For Stratford-upon-Avon, the site of New Place provided the fullest opportunity yet to investigate, in the context of a large-scale excavation, the remains of a prehistoric settlement anywhere in the town.

What did we find? When asked this question by a casually interested visitor, we came to realise that the most desired answer was probably 'a Shakespearian manuscript preserved in peat', 'the nib of a quill from the early seventeenth century' or even something as theatrical as 'a sword'. When considered by archaeologists, that same question is enriched by the many artefactual answers that the excavations have yielded to us: foodstuffs of many periods (and signifying a high-status diet in Shakespeare's own time), evidence of the Shakespeare family's games and pastimes (Shakespeare, it seems, probably enjoyed a game that involved scoring pegs), their household stuff, and the remains of their cottage industries. Crucially, Dig for Shakespeare (as the project was known) has enabled us to form a compelling understanding of what New Place was like in Shakespeare's time, its size and its layout. Philip Watson's specially commissioned drawings, painstakingly based on archaeological and comparative architectural evidence, help to convey the excitement of what we have learned. They represent the best rendering of what Shakespeare's family home looked like – for the time being. Kevin Sturdy's drawing enables us to understand what the site was like in its earliest times.

Bringing together a range of different expertise means that this book has been co-authored across its chapters, and sometimes within the chapters themselves. Chapter 1, 'Ancient beginnings', covers the first 6,000 years of the site, from its prehistoric beginnings through its development into a plot within the economic context of early medieval Stratford-upon-Avon, and the construction of the first timber-framed building. Chapter 2, 'The origins of New Place', describes the construction and distinctive features of Hugh Clopton's brick-and-timber house, the first New Place, and provides a detailed account of it. Chapter 3, 'Shakespeare and Stratford-upon-Avon, 1564–96', provides a cultural, religious and economic context for Shakespeare's upbringing; education; work; marriage; and early investments up to his son, Hamnet's death, and his father, John Shakespeare, being made a gentleman. Chapter 4 discusses the importance of New Place to Shakespeare and his family during the nineteen years he owned it and spent time there. The chapter takes us to just beyond the death of Shakespeare's granddaughter, Elizabeth, Lady Bernard, the last direct descendant of Shakespeare to live in the house. Chapter 5 considers what Shakespeare's New Place was like, its appearance and layout, and describes artefacts and objects that relate to the Shakespeare family's time there. Chapter 6 describes the house that, by 1702, had replaced the one that Shakespeare knew. Chapter 7 gives an account of James Halliwell's acquisition of the site, his archaeology and how New Place has become an important focus for the local community, not least during the 'Dig for Shakespeare'.

Our project deliberately turned archaeology on its head. The discipline is normally used in order to uncover truths about entire peoples, cities and civilisations. We used archaeology as a tool in an ambitious attempt to find out more about the life of William Shakespeare. The discovery of the body of Richard III under a Leicester car-park, has demonstrated what archaeology can teach us about individuals. By uncovering the remains of New Place, its features and artefacts, we can begin to learn more about its inevitable importance to Shakespeare.

It is our hope that we have played our part in rebuilding the house and home Shakespeare knew – in imagining it – and that we have helped to return New Place to its rightful place in history and Shakespearian biography.

References

Gurr, A. (1996). *The Shakespearian Playing Companies* (Oxford: Clarendon Press).

1

Ancient beginnings: the site of New Place from the prehistoric to the early medieval period

William Mitchell and Kevin Colls

The complex history of Stratford-upon-Avon can be chronicled through the fortunate survival of its early records. The wealth of preserved material available is partly due to chance, but also to the town's association with Shakespeare and the desire of successive generations to preserve and collect anything of relevance to the playwright. These records do not, however, tell the entire story, which can be augmented by archaeological investigation, including 6,000 years of history, and four successive centres of settlement located on both sides of the River Avon. The site of New Place presents us with a microcosm of the wider Stratford-upon-Avon area with almost the entire settlement period represented in its archaeological record.

The prehistoric origins of Stratford-upon-Avon

The site of New Place is situated in the lower Avon Valley close to a natural fording point along the River Avon. It lies on the north side of the Avon flood plain, on the edge of the Second River Gravel Terrace, around 9–12 m above sea level (BGS, 1974). This provides a dry site for construction, with easily cultivated and well-drained soils. Fresh water is supplied from the river and wells sunk into the sands and gravels (Slater and Wilson, 1977: 1). The river provided an easily navigable transport route and the presence of the ford was significant, allowing people, animals and goods to cross safely.

An introduction to prehistoric archaeology

Within urban environments, the survival of prehistoric features is much more uncommon than in rural settings. Any remains that do survive can be difficult to characterise and interpret. Most buildings were timber-and-thatch, and only the foundation holes of the posts and beams of these constructions could potentially survive. Typically, little or nothing would have been left above ground, having decayed or been removed. The pits, ditches and gullies that belonged to the settlement are more frequently preserved. These provide evidence of the usage and extent of the long-vanished settlement (Darvill, 2010: 77–188).

We can find out about various aspects of prehistoric life such as climate, environment and food production from the analysis of surviving archaeological evidence. Amid this, analysis of pollen from plant remains in waterlogged deposits, studies of animal bone assemblages, insect remains, and the tools and physical remains left by man all produce a varied picture of life at the time. Pits, for example, can often represent an important later prehistoric resource for archaeologists and historians, as frequently, upon disuse, the pits became used as repositories for a wide range of material culture. The relatively small number of archaeological features and artefacts that have been recovered on site tell us much about what life was like in Stratford-upon-Avon when compared with other evidence from the period (Cunliffe, 1991, 371–2).

Agricultural and societal development in the Neolithic period

At the beginning of the Neolithic period (*c.* 4000 BC–2400 BC) there was a rapid growth in trade, technology and commerce. The domestication of cattle and cereals (such as wheat and barley) was adopted by the people of Britain, and modelled on techniques from the Continent. Agricultural practices were developed, and settlement locations, where water, farm land and sources of food were abundant, were sought after. There was, too, a significant investment of time, labour and resources in the construction of ceremonial and funerary monuments, obtainable only through an organised complex social and cultural system and hierarchy (Cunliffe, 1995: 112).

Several of these monuments are known from crop marks in the area around Stratford-upon-Avon, and find-spots of Neolithic-worked flint and pottery sherds are known. Many of these may represent accidental deposition and could be present as a result of intermittent visitation of nomadic groups across the area, but others may be the result of more permanent occupation by these Neolithic communities. (PAS, 2003–; Slater and Wilson, 1977: 19).

The Neolithic inhabitants of Stratford-upon-Avon

What we know of the prehistoric origins of Stratford-upon Avon is based upon sparse, fragmentary evidence, occasionally recovered from the area during modern archaeological investigation. Our knowledge of the period is under constant revision, but evidence from the New Place site, and others in the surrounding area, suggests an increased human presence beginning in the Neolithic period.

Although, as yet, there has been no definitive Neolithic occupation evidence recovered within Stratford-upon-Avon, there is good indication that this location was visited and is likely to have become settled. It is highly probable that the area was carefully chosen for settlement several thousand years ago, because of its close proximity to the important natural resources of the river and the associated fertile grazing and crop lands. Physical evidence was gathered from the site to support the idea of an increased Neolithic presence and possible settlement within the locality of Stratford-upon-Avon. Several flints were recovered, the finest of which was a probable Neolithic, bifacially worked discoidal knife or scraper (Figure 1.1). A number of other retouched flint flakes, possibly Neolithic in origin, were also recovered. The flints identified on site had a multitude of uses but may have primarily been used for

Figure 1.1 One of the Neolithic artefacts recovered from the site. This example represents a Neolithic, bifacially worked discoidal knife or scraper.

animal butchery and preparation. Four small sherds of pottery from two separate layers were of Neolithic date. These belong to the early Neolithic bowl tradition and represent a rare occurrence of this pottery. Other comparable examples are known from elsewhere in the Avon Valley, including Barford and Wasperton (Mullin, 2011–12). This pottery represents clear evidence of a Neolithic presence in this area, but because of the very weathered nature of the examples, and the fact that they were recovered from alongside Iron Age material, it is likely they did not originate from this location.

The Bronze Age in Stratford-upon-Avon

The Bronze Age (*c.* 2400 BC–700 BC) is not represented on the site by either physical or artefactual evidence. There is, however, evidence from this period within the Stratford-upon-Avon and Warwickshire areas generally, although the exact nature of the activity is difficult to characterise. Several settlement sites have been identified as crop marks from aerial photographs, and locally there are ploughed-out roundbarrows (Slater and Wilson, 1977: 27). Excavations at Barford Quarry, Glebe Farm and Waverly Wood Quarries in Bubbenhall, have contained Bronze Age settlement evidence.

Societal change in the Iron Age

The Iron Age (700 BC–AD 43) was a period of immense social, technological and agricultural change. The new social systems and food-producing strategies enabled groups to come together and collaborate on building projects such as the construction of hillforts. New varieties of crop were established and produced. Different cereals could be sown, and in locations and at times of year once thought unviable. The intensification and diversification of crop production was driven by the demands of an increasing population. Environmental change and the alluviation of river valleys altered the productive potential of the land. Many farmsteads sprang up as a result (Cunliffe, 1995: 112). Within the area of the Avon Valley, new locations along the gravel terraces were chosen for their fertile, easily worked soils.

Iron Age settlement within Stratford-upon-Avon

During the Early to Middle Iron Age, settlements consisted of individual farmsteads scattered across the Avon Valley rather than planned, nucleated settlements. The archaeological evidence recovered on the New Place site confirms the existence of a small settlement or farmstead. Numerous small settlements and around sixteen Iron Age hillforts, such as Meon Hill near Stratford, or Oldbury near Nuneaton, are known to have existed across the Warwickshire area (Figure 1.2). The settlements consisted of groups of farmsteads, occupied by family groups: for example Wasperton, Tiddington and elsewhere (Palmer, 2010a, b; Hurst, 2011). Their populations may have taken refuge in the nearest hillforts in times of trouble. The individual farmsteads would have

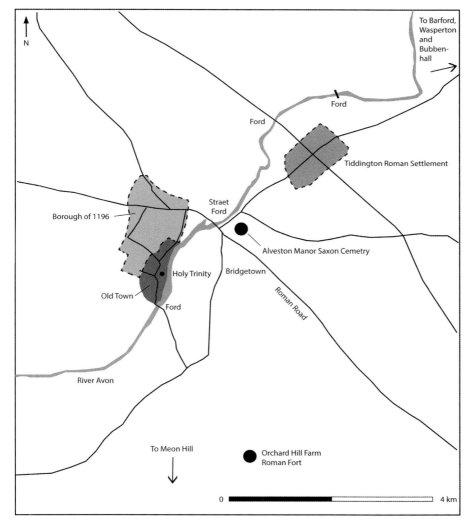

Figure 1.2 Map of Stratford-upon-Avon and the immediate region, showing location of prehistoric, Roman and Saxon sites. The figure also illustrates the locations of the crossing points (fords), settlements (Tiddington and Old Town) and the borough boundary of the twelfth century.

generally contained a main building, being a thatched round house, where the family and some of the livestock would have lived. Around each house there may have been livestock pens, workshops and storehouses. The wider settlement would have been surrounded by a deep ditch for defence from wild animals. Further ditches and gullies were used for drainage and to demarcate areas of land ownership.

Three natural fording points along the Avon created a convergence of routeways connecting smaller farmsteads to larger settlements and hillforts. The first larger, nucleated settlement to emerge developed at the furthest north of these fords at Tiddington, during the later Iron Age. Significant archaeological excavation has been undertaken in and around Tiddington, one mile away on the eastern side of the river. Evidence suggests that the village became a focal settlement towards the very end of the Iron Age, about AD 30–70, in the period spanning the Roman conquest. It continued to prosper for the next 300 years. This settlement at Tiddington would certainly have influenced the surrounding environment, and its food-producing activities would have necessitated the use of the outlying agricultural land. It was essentially a large farming community that also survived on being the focus for a marketplace serving the local area (Palmer, 1997: 21).

The New Place site in the Iron Age

Significant evidence dating to the Iron Age was recovered from beneath the foundations of New Place. The evidence suggests the presence of a small farmstead on this, the western side of the River Avon. The settlement perhaps existed just prior to and contemporaneously with the Tiddington settlement on the opposite side of the river.

Several storage pits, a truncated occupation layer and a gully were identified. These were extremely well preserved and relatively undisturbed. There are no other recorded examples of Iron Age (or prehistoric) cut features within the centre of Stratford-upon-Avon. As such, they represent an unusual survival within a developed urban town and have contributed significantly to our understanding of the historic development of Stratford-upon-Avon (Figure 1.3).

What was found on site?

Individually, each of the Iron Age features found on the site was a significant discovery; taken together they can build a substantial picture of life within the later Iron Age Stratford-upon-Avon (Figure 1.4). Eight storage pits were found in close proximity to one another (pits 1 to 8; Figure 1.5). Most of these storage pits were relatively uniform in nature because they were similar in size, shape and contents. There were two main variations, but it is clear these were dug relatively contemporaneously. One linear

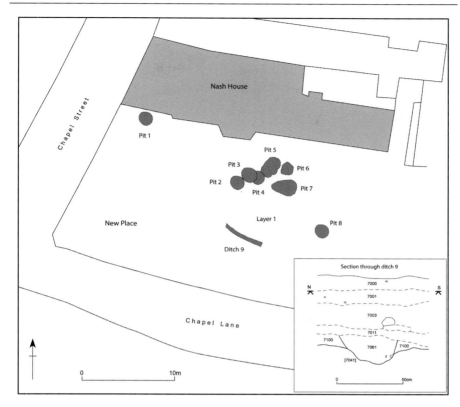

Figure 1.3 Archaeological plan showing the Iron Age archaeology identified across the site. Eight storage pits and one ditch were encountered. An illustrated section through ditch 9 is also included.

gully (ditch 9) was found to the south of these storage pits. It was difficult to identify, but it had survived to 5 m in length and 0.2–0.3 m in depth. This gully was most likely to represent part of a field or settlement boundary, or perhaps a delineation between the area of storage pits and the rest of the settlement. In a domestic context, ditches and gullies were usually required for defence, to mark a settlement or field boundary, or to act as drainage.

The remains of an Iron Age occupation layer (layer 1; Figure 1.3) were located to the south of pits 4 and 7. This layer sat directly over the natural sand and gravel deposits, had been cut by several later medieval features, and may be associated with the excavation of the pits. Although no structural evidence was encountered (such as round-house post-holes or drip gullies), the site itself would have provided the ideal location for early habitation, and the presence of grain storage pits suggests the main nucleus of the settlement could have been located within the vicinity of the New Place site.

Figure 1.4 Artistic reconstruction of the site during the Iron Age period.

Figure 1.5 Photograph of the main concentration of the Iron Age grain storage pits. The pits were large yet shallow in size with near-vertical sides.

Sowing and harvesting of crops

Agricultural and technological advances were a feature of this period as the increasing population meant that demand for reliable sources of food soared. The occupiers of this farmstead would have used the land in the surrounding areas to grow their crops. The grain was ploughed into the soil using oxen and iron-tipped ploughing equipment, more productive and durable than previous methods, and these improved cereal production (Cunliffe, 1995: 113). The crops are likely to have been harvested by hand using reaping hooks (examples of which have been found across the country) and then taken back to the farmstead for processing (Cunliffe, 1991: 373).

Drying of corn, pot-boilers, and the use of fire-cracked stones

Once the grain was gathered from the farmed fields, two alternative methods of preservation and storage were used. The first method required the grain being dried. If a damp or unripe crop was harvested, some form of drying process was employed by the Iron Age farmers to prevent it from germinating. Several methods are suggested, including the construction of temporary ovens or the laying of corn on skins spread over pre-heated stones. This would reduce the risk of the corn charring (which was always a possibility, as attested to by the examples of charred grains found on other sites). This explanation also partially explains the vast quantities of fire-cracked river cobbles (also known as 'pot-boilers') recovered from the site, especially when these were found in association with the storage pits (Cunliffe, 1991: 374).

Crop storage

Burial of grain provided a further method of preservation and storage. The pits were used for the storage of grain or other crops, and were filled in at the end of their useful life. Pits of this type often survive in Iron Age settlements. Grain required for planting the following season was stored damp in underground pits, which were sometimes lined and sealed with a clay or earth top. The release of carbon dioxide by the top layers of sprouting grain inhibited further growth and prevented bacteria. Experimental archaeology has shown that 75 per cent of grain will germinate the following season, after being stored a year in these pits (Mulville, 2008: 235; Reynolds, 1974).

The pits encountered on site were aligned northeast to southwest. They continued beneath the trench edge on the northern side of the site, and into the neighbouring property (Mitchell, forthcoming). Several of these pits had been truncated by successive periods of occupation. On the whole, they were extremely well preserved, perhaps as a result of their location, which later became the central courtyard of the fifteenth-century house. Samples of the layers within these pits were taken for analysis. These data can often be used as a guide to the economic and environmental factors on a site at a given time. The pits would have drained freely, and their sandy nature, along with their deeper natural gravels, meant they failed to produce any environmental data. Experimental archaeology has shown that, despite the often considerable difference in detail, shape and size of the preserved examples, a large number of these pits were probably used for storage. There were two main types of pit. The first (pits 1 to 4, 6 and 8) was rounded and relatively uniform in size, being around 1.5–1.6 m in diameter and 0.2–0.6 m in depth. Pits of this type had vertical profiles; extremely compacted, flat bases; and contained distinctive, sterile, homogeneous deposits. Each was filled with one or two layers, primarily composed of sands and silts. Artefacts such as pottery, quernstone fragments and fire-cracked stones were recovered. These appeared to be incidental and not a result of deliberate deposition. These pits did not, however, contain any metalwork, slag, worked-stone tools or building materials.

There was evidence that the pits may once have had linings such as timber or wicker, as several of them had darker lenses of sandy clay around their edges and on their bases. Their stratigraphic relationship was observed. These pits were not excavated contemporaneously, as it was clear that some of them had cut through the filled contents of others. Their life-span is known to have been relatively short, and regular re-cutting and renewal were necessary (Reynolds, 1974, 1988). Examples of a similar type have been found at other local sites such as High Cross, Burton Dassett, Tiddington and Barford. These pits may have been used to store vegetables (Palmer, 2005, 2010).

A second type of pit was identified (pits 5 and 7). These were different, being more ovoid in shape, and had been excavated to a greater depth (1 m). The bases of pits of this type slightly undercut their profile, and the pit-fills resembled those recovered from within the other Iron Age examples; like those, they were almost devoid of artefactual evidence. The deliberate undercutting profile of these pits has been shown to aid the preservation of cereal crops over the winter ready for sowing in the spring (Reynolds, 1974). Comparative examples of undercutting pits such as these are known from local sites such as Tiddington, Barford, Ryton-on-Dunsmore and Hampton Lucy.

Later prehistoric pit alignments and pit clusters

The increase in the settled population and more complex knowledge and use of advanced intensive farming techniques led to land in the Iron Age becoming increasingly subdivided. A new type of boundary was introduced at this time, represented by alignments of post-holes and pits and natural geological features (Hurst, 2011: 106).

The number of pits in close proximity created an alignment or cluster, a common feature of the period, and many comparable examples are known. Often pits such as these are associated with other settlement features or are discretely in isolation. Similar pit alignments and clusters are known from other sites across the Midlands and the rest of the country. They were used as boundary features and there are surviving examples that show these were created on a vast scale, requiring a large communal effort. Many pit alignments, which have been recorded through aerial photography in rural locations, can be traced for hundreds of metres and may have served the purpose of dividing up land and demarcating territory (Cunliffe, 1991: 393). They are often located on the periphery of the known settlements, as may be the case on the New Place site.

The grinding of corn and use of rotary quernstones within the home

Two fragments of a rotary quernstone were recovered and provide firm evidence of the use of grain in this location. Once the grain had been harvested and prepared or removed from storage, it was ground to flour to make bread or griddle cakes, by crushing and grinding in between two stones. From the second century BC this involved the use of a rotary quern, in which the upper stone revolved on the lower.

The pottery

These storage pits yielded examples of handmade pottery (Plate 1). These were very abraded, and it was difficult to identify their form and function. Most are likely to have been general cooking wares and vessels used for serving and dining. At this time pottery varied from one region to another. It was predominantly homemade by individual families or within the community, but a greater distribution of comparative vessels began to occur during the later Iron Age, suggestive of the commencement of a pottery trade and the origins of industrial centres.

The urbanisation of Stratford-upon-Avon

Following the abandonment of the Iron Age features, the site appears to have slowly reverted back to a rural character. There was a gradual silting of the features followed by an accumulation of layers above. The layers, which perhaps originated because of a natural widening of the River Avon at this period, sealed the prehistoric features beneath. Small fragments of abraded prehistoric pottery contained within appear to have acquired their appearance from being rolled around in water.

The site of New Place was not then permanently settled again for a further 1,200 years. Occasional residual fragments of pottery were recovered from the site of New Place, dating to the Roman and Anglo-Saxon periods. These demonstrate a continued human presence in the general area, but archaeological evidence confirms that there was no nucleated settlement on the New Place site during the Roman or Anglo-Saxon periods. Perhaps, because of the evolving course of the River Severn, the area became unsuitable for sustaining a settlement. Around the time of the Roman occupation, the course of the river had probably settled close to its present position, upon which the surrounding flood plains became sought after, as fertile agricultural land.

The Roman and Anglo-Saxon presence

No definitive trace of a Roman fort has yet been discovered in the area, but the settlement at Tiddington continued into the Roman period and was occupied until the late fourth to the fifth century (Figure 1.2). Outlying Romano-British farmsteads that also existed throughout this time are likely to have been scattered across the landscape; many of these are known as crop mark sites (Slater and Wilson, 1977: 28). A further ford existed south of the village of Tiddington. This appears to have risen in importance, leading to the abandonment of the settlement following the departure of the Romans from Britain.

A second settlement of the area rose to prominence in the fifth and sixth centuries, half a mile to the southeast at Bridgetown, on a site now known as Alveston Manor (Figure 1.2). It is at this site that the name Stratford rose to prominence. The name 'Streat-ford' is Saxon in origin and means 'where the Roman road crosses the river'. The Anglo-Saxon migrants deliberately settled near to this strategic routeway finding that it joined the major Roman routes of the Icknield Street going north and the Fosse way going south (Fogg, 2014: 7).

The site at Bridgetown has revealed the presence of a significant Anglo-Saxon cemetery that contained over 100 inhumation and cremation burials with grave goods, including jewellery, pottery vessels and weapons belonging to individuals from all echelons of society (WCC, 2008). There is limited evidence for settlement associated with this cemetery but a series of palisaded boundaries and sherds of Anglo-Saxon pottery are suggestive of its location.

The origins of modern Stratford-upon-Avon and 'Old Town'

The settlement at Bridgetown had probably disappeared by the late tenth century because a third shift of settlement occurred. Much of the evidence for the establishment of this new settlement is topographical or documentary but archaeological evidence supports the established story (Figure 1.2).

The Anglo-Saxon settlement that we know to be the forerunner of modern Stratford-upon-Avon was established on the west bank of the River Avon south of the *Streat*-ford, when a minster-church was constructed in the late eighth century at the centre of a large estate owned by the Bishop of Worcester (Palmer, 1997: 27). This church, its estate and the village that clustered around it were located on the higher ground above the river and became known as 'Aet-Stratford': 'the isle of the Ford' (Fogg, 2014: 7). It was probably located at this position to distance it from the Bridgetown settlement. The Domesday survey of 1086 found a small rural settlement occupied by forty-four households with a minster church and mill, which formed part of an estate owned by Wulfstan, the Saxon Bishop of Worcester. It continued to be held by his successors until the fifteenth century (Carus-Wilson, 1965: 47). The location of this early medieval village is still referred to as 'Old Town' today.

Stratford-upon-Avon: an example of medieval town planning

The next chapter in the long history of Stratford involves town planning, urbanisation and increased agriculture. Throughout the early medieval period, the area surrounding Stratford-upon-Avon became more extensively farmed. During the eleventh and twelfth centuries, the general population was increasing and the resource of the Forest of Arden became more intensively used. There was continued, deliberate deforestation for the purpose of ploughing and cultivating the soil. All of the area north of the early medieval settlement centre became used as open fields for farming (Figure 1.6). This agricultural development yielded increased harvests and grazed land, which was particularly suited to corn-growing, sheep and cattle (Carus-Wilson, 1965: 47–8). The land around Stratford-upon-Avon proved very productive and a surplus began to be produced and traded.

As a result, the present town centre was established as a planned borough in 1196. King Richard I granted a market to John de Coutances, the Bishop of Worcester,

Figure 1.6 Map of Stratford-upon-Avon showing the site in relation to the open field systems that were in use before the town planning and the laying of the burgage plots in the late twelfth century. For reference, the modern road system has been shown, although not all of these roads would have existed during this period.

who then set out his plan for the town under another charter (Bearman, 1997: 1–12). The new town was laid out on a grid system, with intersecting streets lined with plots of land (burgages). This newly planned town was laid over part of the open field land of the earlier community, half a mile north of the original Saxon settlement (Carus-Wilson, 1965: 49). Within this new plan, areas were set aside for housing and marketplaces (of which there were four in total).

The frontages of the intersecting streets were lined with plots of land that were occupied by buildings, workshops and gardens, with allotments behind. The measurements of these burgage plots were defined in the borough charter, 3½ perches (17.60 m or 57.75 ft) in width and twelve perches (60.35 m or 198 ft) in depth (Slater, 1997: 37–8). As often in medieval town foundations, these burgages were laid on the already established orientations and divisions that were present as a result of ancient field boundaries and the underlying ridge and furrow of the earlier open fields. The plots were not simple rectangles; they were distorted in order to fit into these earlier field systems and keep them off the flood plain (Figure 1.7). This created a more parallelogram-shaped street grid plan (Slater, 1980: 55). This layout can be traced up to the present day, as Stratford-upon-Avon was not subject, as other towns were, to the intense redevelopment of the nineteenth and twentieth centuries.

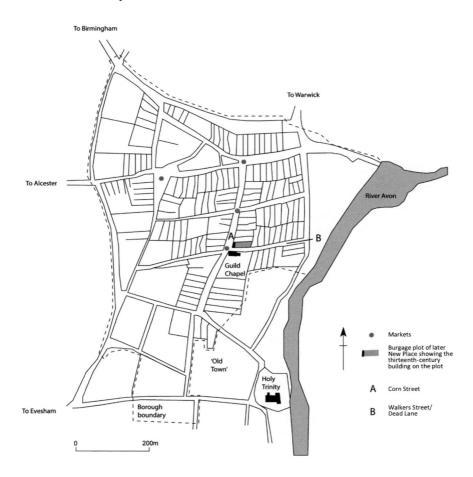

Figure 1.7 Map of Stratford-upon-Avon in the late thirteenth century, showing the layout of the burgage plots and markets. The precursor house on the New Place plot is marked, as are the Guild Chapel and Holy Trinity. Corn Street and Walkers Street/Dead Lane will later become Chapel Street and Chapel Lane respectively.

What trades were established in the newly established borough market town?

The wealth of medieval towns was usually owing to their success in using local produce and redistributing it, either as ready manufactured goods or as raw materials. Not all towns traded the same products, and some towns specialised. As an example, the two largest local towns, Coventry and Worcester, were built upon the fortunes made from woollen cloth production and distribution (Schofield and Vince, 2003: 151).

A large number of documentary sources exist from this period, recording the trades and trading details of the townspeople of the time. Stratford-upon-Avon appears not to have specialised, but the most prominent of the trades and industries within the town were, as in the nearest large urban centres, to do with clothing. A survey of the borough of Stratford-upon-Avon of 1251–52 records a wide range of occupational names from tanners to tailors, because of the availability of raw materials (Carus-Wilson, 1965: 55).

The location: what was in the surrounding area?

The site of New Place is located on the corner of Chapel Street and Chapel Lane. Chapel Street featured prominently in the layout of the town from its inception, and it made up part of the roadway that linked the newly formed town with the old settlement around the church. During this period Chapel Street was known as Corn Street, as a corn market was held further north at the junction with High Street. The Chapel Street name came into existence in the latter part of the fifteenth century, and became consistently used after the reconstruction of the Guild Chapel nave and tower. There was also a market area directly opposite the Guild Chapel (Figure 1.7). A cross known as the 'White Cross' was located here from about 1275 to at least 1608. In later years this was the location of the butter and cheese market (Bearman, 2007: 30). Chapel Lane (formerly known as Walkers Street or Dead Lane) had an altogether different appearance. Chapel Lane was not a well-used thoroughfare as Chapel Street was, and it ran alongside gardens and barns belonging to the properties along the frontages. A brook that ran from Old Town along Church Street continued along Chapel Lane, to join the River Avon. There are frequent references to this brook becoming polluted and full of dirt and debris from the surrounding properties. 'Fulling' (or 'walking') was known to have taken place along the street; this was the process of cleansing woollen cloth by pounding it either by feet, hands or clubs (and later by mechanical means within mills) to remove all impurities. A second preparatory process involved stretching the cloths out on tenters to dry. From the thirteenth century there was a fulling mill towards the bottom of Chapel Lane (Carus-Wilson, 1965: 61).

The street is first mentioned in a record of 1553 where the tenants of the lane were asked to keep it clean: 'Item, that every tenaunt in Chapell lane or Ded lane do scour and kep cleane ther gutteres or dyches in the same lane befor thassencyon day, and so from thensfurthe from tyme to tyme to kepe the same, in peyn of every offender to forfet for every deffalt' (Halliwell-Phillipps, 1883: 486). In latter times this stream became a wide ditch before becoming covered over in the eighteenth century.

The construction of the Guild Chapel and the possibility that there are associations with the New Place site

To the south of the New Place site on the corner of Church Street and Chapel Street is the Guild Chapel complex. It is today regarded as one of the most important extant examples of purpose-built medieval guild chapels in the country and in its time it would have played a highly influential role in the governance of Stratford-upon-Avon.

In 1269 Robert de Stratford and the Guild of the Holy Cross were granted a charter to construct an oratory and a hospital for the use of priests of the diocese of Worcester, within Stratford-upon-Avon (Macdonald, 2012: 13). A large site was chosen, on a road crossing, within the newly laid-out town. The chapel itself contains fragments of thirteenth-century fabric in parts of the east wall of the chancel and the south of the building. This is likely to represent the surviving elements of the earlier infirmary and oratory building (Giles and Clark, 2012: 161). Given the close proximity and presence of high-status remains on the site of New Place, it is plausible that the buildings that once occupied the site had an association with the construction of the Guild in 1269.

The site of New Place in the thirteenth century

There was no archaeological evidence to suggest that the burgage plot that New Place occupied had been divided at any point in the past (as was often the case). This site has retained the same basic layout for 800 years. The size of the plot means that a significant property could be constructed.

A survey of the bishop's estates in 1252 records 250 occupied burgages within Stratford. Building location was significant, and several of these burgages were split into two or three tenements. The subdivision of burgage plots often meant that plots had multiple residences built upon them and were often occupied by several tenants. The New Place plot remained in an important and prominent position on the corner of two streets within this newly laid-out town. Corner properties were often grand structures that became local landmarks. They effectively had two frontages and this afforded them an advantage (Schofield and Vince, 2003: 82). The tenant paying rent on this burgage plot would have been able to construct a house of considerable size. At Preston in Lancashire a tenant who held a street frontage of at least 12 ft could qualify as holding burgess status (meaning a privileged landowner or householder who paid their share of communal expenses). Perhaps this was also true in Stratford-upon-Avon (Bateson, 1965: 58).

The building from the 1200s to the 1400s

Aside from a few post-holes, fragmentary stone foundations and occupation surfaces, very few of the physical remains of the building have survived. As a result of site development and the insertion of cellaring in later periods much of the frontage has not survived. Archaeological remains (behind where the main building would have stood)

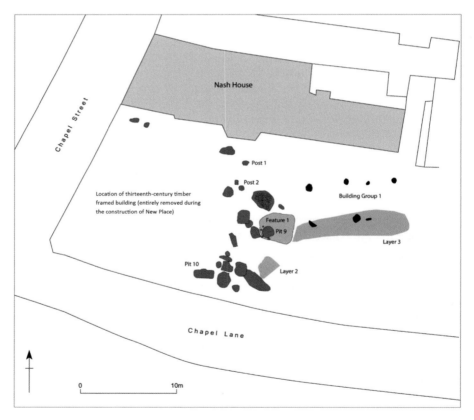

Figure 1.8 Archaeological plan showing the thirteenth-century features identified across the site. These features include one probable building (building group 1), occupation layers, and pits and postholes. The lack of evidence belonging to the main building at the front of the site from this period is a direct result of the later construction of two iterations of New Place on this site.

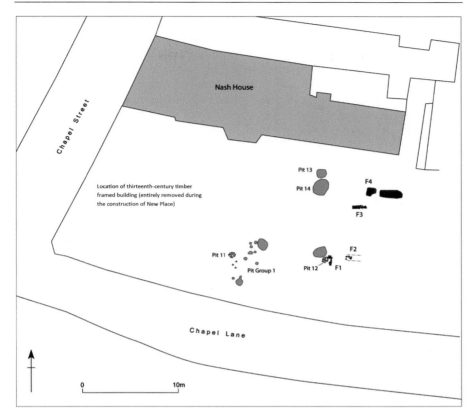

Figure 1.9 Archaeological plan showing the fourteenth-century features identified across the site, including pits, one pit group, and stone foundations (F prefix). Note also the location of the thirteenth-century house (which would still have been present).

can be interpreted through comparative analysis with contemporary building techniques and layout, surviving artefactual remains, evidence from the rear of the property (including possible outbuildings), and the domestic and industrial activity within the backplots (Figures 1.8 and 1.9). The artefacts used to date the structural evidence indicate that the primary date of construction was some time in the early-to-mid-thirteenth century. Elements of this thirteenth-to-fourteenth-century building (materials and substantial foundations) were incorporated into Hugh Clopton's 'grete house' in the 1480s.

The layout of the building

The thirteenth-century building is likely to have been of high status, and occupied the whole width of the plot. Later, it may have been subdivided and occupied by several tenants. The Chapel Street frontage would have followed the pattern of other domestic buildings, containing several rooms, and standing before an open hall, accessed through a passageway. To the rear were the gardens, outbuildings and workshops.

The frontage may have been used for shops (a tradition which developed from semi-permanent, open marketplaces), typical for most houses in town centres. They developed out of necessity as craftsmen and traders began to require permanent workshops and secure storage for their wares (storage space was generally above the shop, or below in a cellar). Shops provided space in which the outlying agricultural community could trade. Frontages were chosen because they were the most accessible element of the building (Clark, 2000: 58–63; Pantin, 1962–63: 205).

The building's appearance

The main fabric was timber, but it also contained stonework. Fragmentary stone foundations and a large assemblage of stone roof and floor tiles from this period were recovered. Some of these foundations were reused within Hugh Clopton's house construction, for example in external structural elements such as stairwells and bay windows (Figure 1.10).

Figure 1.10 Photograph of a large, deep, stone foundation dating to the late thirteenth century. The purpose of this is unclear, although stone remains were added (to the upper courses) during the construction of New Place's hall to form a probable bay-window base.

The majority of the building is likely to have been a timber-frame, post-built construction, which centred around a hall space, open to the roof and heated by a central hearth built on to the floor. Throughout this period, the open halls of the elite were divided into hierachical areas. The upper part of the hall was reserved for the owner of the house, and was often occupied by a dais for the owner's table. The lower part was for the servants.

It was not until the later twelfth century that domestic buildings began to be constructed of more permanent timber framing. Only the houses of the very rich were built entirely in stone. Prior to the twelfth century, a semi-permanent wattle-and-daub construction with thatched roofs was used, which had a more limited life-span (Milne, 1992, quoted in Slater, 1997: 41). Some of the frontage may have been a two-storey construction, as houses in the centre of towns were under pressure to use all available space (Harrison, 2014: 19). The walls would have been constructed of upright posts set into holes or upon pad-stones at regular intervals, parallel to the plot boundary. Although the majority of the frontage had been removed, examples of its well-preserved post-holes and post-pads had survived.

Towards the rear of the property there was increased survival of these features. There were post-holes distributed across the site at regular intervals and some were laid in rows. Some of the rows of posts may have represented fence lines, or small out-buildings and workshops (building group 1, Posts 1 and 2; Figure 1.8). Alternatively these post-holes could represent lines of posts used to support racks to dry processed textiles and cloth (tenter racks).

Several of the occupation layers had survived towards the rear of the site (layers 2 and 3; Figure 1.8). These surfaces would have been within or immediately out-side the buildings and were typically made up of beaten earth covered with rushes or straw to reduce dust. As these surfaces became worn they were patched up and replaced, sometimes with flagstones. This resulted in a build-up of thin floor layers and occupation deposits containing fragmented pottery and other artefacts. As late as 1539 the practice was still common, as Erasmus observed when visiting England: 'the floors are commonly of clay, strewed with rushes; under lies unmolested an ancient collection of beer, grease, fragments, bones, spittle, excrements of dogs and cats and everything that is nasty' (Steane, 1985: 202).

The building materials

At least part of the roof was made up of stone tiles (Plate 2). These were recovered from several locations across the site where they had been deliberately discarded in pits. Fragments of roof tile were also found within occupation layers relating to the alteration of the house. They were also recovered from elsewhere, showing that these roof tiles were highly regarded and reused in later buildings.

The tiles varied in size and graduated courses were used, with larger stone tiles located around the eaves and smaller, thinner tiles towards the ridge. The top of each tile was rounded off, probably to reduce the accumulated weight, and was pegged through holes on to the roof with an oaken peg to a lath. This was in turn pegged or nailed to the rafters, a method of construction widely used in the Cotswolds and found elsewhere in England and Wales. These stone tiles could be laid at a relatively steep pitch, at 50 degrees or more (Brunskill, 1976: 84).

Industrial and domestic activity on the site

Towards the rear of the property, there were dense concentrations of activity. Groups of well-preserved pits dating to the thirteenth and fourteenth centuries were identified (Figures 1.8 and 1.9). These contained discarded waste such as high-status pottery, animal bones, building materials and personal artefacts. Whilst the majority of these pits were domestic in origin, the evidence suggests that many were created for light industrial purposes. Several of these pits were found in close proximity, to the rear of the frontage's presumed location.

One of these features appeared to be a self-contained working area (feature 1; Figures 1.8) consisting of a sub-rectangular sunken area, which contained a deep, clay-lined pit (pit 9; Figures 1.8), and had several small stake-holes regularly spaced at 0.35 m around it. This was adjacent to a possible workshop building (building group 1; Figures 1.8) and occupation layers (layers 2 and 3; Figures 1.8). The presence of stake-holes suggests a temporary structure was built over the pit, perhaps a wooden frame from which something was suspended as part of the industrial process – possibly a mixing-pit for bleaching or dyeing. Very few of the pits contained large numbers of artefacts, which suggests they were used for storage or industrial processes. One pit (pit 10; Figure 1.8) contained the remnants of a clay lining, so perhaps it was used to hold liquid.

Activity changed dramatically in the fourteenth century. A discrete group of pits and post-holes were present in this period (pit group 1; Figure 1.9). Pit Group 1 consisted of pits that were smaller in size and fewer in number than in the previous century, suggesting that industrial processes were scaled back, changed or ceased. The presence of large pits (pits 13 and 14; Figure 1.9) excavated and backfilled in the fourteenth century suggests that the building in this location fell into disuse (building group 1; Figure 1.8). Pits 11 and 12 (Figure 1.9) had secondary, reused stone tile linings set into clay (Figure 1.11) that would have provided waterproofing. Storage in subterranean pits or buried ceramic pots was common and meant the contents could be kept at lower temperatures.

Several of these pits may have been used for the disposal of cess or refuse. The fill of pit 13 (Figure 1.9) was greenish in colour, suggesting organic waste. A large majority of this material would have been taken away from the urban centre and used as fertiliser on agricultural land, but there was continuous demand for places in which to dispose of domestic refuse within a property's boundaries.

Several stone foundations dating to the fourteenth century were located towards the rear of the property (F1, F2, F3 and F4; Figure 1.9). These remains suggest the presence of a more permanent structure that potentially replaced the timber structure that had been there previously (building group 1; Figure 1.8).

Figure 1.11 Photograph of pit 12. Reused stone roof tiles were used in conjunction with clay to line the pit. Subterranean storage pits were common during the fourteenth century.

The finds of the twelfth and thirteenth centuries

Belt buckles and copper alloy aiglets or lace chapes, which were used to bind the ends of the laces that adorned medieval clothing, were found among the discarded pottery, animal bone and building materials. Trading currency was also recovered in the form of the clipped half of a silver short cross penny, dating to 1180–1247, and a silver farthing.

The pottery of the thirteenth and fourteenth centuries

The pottery assemblage confirms occupation from the beginning of the thirteenth century that increased after 1250. There was a surprisingly large amount of pottery dating from the thirteenth and into the fourteenth century. Some was found residually in later features, but the majority came from the scattered, backfilled pits and post-holes dated to this period. The good quality of this pottery, including many sherds from highly decorated jugs, indicated a relatively high-status domestic occupation.

The earlier medieval pottery came from a variety of sources including Buckingham (Brill-Boarstall wares; Plate 3), Oxford (Oxford medieval wares), Birmingham (Deritend jugs and cooking pots), Worcester, Lyvden-Stannion, the Nuneaton area (North Warwickshire ware, Chilvers Coton; Plates 4 and 5), and the East Midlands (shelly wares) and the Malverns. The reasonably high component of reduced Deritend-ware cooking pots suggests these were containers used to transport a commodity rather than being traded for the pots themselves (Rátkai, 2013).

Continuation of occupation into the later fifteenth century

Occupation of the site continued throughout the 1300s and 1400s, though buildings throughout this time are likely to have been renewed and developed. Then, in the 1480s, came Hugh Clopton. In constructing his 'grete house', he reused some of the substantial stone foundations of the previous buildings, remodelling and incorporating them into his new home.

References

Bateson, M. (1965). 'Victoria County History of Warwickshire III', in E. M. Carus-Wilson, 'The First Half-Century of the Borough of Stratford-upon-Avon', *The Economic History Review*, 18.1: 46–63.

Bearman, R., ed. (1997). *The History of an English Borough: Stratford-upon-Avon 1196–1996* (Sutton: Shakespeare Birthplace Trust and Sutton Publishing).

Bearman, R. (2007). *Stratford-upon-Avon: A History of Its Streets and Buildings* (Stratford: Stratford-upon-Avon Society).

British Geological Survey [BGS] (1974). *Geological Survey of Great Britain, England and Wales*, Stratford-upon-Avon, Sheet 200.

Brunskill, R. W. (1976). *Illustrated Handbook of Vernacular Architecture* (London: Faber and Faber).

Carus-Wilson, E. M. (1965). 'The First Half-Century of the Borough of Stratford-upon-Avon', *The Economic History Review*, 18.1: 46–63.

Clark, D. (2000). 'The Shop Within? An Analysis of the Architectural Evidence for Medieval Shops', 43: 58–87.

Cunliffe, B. (1991). *Iron Age Communities in Britain: An Account of England, Scotland and Wales from the Seventh Century BC until the Roman Conquest* (London: Routledge).

—— (1995). *Iron Age Britain* (London: Batsford/English Heritage).

Darvill, T. (2010). *Prehistoric Britain* (Abingdon: Routledge).

Fogg, N. (2014). *Stratford-upon-Avon: The Biography* (Stroud: Amberley Publishing).

Giles, K. and J. Clark (2012). 'The Archaeology of the Guild Buildings of Shakespeare's Stratford-upon-Avon', in J. R. Mulryne (ed.), *The Guild and Guild Buildings of Shakespeare's Stratford: Society, Religion, School and Stage* (Aldershot: Ashgate), 135–70.

Halliwell-Phillipps, J. O. (1883). *Outlines of the Life of Shakespeare* (London: Longmans, Green).

Harrison, J. (2014). 'Changing Approaches to the Analysis and Interpretation of Medieval Urban Houses', *The Post Hole*, 42, available at http://www.theposthole.org/read/article/312 (accessed 19 February 2016).

Hurst, D. (2011). 'Middle Bronze Age to Iron Age: A Research Assessment Overview and Agenda', in S. Watt (ed.), *Archaeology of the West Midlands: A Framework for Research* (Oxford: Oxbow Books), 101–26.

Macdonald, M. (2012). 'The Guild of the Holy Cross and Its Buildings', in J. R. Mulryne (ed.), *The Guild and Guild Buildings of Shakespeare's Stratford: Society, Religion, School and Stage* (Aldershot: Ashgate), 13–30.

Milne. G. (1992). *Timber Building Techniques in London AD 900–1400*. London and Middlesex Archaeological Society Special Society Paper no. 15 (London: London and Middlesex Archaeological Society)

Mitchell, W. (forthcoming). *Nash's House, Stratford-upon-Avon: Archaeological Excavations 2015* (Centre of Archaeology, University of Staffordshire).

Mullin, D. (2011–12). *Prehistoric Pottery from New Place* (unpublished).

Mulville, J. (2008). 'Foodways and Social Ecologies from the Middle Bronze Age to Late Iron Age', in J. Pollard (ed.), *Prehistoric Britain* (Oxford: Blackwell), 225–47.

Palmer, S. (1997). 'Origins: The Romano-British and Anglo-Saxon Settlements', in R. Bearman (ed.), *The History of an English Borough: Stratford-upon-Avon 1196–1996* (Stroud: Sutton), 13–29.

—— (2005). *Archaeological Investigation at 119 Tiddington Road, Stratford-upon-Avon, Warwickshire*, Report 0539 (Warwickshire County Council).

—— (2010a). *Archaeological Evaluation at 69 Tiddington Road, Stratford-upon- Avon Warwickshire*, Report 1001 (Warwickshire County Council).

—— (2010b). *8000 Years at Barford: The Archaeology of the A429 Barford Bypass, Warwickshire, 2005–7*, Report 1046 (Warwickshire County Council).

Pantin, W. A. (1962–63). 'Medieval English Town-House Plans', *Medieval Archaeology*, 6–7: 202–39.

Portable Antiquities Scheme [PAS] (2003–). https://finds.org.uk (accessed 19 February 2016).

Rátkai, S. (2013). Unpublished pottery report for the Dig for Shakespeare Project.

Reynolds, P. J. (1974). 'Experimental Iron Age Storage Pits: An Interim report', *The Prehistoric Society*, 40: 118–31, available at www.butser.org.uk/iafhist08_hcc.html (accessed 19 February 2016).

—— (1988). 'Pit Technology in the Iron Age', *British Archaeology Magazine*, 10: 24–6, available at www.butser.org.uk/iafhist08_hcc.html (accessed 19 February 2016).

Schofield, J. and A. Vince (2003). *Medieval Towns: The Archaeology of British Towns in Their European Setting* (London and New York: Continuum).

Slater, T. (1980). *The Analysis of Burgages in Medieval Towns: Three Case Studies from the West Midlands* (University of Birmingham, Department of Extra-Mural Studies).

Slater, T. R. (1997). 'Domesday Village to Medieval Town: The Topography of Medieval Stratford-upon-Avon', in R. Bearman, *The History of an English Borough: Stratford-upon-Avon 1196–1996* (Sutton: Shakespeare Birthplace Trust and Sutton Publishing), 30–42.

Slater, T. and C. Wilson (1977). *Archaeology and Development in Stratford-upon-Avon* (University of Birmingham, Department of Geography).

Steane, J. M. (1985). *The Archaeology of Medieval England and Wales* (London and Sydney: Croom Helm).

Warwickshire County Council [WCC] (2008). *Stratford on Avon District: Local Development Framework Core Strategy. Historic Environment Assessment of Proposed Strategic Sites* (Warwickshire County Council).

2

The origins of New Place: Hugh Clopton's 'grete house' of c. 1483

William Mitchell and Kevin Colls

Some time in the later fifteenth century (*c.* 1483), the plot of land at the corner of Chapel Street and Walker's Street (later Chapel Lane) had come into the possession of Hugh Clopton. He removed almost every trace of the previous buildings and erected his own extensive residence. Hugh Clopton's 'grete house', which soon became known as 'New Place', was to become one of the most celebrated and striking houses in Stratford-upon-Avon, both within Hugh Clopton's lifetime and beyond.

Hugh Clopton

Hugh Clopton (1440–96) was a wealthy mercer, benefactor and public official. He was the youngest son of John and Agnes Clopton and was born near Stratford-upon-Avon at Clopton House, his ancestral home, in 1440. The Clopton family first came into possession of the land upon which Clopton House was built in the thirteenth century and subsequent family members played an influential role in the prosperity of Stratford-upon-Avon. Being a member of a prosperous manorial family, opportunity permitted him to leave his home in 1456, when he became apprenticed to a London mercer, John Roo. There he rapidly learned his craft and earned his living by trading in wool and cloth out of London (Giles *et al.*, 2012). He gradually gained influence, and, in 1464, he became a member and then warden (1479, 1485 and 1488) of the company of mercers. In 1469–70, he was admitted to the Stratford-upon-Avon guild as a merchant of London, serving as a master for two years. Throughout the latter half of the 1400s, Hugh Clopton became established within the mercantile profession, and as one of the merchants of the Woolstaple (an English corporation that dealt in wool and also, it is believed, skins, lead and tin) he was able to trade freely and amass his fortune. The Woolstaple was an influential corporation and it had controlled the export of wool from across England to the Continent, from as far back as 1314. Hugh Clopton's name is recorded in the Exchequer Customs accounts for 1480–81, and he is named among the merchants of the Staple, who were shipping wool and animal hides to Calais from London. Through hard work and influence he quickly amassed his own fortune and established himself as a person of notable authority. In 1485 he was chosen to be Alderman of the Dowgate ward in London, and a year later he became the Sheriff of London. He was also, at various times, a Member of Parliament and an ambassador to Maximilian of Flanders (and on one occasion to Richard III). The peak of his career occurred in late 1491, when he was elected Lord Mayor of London.

Hugh Clopton died in 1496. His will confirms he had achieved a success-ful career and wealthy status, and reflects his loyalties both to London and to Stratford-upon-Avon. His house in Stratford was described by Clopton in his will as 'my grete house' (Halliwell, 1864:1), and upon the inquest into his will in 1497 the loca-tion of New Place is established: 'de uno burgagio jacente in Chapell Strete in Stretforde predicta ex oposito Capel ex parte boriali' (that is 'of a burgage in Chapel Street to the north of the Chapel opposite', Shakespeare Centre Library and Archive, ER1/121).

Having remained unmarried, he bequeathed the house and 'all other my landes and tenementes being in Wilmecote, in the Brigge Towne and Stratford' (Halliwell, 1864: 1) to his great-nephew William Clopton (1481–1521), the grandson of his elder brother, Thomas. Furthermore, considerable sums were left to his extended family, his merchant colleagues of London and charitable causes around Stratford-upon-Avon.

Hugh Clopton's affinity with the town meant that he invested in it. He com-missioned the rebuilding and redecoration of the Guild Chapel around 1495, which centred on the reconstruction of the nave and the installation of new religious wall-paintings. Virtually next door to his 'grete house', Clopton probably thought of the Guild Chapel as his own private place of worship. The developments that were being undertaken were ultimately paid for by the money left in his will (Bearman, 2007: 57). In the 1490s, Clopton commissioned the construction of a stone bridge over the River Avon, replacing its wooden predecessor, which dated back to at least 1235 and was said by the poet and antiquarian John Leyland (1503–52) around 1542 to have been 'but a poore Bridge of Timber, and no causey [causeway] to come to it', 'very smaulle and ille, and at hygh waters very harde to passe by' (Toulmin-Smith, 1910: 49–50). He also donated large sums for the restoration of the cross aisle of Holy Trinity Church (Stratford-on-Avon Preservation Society, 1924: 3).

New Place: Hugh Clopton's 'grete house'

We cannot be sure how much time Clopton spent at New Place – he was a man of prop-erty and influence with many commitments outside Stratford-upon-Avon, especially supervising the trade of his investments in London. This was Clopton's only purpose-built house, and it is likely he carefully designed and planned it as a visible expression of his wealth and status.

No plans of Stratford-upon-Avon survive from before 1759, and no detailed ground plans of New Place remain. Information on the appearance, location and significance of the house therefore comes from later accounts, passing references and official documentation (such as concords, rents and leases relating to the site), as well as archaeological evidence.

The earliest reference to a building on this plot is Clopton's own will of 1496: 'my grete house in Stratford'. This may have differentiated it from other, lesser dwellings on his estate, such as those on the corners of Swine Street (now Ely Street) and Sheep Street. It is generally believed that the house became known as the 'New Place' immediately upon its construction, although the first time it is specifically referred to by this name is in an indenture in 1532 between the son of William Clopton, also named William, and his sister, Elizabeth Cole, for her marriage money, charged on 'a messuage called the New Place' (Halliwell-Phillipps, 2013). In 1542, Leyland, on his journeys around England producing descriptions of libraries and religious buildings for Henry VIII, wrote of the 'right goodly Chapel' and 'the pretty house of brick-and-timber by the North side of it'. This description of New Place is the first recorded use of brick in Stratford-upon-Avon (Toulmin-Smith, 1910).

Following the establishment of the borough, Stratford-upon-Avon, like other towns, underwent several periods of sustained economic and cultural expansion, followed by contraction. One of Stratford-upon-Avon's important industries, cloth-making, had been in decline in the fifteenth century, and initiatives and projects undertaken by the town's elite, such as Hugh Clopton's bridge and the Guild Chapel, can be seen as attempts to rejuvenate urban life during a time of depression (Dyer, 1997: 53). New Place itself can be identified as a statement of the town's desired prosperity. The economy of Stratford-upon-Avon may have enabled Clopton to acquire the plot at a reduced rate.

Hugh Clopton chose a style of house most appropriate to his situation and social stature. New Place was built in the grand medieval style with a great hall around a courtyard plan. It was the largest residence within the jurisdiction of the borough. No other courtyard house is known about in Stratford-upon-Avon. The tradition of a great hall being the large principal room in high-status domestic buildings had existed from pre-Saxon times.

What was Clopton's House like?

What follows is a detailed description of Clopton's New Place based upon a unique schematic of the house (Figure 2.1) created from documentary and archival sources, specialist input, and archaeological evidence. A significant number of features were identified across the site that date to Hugh Clopton's house and occupancy

(Figure 2.2). Altogether, this evidence has culminated in an artistic reconstruction of Hugh Clopton's New Place (Figure 2.3) that was made possible by the following descriptions.

The front range

New Place was accessed through a central gateway within a frontage on Chapel Street. The ground floor probably had two or more rooms separated by a central entranceway. The close proximity of Coventry meant that much of the economy of Stratford-upon-Avon was based upon the preparation and trade of wool and

Figure 2.1 Schematic ground- and first-floor plan of Hugh Clopton's fifteenth-century New Place, based on historical research and archaeological data. The room functions of the ground floor have been identified through archaeological structures found during the excavations. The room functions of the first floor are more conjectural. This depicts New Place as a courtyard-style house with a hall and second courtyard to the rear, and one large cellar within the front and side ranges.

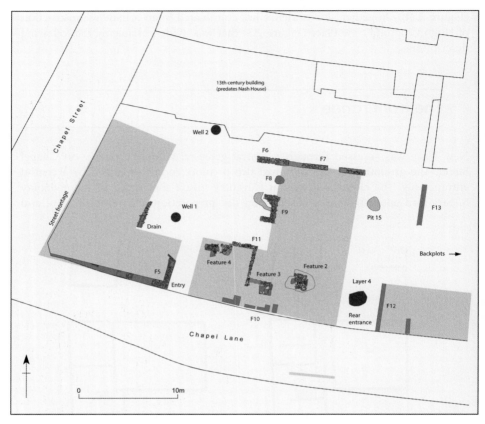

Figure 2.2 Archaeological plan showing all of the fifteenth-century features identified across the site. A significant number of structural remains dating to Clopton's New Place were discovered, including stone foundations (F prefixes), wells, pits, occupation layers and other features (feature 2: oven, feature 3: stone tank or sink, feature 4: hearth or vat bases). The large shaded area represents the New Place building layout as depicted in the schematic plan (Figure 2.1).

wool-cloth. Archaeological evidence suggests that it is likely that Hugh Clopton used the frontage range as shops. Throughout his early career, Clopton's primary income was from wool, and he exported his wares to the Continent. A number of cloth- or bale-seals made from lead, used throughout Europe from the thirteenth to the nineteenth century for identification and regulation purposes, were recovered from the site. Each of these seals was stamped with a unique design to identify its origins (Egan, 1994) and is evidence of Hugh Clopton's mercantile associations (Figure 2.5).

Hugh Clopton also spent time elsewhere, so perhaps he let out the frontage buildings. Pantin notes: 'We cannot tell in most cases whether the shop was actually used by the inhabitant of the house. But it was certainly very common for shops to be let off separately, or even form separate freeholds' (Pantin, 1962–63: 208). This is supported by Leech, who records that in Bristol 'Houses with open halls might

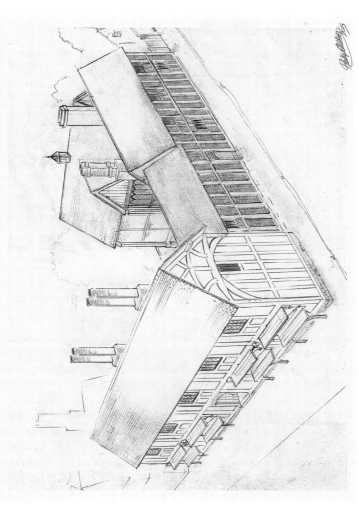

Figure 2.3 The five-bay-front gatehouse range in its original form as built by Hugh Clopton most probably housed merchants' shops with horizontally split timber shutters opening up to form the canopies and the counters. Each shop front would have featured a decorated lintel, supported on curved timber braces creating an arch-like opening. Access was via a smaller central doorway leading to a passage at the rear, servicing all four units. The plain roof surmounts a simple arched, braced-collar end-gable with an unglazed upper window overlooking the Guild Chapel. The close, vertical timber studding signifies high status. Although the herringbone brick of the service range is present, the chimneys show an earlier, simpler design with less embellishment and a less efficient, rectangular stack serving the buttery. The louvre is the only form of smoke extraction serving the central fireplace of the open hall. Several of the windows, particularly in the service-range ground floor, are unglazed with vertical oak bars.

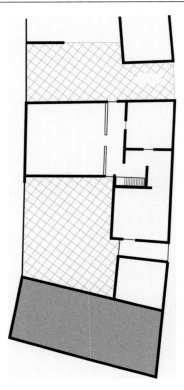

Figure 2.4 Schematic guidance plan 1, showing the location of the front range.

or might not have one or more shops on the street frontage; in the same owner-ship as the buildings behind, these shops might be in separate occupation' (Leech, 2014: 69). Pearson adds that 'Dwellings often inhabited by wealthy merchants lay back from the street front which was reserved for commercial activity' (Pearson, 2009: 4).

The upper floor (or floors) of the front range probably contained bedchambers and additional storage rooms. It was approximately 16 m (52.5 ft) in length by 7 m (22.11 ft) in width. An open passage lay between the northernmost wall of the front-age and the building that existed on the adjacent plot, 22 Chapel Street (later demol-ished) when what would become known as Nash's House was constructed in the early sixteenth century (Mitchell, forthcoming).

Almost all trace of this front range was removed by later developments and the archaeological evidence is limited to only the most deeply stratified foundations. The physical appearance is therefore primarily based on documentary sources, recovered construction materials and architectural comparison.

Figure 2.5 Lead bale or cloth seals recovered from the site. These lead seals were used throughout Europe between the thirteenth and nineteenth centuries for identification and quality control of the article contained within.

The cellar

As with other high-status town houses of this period, Clopton's New Place had a cellar beneath the front range. Less typical is the fact that the cellars were constructed beneath the southern part only, with the remaining, northern part only built up from ground level. These cellars removed all trace of any previous thirteenth- and fourteenth-century buildings. The cellar was probably divided into distinct storage areas for ale, mead and wine barrels (or 'butts'), and goods for the shops above. A stairwell is likely to have been located at the eastern end for quick access to the buttery at the service end of the hall (see below). Several substantial cellar foundations built from limestone were identified at significant depth along the southern Chapel Lane boundary, with the longest surviving section 8 m in length (F5; Figures 2.2 and 2.7). The distance between the easternmost cellar-wall foundation and the westernmost archaeological features of the buttery/brew-house building (see pp. 46–50) suggests that this was the location of a side entrance leading to Chapel Lane.

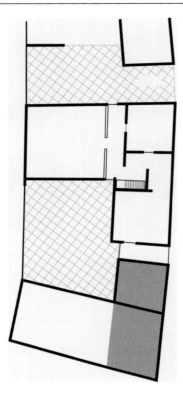

Figure 2.6 Schematic guidance plan 2, showing the location of the cellar.

The courtyard

The courtyard was enclosed on three sides by buildings and completed probably by a low wall against the passage on the northern side (F6; Figures 2.1, 2.2 and 2.3). The courtyard was roughly rectangular and was approximately 14 m × 9m (45.11 × 29.6 ft), and the documentary sources suggest that at some point it became an open space covered by a grass lawn. A well was positioned within the courtyard. The domestic courtyard developed stylistically from both the monastic cloister and castle bailey forms, and 'by the beginning of the fourteenth century the courtyard was the primary shape for most high-status houses' (Emery, 2012: 65). Although no further examples of this house type are known in Stratford-upon-Avon, this style was not unusual and it is considered one of the main types of English medieval house that typify the period. Schofield and Vince support this and suggest that 'in the vast majority of cases where their plans can be ascertained, the houses of religious and noble leaders in north European towns were of courtyard plan' (Schofield and Vince, 2003: 88). Pantin records that a general layout was adhered to when designing town houses. He observes: 'In these houses where the shops occupy the front,

Figure 2.7 Photograph of stone cellar wall foundation (F5) from Clopton's New Place. The brick 'boxes' in the foreground represent eighteenth-century cellar walls belonging to the second New Place surrounded by brickwork built by Halliwell-Phillipps in the 1860s.

the principal dwelling-house, or at least the hall range, will generally be at the back, where it can open on to a courtyard or garden, with greater space and quiet' (Pantin, 1963–64: 205–6). The existence of a courtyard is corroborated by the presence of rubbish pits that were dug and backfilled during the mid-sixteenth century.

The wells

Wells were the most efficient and practical source of water. Three wells are known to have existed on the site, although only two seem to date from Clopton's New Place.

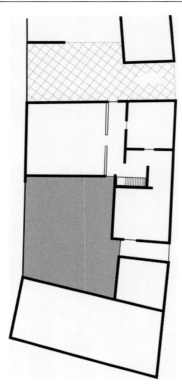

Figure 2.8 Schematic guidance plan 3, showing the location of the front courtyard.

Figure 2.9 Image of the courtyard well (well 1) from Clopton's New Place, as sketched by Halliwell-Phillipps in the 1860s.

The first was located in the courtyard of the house (well 1; Figures 2.2 and 2.9) and the second in the passage between New Place and the property to the north (well 2; Figure 2.2). The wells were constructed of limestone bonded with clay and dug down to the natural sandstone. Both were excavated in 1862 and have since been cleared on a number of occasions. A third well, located further to the rear of the plot, was probably associated with the later, eighteenth-century house.

The passage

A passageway ran along the northern side, between New Place and the neighbouring buildings, from Chapel Street in an easterly direction. It was approximately 2 m (6.6 ft) wide. Limited archaeological investigation along its length did not expose any buried features dating to the medieval period, suggesting it had remained an open passageway from the late twelfth century onward. It was probably bound on both sides by a low mud brick wall, and the well within the passageway may have been shared

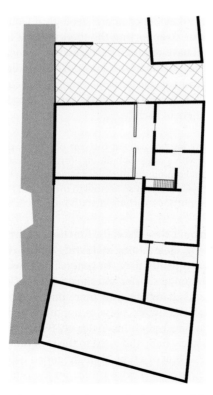

Figure 2.10 Schematic guidance plan 4, showing the location of the passage that would have been located between New Place and the neighbouring property (Nash's House).

between the two properties. The majority of the buildings along Chapel Street retain irregular passageways along their northern side, shared by properties to gain access to the rear. Passages are known to have existed within medieval towns from their origins, and they would have been factored into the town planning of the late twelfth century. They are often identifiable in the archaeological record as unused and undug strips between property boundaries (Schofield and Vince, 2003: 80).

The hall building

Across the back of the courtyard, to the east of the plot, was the hall building (Figures 2.1–2.3). Archaeologically, timber-framed buildings such as this would not necessarily leave substantial structural remains, and the evidence for Clopton's hall is minimal. This is due partly to the construction methods but also to the substantial redevelopment of the site in the eighteenth century. However, several important archaeological structures and features from the hall building were identified during the excavations that, with documentary research, enable conclusions. Also of importance are the areas where no archaeological remains were present. Across the location of the hall there was no evidence of archaeological features that post-dated the mid-to-late fifteenth century, supporting the theory that a large open building was present. As the hall would have required permanent flooring, probably stone flags, it would have been impractical to dig in this area once the building had been erected.

The hall played a prominent role in the planning of the courtyard house throughout the medieval period. Schofield and Vince report that this style of house was favoured by certain members of society:

> The hall of the property lay normally at the rear of a yard, though occasionally to the side on restricted sites, with a range of buildings (often separately let) fronting the street. Leaders of the merchant community in major towns, such as those who dealt in wine or some other aspect of royal service, also aspired to the style of house with a courtyard and an open hall of lofty proportions. (Schofield and Vince, 2003: 88)

Around the time Clopton built New Place, the functions of the hall were evolving from its being primarily the living, entertaining and eating room to becoming a largely symbolic space that was less frequently used. In general, halls of the fifteenth century or later decreased in size, becoming shorter and square in plan (Wood, 1990: 193), whilst rooms such as parlours and chambers grew more important as living spaces (Leech, 2014: 71–2). The open hall did not decrease in importance, however, as it developed into a symbol of social standing rather than necessity (Quiney, 2003: 186). Halls of this period were often impressively built and open to the roof timbers (Plate 6).

The New Place hall was that of a typical single-ended hall house, with the hall on one side of a screens-passage and service rooms on the other (Brunskill, 1971: 98). With the inclusion of the service rooms at the southern end, the hall range was

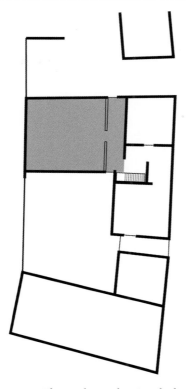

Figure 2.11 Schematic guidance plan 5, showing the location of the hall.

approximately 16 m × 8.5–9 m (52.5 ft × 27.9–29.5 ft), and like other halls of the period, the width was approximately two-thirds the length (Wood, 1990: 51). The screens-passage, the purpose of which was to shield the view of the service rooms from the main hall, would also have been constructed to established dimensions, with a width of, on average, 2 m (6.6 ft). The absence of substantial physical evidence for the screens-passage may suggest it was separated from the main hall by a moveable wooden screen or spere (a partial screen). The building ran parallel to Chapel Street (north to south) to fill the width of the plot, leaving the access passage between New Place and the adjacent property intact. Several stone features had survived that are likely to represent sections of the external foundations of the hall. One such feature, consisting of multiple sections of limestone blocks, bonded with clay and mortar, ran for 10 m and represents the foundations for the northern hall elevation (F7; Figures 2.2, 2.12).

There was evidence of rebuilding using brick at the eastern end of the wall, perhaps as a result of later remodelling during Shakespeare's occupancy (see Chapter 5). A small rounded depression filled with compacted gravels (F8; Figure 2.2), located towards the northwestern corner of the hall, may have been the location of a large padstone within the western wall of the hall to support timberwork.

Figure 2.12 Photograph of the stone foundations for the northern wall of the hall. This feature was identified by Halliwell-Phillipps during his excavations and he built brick boxes around the fragile remains to protect them.

In his comprehensive study of medieval town houses, Leech records that 'at the beginning of the fifteenth century houses of middling men, in cities such as Winchester, Exeter and York, may have contained no more accommodation than a hall and chamber, together with a cellar, buttery, pantry kitchen and brew-house' (Leech, 2014: 90). The provision of food and drink to the household provided the basis for the architectural arrangement of the buildings and rooms around the hall. The chosen layout was dependent on access to water, food- and drink-production, and storage (Woolgar, 1999: 144). Food reached the hall, and the rest of the house, from the service rooms and kitchen through the screens-passage, and the well in the courtyard provided the house with immediate access to water. Within the hall building, evidence suggests the service rooms to the south of the screens-passage were functional as the buttery or bake-house and the pantry.

First-floor apartments, probably including some of Clopton's personal chambers, would have been located above the service rooms at the southern end of the hall building and accessed from stairs off the screens-passage (Figure 2.1). The great chamber (or solar) was the room set aside for Hugh Clopton and probably doubled as a living room and bedchamber. These are probably the rooms that Shakespeare would have taken over as master of the house. To span the roof of the 8.5–9 m (27.9–29.5 ft) hall, the builders would have needed to source significantly large timbers. Beams of this size, however, were not uncommon at this period. The roof would have been of an arch-braced collar or hammer-post type to span it adequately. This type of roofing construction would have obviated the need for any internal pillars or posts for roof support as all the weight is spread to the external walls.

The hall was probably lit by elaborate windows. A section of substantial stone foundation constructed in the thirteenth century was redeveloped during the latter part of the fifteenth century (F9; Figures 2.2 and 2.13), perhaps forming the foundations of a full-height bay window in the western elevation of the hall. Like the other fifteenth-century foundations on the site, it was constructed of rough-cut limestone blocks bonded together with clay that had almost completely degraded. The foundations survived to around 2.9 m in length and a height of five courses. A large window would have been a clear statement of Hugh Clopton's wealth and would have allowed extra light on to the high-status end of the hall. Further smaller windows may also have been present set high at the southern end of the hall. There was no clear evidence to suggest how the hall was heated. Large, central hearths were common throughout the medieval period, with the smoke escaping through a louvre (smoke turret) in the hall roof. Louvres were set on to the ridge of the roof and were often elaborately constructed (Wood, 1990: 277). However, the fifteenth century witnessed the development of the wall fireplace and flue (Steane, 1985: 196; Wood, 1990: 257) which were adopted as alternatives to the central, open hearth.

Figure 2.13 Photograph of the stone foundations for a probable bay window located on the western wall of the hall. The deeper stone foundations to the left of the photograph represent the structural remains from an earlier stone feature that dates to the thirteenth century. The builders of the hall utilised these solid foundations for their bay-window foundations.

The hall service rooms: buttery/bake-house and pantry

At the southern end of the hall, and accessed from a doorway obscured by the screens-passage, were the service rooms (buttery/bake-house and pantry) with chambers above. 'Buttery' comes from the French word for bottle (*bouteille*). Beverages like ale, mead and wine were kept in barrels and stored in the cellar. These barrels were brought up from the cellar and transferred to the buttery to allow them to settle before being transferred into jugs for serving. The buttery was often the bigger of the two rooms (buttery and pantry) as beer (and/or wine) could be kept for a longer duration and in larger quantities than foods such as bread. It also appears that for some of the life of this room, it doubled as a bake-house. An oven (F2; Figures 2.2 and 2.16, Plate 7), probably for baking bread, was identified. This oven comprised two substantial stone walls with a surface, made up of stones laid on their edges, in between. The surface and walls had been subjected to intense heat, and large amounts of ash

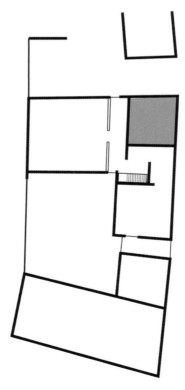

Figure 2.14 Schematic guidance plan 6, showing the location of the buttery/bake-house.

Figure 2.15 Schematic guidance plan 7, showing the location of the pantry.

and charcoal were present. A substantial limestone slab had been used for the eastern threshold and the oven would have been accessed from this eastern side.

The pantry's primary function would have been temporarily to store cold, cooked food prior to use in the hall. The word 'pantry' comes from the French word for bread (*pain*). Other items of tableware to be used in the hall may have been stored here. It is also likely that the stairs to the first floor were located at the northern end of this room. At the western end, a large, square, stone-built structure (F3; Figures 2.2 and 2.18, Plate 7) was identified. This squared structure would have been sunken below the floor level of the pantry, and comprised a stone wall on its north and east sides and large stone slabs set on edge on its south and west sides. The base was made up of stone flags and there was a sloping stone slab in its southeast corner. The function of this feature is unclear, but it may have been used as a cold storage tank or a drainage tank or sink for the disposal of waste water produced throughout the household. The water could be thrown into the tank and would gradually drain away through the cracks between the stones into the gravels beneath (Slim, 2010: 50). A series of wall foundations running down Chapel Lane, which presumably made up the outer southern elevation of this range (F10; Figure 2.2), was identified by Halliwell-Phillipps.

Figure 2.16 Photograph of an oven located in the service rooms of Clopton's hall. Built of stone, this may represent a bread oven rather than the main kitchen hearth/oven, suggesting this area was also used as a bake-house.

The kitchen/brew-house

To the west of the buttery and pantry was the kitchen and brew-house. In a large household such as this, food production was an almost continuous task: for example the production of bread and small beer (the well water was not safe enough to drink). This room was slightly wider than the pantry and buttery. Kitchen buildings had become an integral part of the medieval household (Wood, 1990: 247). Prior to this, food preparation and cooking were undertaken within the hall or in separate ephemeral buildings nearby. Kitchens of great houses contained one or more fireplaces and ovens, and often had a fireproof roof made of stone (Wood, 1990: 253). The northeastern corner of the kitchen building had survived in the form of a substantial wall foundation (F11; Figures 2.2 and 2.19). This foundation functioned as a plinth upon which the timber framing would have sat. Forming a right angle, these foundations were 0.4 m in width and were constructed from roughly cut, local limestone blocks with up to four courses remaining. The northernmost foundation made up the external wall of the kitchen building next to the courtyard. It is also highly likely that a small servants' entrance was present off Chapel Lane, leading to the kitchen and other service rooms (Figure 2.2).

Inside the kitchen building, further archaeological features were identified that comprised large groups of laid stones (F4; Figures 2.2, 2.19 and 2.20). These appeared

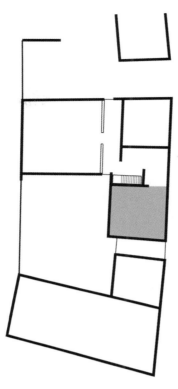

Figure 2.17 Schematic guidance plan 8, showing the location of the kitchen/brew-house.

Figure 2.18 Photograph of a stone-built feature located in the service rooms of Clopton's hall. Sunken below floor level, this feature may represent a stone sink for drainage, or a cold storage tank.

Figure 2.19 Photograph of the archaeology within the kitchen/brew-house area of Clopton's New Place. The remains include the limestone foundations for the building itself (left of the picture), and a number of internal features including areas of stone flooring and cobbling (right of the picture), which may represent platforms for vats, hearths or cauldrons.

to be discrete features that were not associated with the foundations of the kitchen. It is likely that they functioned as platforms to support the hearths and the vats or cauldrons that would have been above. The platforms were oval or sub-square in shape and each was over a metre in width. Charcoal fragments and large deposits of animal bone were present around these platforms, which supports the suggestion that cooking and food processing took place in this room.

The parlour

Across the entry passage to the west of the kitchen/brew-house was a room that may have been a parlour. This room, which may have afforded greater comfort and privacy than the hall, would have been used as a reception room for the receiving of guests prior to their being shown into the main hall. Pantin noted that often 'the ground floor room at the service end of the hall was used as the parlour … where space across the rest of the house was at a premium' (Pantin, 1962–63: 205). No archaeological evidence was recovered to confirm this hypothesis.

Figure 2.20 Close-up photograph showing the stone and cobble surfaces in the kitchen/brew-house. These platforms may have supported vats or cauldrons, and in this picture are surrounded by brickwork constructed by Halliwell-Phillipps in the 1860s.

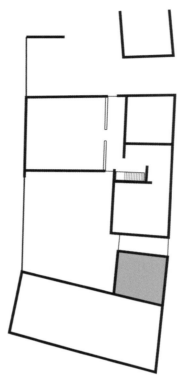

Figure 2.21 Schematic guidance plan 9, showing the location of a possible parlour.

Rear entrance, courtyard and outbuildings

The remains of a compacted floor surface were identified outside the eastern end of the main buildings, which suggests that a rear courtyard was present (layer 4; Figure 2.2). Several examples of trampled pottery sherds dating to the early sixteenth century were recovered from within this surface. The presence of a large pit (pit 15; Figure 2.2) in this area dating to the late fifteenth century confirms that it is highly likely that the area was open, with no standing buildings. There was tentative evidence that there were further buildings towards the east of the house running down Chapel Lane (F12 and F13; Figure 2.2). Foundations were identified in this area during the nineteenth-century archaeological investigations by Halliwell-Phillipps (see Chapter 7). Barns and stables would be expected at a house such as New Place, and it is likely that these outbuildings functioned as such. It is also highly likely that a large entrance would have been present leading to the courtyard and buildings from

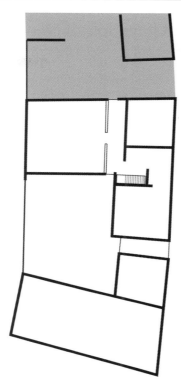

Figure 2.22 Schematic guidance plan 10, showing the location of the rear entrance and courtyard

Chapel Lane, as well as to gain access to the hall screens-passage on the eastern side of the hall building.

The backplots (gardens)

The backplot was often used for the accumulation of middens, rubbish disposal, industrial and domestic processes, and cess pits (Figure 2.2). A small excavation was carried out in the backplot area to identify evidence of these activities and processes. Archaeologically, there was increased activity in the backplots in this period, which coincided with the construction of New Place. Several features and layers were identified, including pits of varying sizes. Part of the backplot is likely to have been given over to gardens. The majority of the plants grown would have provided food and medicine. Vegetables, fruits, herbs and cereals would all have been grown. In households of higher status, gardens also provided space for entertainment, pleasure and relaxation (Steane, 1985: 214).

The construction materials of New Place

Periodic repairs or complete rebuilding appear to have been cyclical events, often undertaken on several houses simultaneously or over a short period of time. In the medieval period building materials were usually locally sourced. Within Stratford-upon-Avon, the overwhelming majority of the buildings were timber-framed (usually oak, which was easily transportable and plentiful in the nearby Forest of Arden). The other main building material was stone: durable, visually impressive and costly. Stone was often only used sparingly for architectural features such as fireplaces, doorways and window mouldings. The stone used was quarried locally and consisted of Arden and Warwickshire sandstones, blue Lias limestones from the local quarries of Wilmcote and Binton, and white Lias limestone from Moreton Morrell. Cotswold limestone was used only in the finest properties.

Hugh Clopton's New Place is known to have been built of brick and timber, and it is assumed that brick was used to infill the timber framing (nogging) and for various architectural details (for example chimneys and fire surrounds) rather than for significant structural elements. The filling of timber framing with brick was in use by the mid-fifteenth century and the panels usually formed simple patterns by containing bricks laid horizontally, diagonally or in a herringbone pattern (see Figure 2.3). Throughout the Tudor period bricks were frequently used as a building material, and this brick infill method continued into the seventeenth century (Ward, 2008: 63). It is highly likely that Clopton became aware of this building technique, in particular the use of brick, whilst he was Lord Mayor of London, and brought this taste back to Stratford. There is evidence that from the beginning of the fifteenth century, the use of bricks increased in the southeast of England, beginning in London, gradually moving out to the periphery and ultimately across the country (Schofield, 1991: 21–2). In Stratford, it became a more common practice to construct brick walls and tiled roofs after the devastating fires of the sixteenth and seventeenth centuries (1594, 1595, 1614 and 1641), which had caused so much damage to the timber frames and thatched roofs (Bearman, 1997: xvii). It is important to note, however, that, when New Place was built, the use of brick was still mostly associated with high-status buildings of the elite and did not really become fashionable with the merchant class until the early sixteenth century.

Evidence of construction materials, such as roofing, floors and window glass, was recovered. It is likely that materials from the earlier property on the site were reused by Hugh Clopton: that former building, too, was of high status. A quantity of fragmentary, rectangular Malvern Chase ceramic nibbed peg tiles were identified and it is likely that the roof of New Place was given a very distinctive appearance from the use of olive-green-glazed and decorative ridge tiles (Plate 8) at the apex. Examples of coxcomb crestings (Plate 9), which had been cut using a knife before firing (a type associated with the later medieval period) were also recovered (Steane, 1985: 199). Such crestings would probably have remained during Shakespeare's occupancy.

Several fragments of flagstone flooring were recovered from across the site, although none were found *in situ*. It is likely that these flagstones were reserved for the high-status elements of the building, such as the hall, with other types of flooring (timber or beaten earth and rushes) used elsewhere. Smaller stone floor tiles were found across the site at various stratigraphic levels, which confirms that these were also used in the later buildings on the site. Fragments of glazed floor-tiles suggest that New Place would have had at least one high-status tiled floor. The majority of the other flooring was probably covered with rushes or 'thresh', which soaked up spillages and could be easily replaced when soiled.

With the exception of the large bay window in the open hall, the majority of the windows are likely to have been relatively small openings framed with either stone or timber and divided into lights by the use of mullions. Shutters attached to the windows would have provided security and draught protection. Glazing was unusual within these lights at this period; however, some small fragments of decorated window glass recovered from layers attributed to this period confirm the assumption that this property was of high status. These may have come from large, oriel windows, which were typical of larger high-status houses of the period; these sometimes took up an entire floor or even extended from the ground floor to the roof line (for example Gainsborough Old Hall in Lincolnshire, and the Commandery in Worcester). As glass was an extremely expensive commodity in the fifteenth century, linen coated with sheep fat and wax could be used as an alternative. During bad weather these would have been supplemented with wooden shutters.

The artefacts

Apart from these building materials, the majority of the artefacts recovered were fragments of pottery. Pottery is extremely useful as it can be used to date the features and deposits that it resides in. Unsurprisingly, it indicated high-status occupation, with examples of Tudor Green and Cistercian tablewares, as well as more specialised cooking equipment such as chafing dishes (Plate 10) and dripping trays (Rátkai, 2011). However, there were no obvious continental imports, which seems unusual for a prestigious, urban building in the West Midlands. One of the chief suppliers was the Malvernian industry (producing what is sometimes known as Malvern Chase ware), which was in operation from *c.* 1350/75 to 1600. Late medieval oxidised wares represent a second major group of ceramics recovered. Although sourced from numerous locations, several sherds share characteristics with pottery produced at Wednesbury in the Black Country. Wednesbury products are known to have been widely traded. Blackware and yellowware ceramics, which date from at least the final quarter of the sixteenth century, were poorly represented. Fragments of Cistercian ware (dating from *c.* 1480 to 1550/75) were sparse within the ceramic assemblage, which again is unusual for a prosperous urban site of this period. One explanation is that Tudor Green ceramics may have retained their popularity within this household, which kept down the numbers of Cistercian ware vessels brought in. Although Tudor Green is known to have been copied by potters in the West Midlands, the sherds from New Place appear to have been the genuine article originating in Surrey or Hampshire. Therefore, the presence of true Tudor Green ware may be a direct result of Hugh Clopton's intimate associations with London (Rátkai, 2011).

Two small, unique artefacts were recovered from the excavation work. The first was a curved fragment of worked bone with a shallow groove carved on the inner circumference, thought to be part of a spectacle frame (Figure 2.23). Dated examples of bone spectacle frames in Britain date from the early fifteenth to the seventeeth century and they are also mentioned in the inventory of personal effects of the Bishop of Exeter on his death in 1326 (Hingeston-Randolph, 1892: 525). A pair of spectacles of very similar dimensions to the fragment recovered was found at Trig Lane, London in a context dating to *c.* 1440 (Rhodes, 1982). The frame is likely to have held a convex lens for use by a long-sighted person engaged in close-up work. Contemporary images use spectacles to give a scholarly air, as they would have been mainly used by literate males such as merchants, illuminators and lawyers. A bone die was recovered of a type dated from the thirteenth to fifteenth centuries (Plate 11).

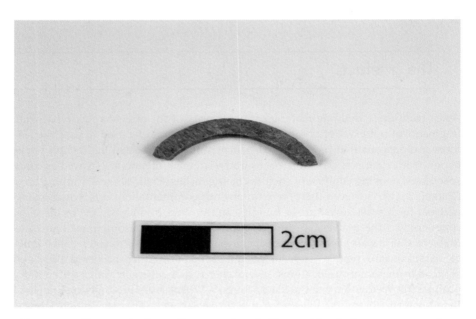

Figure 2.23 Photograph of a small section of worked bone with a shallow groove carved on the inner circumference, thought to be part of a spectacle frame. Dated examples of bone spectacle frames in Britain date from the early fifteenth to the seventeenth century.

Comparable dwellings in and around Stratford-upon-Avon

Only three domestic buildings that date from the late fifteenth century remain in a condition close to their original form. These are the White Swan and Mason's Court (both in Rother Street), and what became the Falcon, opposite New Place, on Chapel Street (Figure 2.24). Each of these buildings was differently arranged from

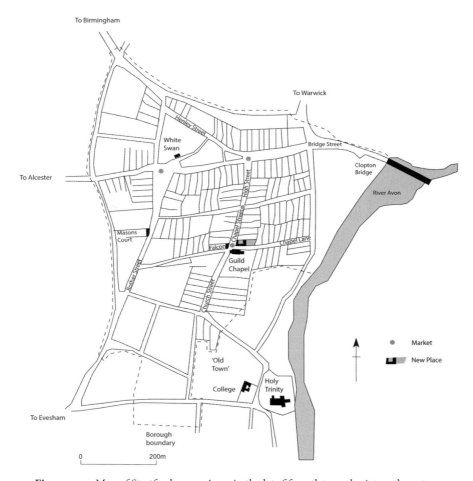

Figure 2.24 Map of Stratford-upon-Avon in the late fifteenth to early sixteenth century, showing buildings mentioned in the text including Mason's Court, the Falcon, the White Swan, Holy Trinity, the Guild Chapel, the College, and of course Clopton's New Place. Corn Street and Walkers Street/Dead Lane have changed to become Chapel Street and Chapel Lane respectively.

New Place, being of a lesser status. Their halls were aligned parallel to the street, along the frontage, but their general appearance provides an idea of how New Place may have looked.

Extant and excavated examples of comparable medieval courtyard houses can be found further afield. Hugh Clopton is likely to have encountered this type of building during his time living and working in London and travelling across England. The limitations of the plot sizes meant that this 'courtyard' plan did not follow a predetermined pattern, but made best use of the available space. Usually, the house's hall lay parallel to the street towards the rear of the courtyard, very often behind shops located along the frontage. The courtyard was enclosed by a further range (or ranges). These courtyard houses exemplify the 'parallel' house form as defined by architectural historians such as Pantin (1962–63), Faulkner (1967) and Schofield (1991).

The late-fourteenth-to-fifteenth-century examples of Marshall's Inn (Oxford), Bucklersbury House (London), Strangers' Hall (Norwich), Courtenay House (Exeter), Suckling's House (Norwich) and The Nag's Head Inn (Shrewsbury) are all notable specimens of the courtyard house form (Pantin, 1962–63: 223–8). In several of these cases, there are many similarities to the New Place ground plan, which supports and confirms the archaeological evidence (Figure 2.25). Other houses that share similarities of architectural form, layout and date, but that are not courtyard houses, are Gainsborough Old Hall in Lincolnshire (c. 1480) and Hams Barton in Devon (Figures 2.26 and 2.27), also constructed in the late fifteenth century.

The Commandery in Worcestershire, primarily constructed between 1468 and 1473, bears careful comparison with New Place (Figure 2.28). This building is traditionally believed to have been founded in the early eleventh century as a hospital by Saint Wulfstan, but the first documentary evidence dates from the thirteenth century. The majority of the surviving timber-framed buildings date from the later fifteenth century, probably around 1468–73, within a decade of the construction of New Place. The buildings are centred on the great hall, which is architecturally significant in both size and detail. The hall has a timber-framed solar and service ranges at opposing ends. The service range is accessed through a timber spere screen and the cross passage at the lower end of the hall and has a protruding oriel window on its long elevation. The hall is spanned by a large hammer-beam roof that uses arch braces (Plate 6). There have been many alterations in the following centuries, including, within the great hall, the creation of a gallery above the spere and cross passage, and the insertion of a staircase leading to the upper floor (Arnold et al., 2006: 1).

The sixteenth-century Lord Leycester Hospital in Warwick and nearby thirteenth-century Baddesley Clinton Hall are two further, local examples of houses built around a courtyard. These, however, cannot be directly compared to New Place because of differences in construction date, form, status and function.

Figure 2.25 Illustration of the ground-floor schematic of New Place in comparison with three other examples of courtyard house plans: Suckling's House, Strangers' Hall and Courtenay House. Each shows similarities in terms of the presence of a central courtyard, a hall and service rooms.

Figure 2.26 Photograph of Gainsborough Old Hall in Lincolnshire. Like New Place, this house was built around 1480 and shares many similar features, including stone and brick plinth foundation, timber framing, and a full-height bay window.

After Hugh Clopton

Within sixty years of the death of Hugh Clopton, the fortunes of New Place changed. Despite being described as a 'praty House of Bricke and Tymbre' by Leyland in 1540 (Toulmin-Smith, 1910. Vol. II: 47–50), just nine years later, upon the death of a subsequent tenant (leaseholder), Dr Thomas Bentley, New Place was described as being 'in great ruin and decay and unrepaired' (Schoenbaum, 1987: 232). It seems likely that the explanation for this sudden change is the delay between Leyland's actually seeing New Place and the publication of his eyewitness account – Leyland may have seen the house some years before 1540. New Place was Hugh Clopton's grand vision; it is doubtful that his house ever looked as 'grete' as it did at the turn of the fifteenth century.

Figure 2.27 Illustration showing the close resemblance of the hall and service rooms of New Place and Hams Barton in Devon. Both were constructed at the end of the fifteenth century.

Figure 2.28 Photograph of the Commandery in Worcester. Built between 1468 and 1473, this house has many similar features to New Place, including a hall, service rooms and a bay window.

References

Arnold, A., R. Howard and C. Litton (2006). *The Commandery, Worcester: Tree-Ring Analysis of Timbers*, English Heritage Research Department Report Series 71/2006 ([Portsmouth:] English Heritage).

Bearman, R., ed. (1997). *The History of an English Borough: Stratford-upon-Avon 1196–1996* (Stroud: Sutton Publishing and the Shakespeare Birthplace Trust).

Bearman, R. (2007). *Stratford-upon-Avon: A History of Its Streets and Buildings* (Stratford: Stratford-upon-Avon Society).

Brunskill, R. W. (1971). *Illustrated Handbook of Vernacular Architecture* (London: Faber and Faber).

Dyer, C. (1997). 'Medieval Stratford: A Successful Small Town', in R. Bearman (ed.), *The History of an English Borough: Stratford-upon-Avon 1196–1996* (Stroud: Sutton Publishing and the Shakespeare Birthplace Trust), 43–61.

Egan, G. (1994). *Lead Cloth Seal and Related Items in the British Museum*, British Museum Occasional Paper 93 (London: British Museum).

Emery, A. (2012). *Discovering Medieval Houses* (Oxford: Shire Publications).

Faulkner, P. A. (1967). 'Medieval Undercrofts and Town Houses', in P. Faulkner (ed.), *Medieval Undercrofts and Town Houses* (London: The Archaeological Journal), 118–33.

Giles, K., A. Masinton and G. Arnott (2012). *Visualising the Guild Chapel, Stratford-upon-Avon: Digital Models as Research Tools in Buildings Archaeology*, http://intarch.ac.uk/journal/issue32/1/toc.html (accessed 2 June 2015).

Halliwell, J. O. (1864). *An Historical Account of the New Place, Stratford-upon-Avon, the Last Residence of Shakespeare* (London: J. E. Adlard).

Halliwell-Phillipps, J. O. ([1887] 2013). *A Calendar of the Shakespearean Rarities, 1887* (London: Forgotten Books).

Hingeston-Randolph, F. C., ed. (1892). *The Register of Walter de Stapeldon, Bishop of Exeter, AD 1307–1326* (London and Exeter: G. Bell and Sons).

Leech, R. (2014). *The Town House in Medieval and Early Modern Bristol*, Vol. I (London: English Heritage).

Mitchell, W. (forthcoming). *Nash's House, Stratford-upon-Avon: Archaeological Excavations 2015* (Centre of Archaeology, University of Staffordshire).

Pantin, W. A. (1962–63). 'Medieval English Town-House Plans', *Medieval Archaeology*, 6–7: 202–39.

Pearson, S. (2009). 'Medieval Houses in English Towns: Form and Location', *Vernacular Architecture*, 40: 1–22.

Quiney, A. (2003). *Town Houses of Medieval Britain* (New Haven and London: Yale University Press).

Rátkai, S. (2011). Pottery report for Dig for Shakespeare. Unpublished report.

Rhodes, M. (1982). 'A Pair of Fifteenth-Century Spectacle Frames from the City of London', *The Antiquaries' Journal*, 62.1: 57–73.

Schoenbaum, S. ([1977] 1987). *William Shakespeare: A Documentary Life* (Oxford: Oxford University Press).

Schofield, J. (1991). 'The Construction of Medieval and Tudor Houses in London', *Construction History*, 7: 3–28.

Schofield, J. and A. Vince (2003). *Medieval Towns: The Archaeology of British Towns in Their European Setting* (London and New York: Continuum).

Slim, A. (2010). *The Tudor Housewife* (Stroud: History Press).

Steane, J. M. (1985). *The Archaeology of Medieval England and Wales* (London and Sydney: Croom Helm).

Stratford-on-Avon Preservation Society (1924). *Clopton Bridge, Stratford upon Avon, Shakespearean and Other Associations* (London: publisher unknown).

Toulmin-Smith, L., ed. (1910). *The Itinerary of John Leland: In or about the Years 1535–1543* (London: G. Bell and Sons).

Ward, G. W., ed. (2008). *The Grove Encyclopedia of Materials and Techniques in Art* (Oxford: Oxford University Press).

Wood, M. (1990). *The English Mediaeval House* (London: Bracken Books).

Woolgar, C. M. (1999). *The Great Household in Medieval England* (New Haven and London: Yale University Press).

3

Shakespeare and Stratford-upon-Avon, 1564–96

Paul Edmondson

Stratford-upon-Avon helped to form William Shakespeare. It is where he was born, brought up and educated, and lived his early adult life into marriage and father-hood. His family, friends and long-standing neighbours knew him differently from the way his London colleagues and friends did. It was in Stratford-upon-Avon that Shakespeare made his most substantial financial investments: freehold property, land and a half share of some of the annual tithes. But, from the early 1590s, something of London, and people's cultural perceptions of it, would have resonated from him while he was at home, when he met friends and acquaintances; a sense of London was probably in people's minds when he was talked about by the neighbours. Although the connections at court that Shakespeare enjoyed through his theatrical work were extraordinary among his Stratford-upon-Avon contemporaries, it is not necessarily the case that the town itself held them, or indeed Shakespeare, in high regard. Ever since Stratford had been refounded as a borough in 1553 (by Edward VI's royal char-ter just eight days before he died), an increasingly shrill puritan voice had begun to dominate its administration. Although there are no references to Shakespeare's the-atrical or literary professions in the Stratford-upon-Avon records, both his writing and his theatrical work are referred to on his memorial bust in Holy Trinity Church. Whilst the town was crucial to Shakespeare's sense of self and livelihood, its religious and cultural climate no doubt made its presence uncomfortably apparent to him, and in contradiction to his art. For all that Shakespeare invested in Stratford-upon-Avon, both personally and financially, he would have appreciated it very differently from London which, by contrast, was a place of expansive, inclusive and creative freedoms. Stratford-upon-Avon gave Shakespeare a deeply rooted love of family, loyal neigh-bours and friends, and although he came to enjoy a prominent social standing there, he probably had little or no time at all for its puritanical side. This chapter considers the town that Shakespeare grew up in – what it was like, who his neighbours were, his schooling, the town's administrative and religious atmospheres and links with London – in relation to Shakespeare's developing reputation.

The Shakespeares of Henley Street

From 1564 to 1596, Shakespeare was identified primarily with one house: his parents' home, a substantial family dwelling on Henley Street. Growing up, he would have come to know other children, played with them, encountered discipline from his parents and noticed the significant arrivals of five siblings: Gilbert (1566–1612); Joan (1569–1646); Anne (1571–79); Richard (1574–1613; and the youngest, Edmund (1580–1607). From 1569, Shakespeare would have been old enough to attend the baptisms of four of his siblings in the same font in which he had been christened when he was around three days old in the large parish church of the Holy and Undivided Trinity on 26 April 1564 (parish registers recording births, marriages and burials were instituted by a mandate of 1538, and in 1597 it was ordained that existing registers should be copied into new parchment volumes from at least the start of Elizabeth I's reign).

He came quickly to learn that life was perilous and that any children were lucky to survive. His parents John (before 1530–1601) and Mary Shakespeare (died 1608) would have told him about the two sisters he never knew, and who died in infancy: Joan (born 1558; the burial records do not survive, the records probably being disrupted during a time of major plague epidemic) and Margaret (christened 2 December 1562; buried 30 April 1563). And his parents probably told him about the great plague epidemic that had hit the town in the year he was born. The parish register – copied out and tidied up retrospectively in 1600 – starts a stretch of entries from 11 July 1564 with the burial of one Oliver Gunne and the marginal gloss 'hic incepit pestis' ('here began the plague'). There were 254 interments overall that year, whereas the average number for the previous six years had been only thirty-eight (Jones, 1996: xviii). Four of Roger Greene's children died of the plague, just three doors away from the Shakespeares. Infant mortality was high even without epidemics: 32 per cent of children died before they were sixteen; 11 per cent before they were a month old, and 9 per cent within a week of their birth (Jones, 1996: 93. Unless otherwise stated, all statistics cited from Jeanne Jones's book should be understood to refer to the sixty-year period from 1570 to 1630.) When he was fifteen, Shakespeare may have attended the funeral of his seven-and-a-half-year-old sister, Anne. John Shakespeare paid 8d to have the bell of the Guild Chapel tolled and for a ceremonial pall (probably black velvet) to be placed over her small bier.

The house on Henley Street was Shakespeare's portal on to the town and into the wider world of the imagination. Much ink has been spilt on whether Shakespeare's parents were literate or not. On the surviving documents, we find that they have signed using their mark, rather than a signature, reminding us of the difference between the ability to read and the craft of penmanship. There are 163 signatures and 126 marks on the town's surviving legal documents, including 25 signatures by women (Jones, 1996: 109). People who could absorb printed texts through private reading or oral transmission were often not able to write more than a shopping-list: not writers, but active in literacy, and perhaps more so than is often supposed. Mary Shakespeare – the youngest child of the prosperous Robert Arden (died 1556) – had inherited most of her father's estate – 'Willmecote cawlide Asbyes' – and was nominated as one of his two executors. Arden had settled his Snitterfield estate on three other daughters in 1550 (Eccles, 1961: 17). She was obviously intelligent, efficient and hugely competent. Like John she had had no extended formal education, but, growing up, both of them are likely to have been taught their alphabet, numbers, the Ten Commandments and the Lord's Prayer at a petty school, or perhaps they learned these basic lessons later as adults. John Shakespeare's several, prominent public offices on the corporation would have required an ability to read.

The population of Stratford-upon-Avon was 2,200 in 1595 (Jones, 1996: xviii) and all adults had to go to church regularly on a Sunday or face a fine. John Shakespeare, who was made bailiff (which after the Restoration became the office of mayor) at Michaelmas (29 September) 1568, would be met each Sunday by the town's beadle, who would come to the door of the Henley Street home and lead the family to church to take their place at the front in the mayoral pew. Most of the rest of the congregation, except perhaps for a few prominent families and householders, and the corporation, would have stood, since pews only became more generally used in James I's time. Shakespeare's father wore his red, civic gown and alderman's ring (Weis, 2007: 16), and perhaps the young William was occasionally allowed to try these on at home, maybe even acting out his father's hopes that his eldest child would be bailiff someday, too.

The family home was the place for storytelling and singing, especially during the long, dark evenings. A middle-class home, like the Shakespeares', may have had a modest shelf of books – a Bible, a prayerbook, and some chapbooks (cheap editions of folk-tales and romances). The oral tradition still dominated, and many stories were told around the hearth, often about legendary figures such as Robin Hood, King Arthur, Guy of Warwick, Gamelyn and Bevis of Hampton. Helen Cooper has demonstrated that casual references to these kinds of stories in Shakespeare's works suggest that they were part of what helped to form his earliest literary imagination (Cooper, 2010: 167–8).

Like most rural towns, Stratford-upon-Avon was full of trees: willows, ashes and around 1,000 elms. The streets were shady and, in some parts, it seemed as though the houses had been built in woodland clearings or among copses. To a casual visitor the trees were part of the town's natural charm; to the locals they were a cherished part of its character. The trees gave the town an atmosphere all of its own. For a young boy with a hyperactive imagination, growing up in Stratford-upon-Avon probably felt like being part of a magical forest (imagine the excitement of the coming spring, the deep leaves in the autumn). The birdsong certainly would be more emphatic than in London, part of the rural feeling that years later would, for Shakespeare the commuter, enhance the contrast between Stratford-upon-Avon and London. But the elms (along with the dividing passageways) helped to mark the boundaries between properties, too (Weis, 2007: 39). The trees also played a vital part in the town's economy.

Figure 3.1 Inspiring the young Shakespeare's imagination, this detail from a mid-sixteenth-century wall-painting in the White Swan illustrates the story of Tobias and the archangel Raphael from the Book of Tobit. Here Tobit and his wife, Anna, say goodbye to Tobias, their son. The painting has been dated to 1555–65 and shows us how wealthy people dressed around the time of Shakespeare's birth.

From time to time, surveys led to some of them being felled for timber, for example during the tenure as bailiff in 1582 of Adrian Quiney, who was the Shakespeares' neighbour from across the street.

What was Stratford-upon-Avon like?

Stratford-upon-Avon's layout and jurisdiction had been determined in 1196, and borough authority did not technically extend into Old Town – the vicinity around Holy Trinity Church and the College, the site of the Anglo-Saxon settlement and the first known church from the ninth century. The twelfth-century grid system (three streets crossed by three streets) remains unchanged to the present day. Bridge Street, Wood Street and Greenhill Street follow the route of the old Roman road. Commerce and traffic to the town increased significantly from 1492 once Hugh Clopton had built the bridge across the Avon. The toll-gate at the bottom of Bridge Street provided a useful source of revenue to the borough.

Strafford Bridge 1803

Figure 3.2 The Clopton Bridge with its fourteen arches, paid for in 1492 by Hugh Clopton, the original builder and owner of New Place.

Figure 3.3 The ten almshouses. Nine of the current buildings are thought to date from the early sixteenth century. It has been proposed that the tenth, which adjoins the Guildhall, was, from 1427, a school-house, with the classroom downstairs and the master's chamber above (Giles and Clark, 2012: 155–6).

The town was divided administratively into six wards: Bridge Street, High Street, Chapel Street, Sheep Street, Wood Street and Henley Street, following on from the model of the Medieval Guild of the Holy Cross (founded in the late thirteenth century and dissolved in 1547). The significant change came in 1553 with a charter that defined a new corporation for the borough, made up of fourteen officers (aldermen), who elected a bailiff and fourteen burgesses. The 1553 charter granted the corporation the estates of the Guild of the Holy Cross in order to supply the necessary revenue to support the school and the almshouses (which had previously been run by the Guild). The corporations was also granted a portion of the annual tithes to pay the vicar.

Together the corporation was responsible for: the Guild Chapel (which dates from 1269, and used to have a hospital attached), the Guildhall next door (where the corporation met, and where some of the visiting acting troupes performed), the Guild estates (the freeholds and land that were rented out), the Clopton Bridge, the almshouses (the current ones date from the sixteenth century) and the King's New School (refounded in 1553, though there is evidence of there having been a school-room from 1427 (Bearman, 1988: 24)).

The corporation was also responsible for the weekly market (held on Thursdays), two annual fairs, and any other feasts and pageants. The vicar and schoolmaster were paid for by the borough: £20 a year for the new master, William Smart, in 1555. This sum is often used to give us a sense of what people were earning at the time. Smart's salary included his having to pay out a pension of 10 marks a year for the former master (who died in 1558), and, after that, allocating £4 a year (from the £20) for an usher, or teaching assistant, and any school repairs (Eccles, 1961: 54). The vicar and the schoolmaster were appointed by the Lord of the Manor, who also ratified the appointment of bailiff.

Figure 3.4 The Upper (or Over) Guildhall, likely to have been used as part of 'the King's new school', established by Edward VI in 1553. The desks and master's chair are eighteenth-century. Visiting acting troupes regularly performed in the Guildhall from 1568 to 1597.

Bridge Street was often the first that a visitor to the town encountered, with Middle Row (old market stalls that had become houses and businesses) running down its centre. Bridge Street itself had four inns – the Swan, the Bear, the Crown and the Angel – but the town had around thirty ale-houses in all (Fogg, 2014: 22). Two streams ran through the town, one along Meer Street and the other opposite New Place, down Chapel Lane, also known as Dead Lane (on account of the masses for the dead in the Guild Chapel) or Walkers Street (for the fullers who ran the mill at the bottom end near the river, last referred to in 1604 (Bearman, 1988: 18)). The High Cross, with its clock and bell, stood at the top of the intersection of Bridge Street, Wood Street and High Street, and, from 1614, a whipping-post was erected there for the public punishment of rogues and vagabonds.

A butter and cheese market was held at the other side of the town, marked by White Cross, which stood outside the Guild Chapel and New Place 'from about 1275 to at least 1608' (Bearman, 1988: 20). On the corner of High Street and Bridge Street stood a dwelling known as the Cage (from 1470), possibly because there used to be an actual cage there, attached to the side of the building for the temporary holding of petty criminals (Bearman, 1988: 39). The Cage, acquired by the Quiney family in 1615, would, one year later, become the home of Shakespeare's daughter Judith and

The Market Cross.
S.E.

Figure 3.5 The Market Cross, or High Cross, where the weekly market was held every Thursday. The base of the cross survives and is usually on exhibition at the Shakespeare Centre.

her husband, Thomas Quiney. They were married for forty-six years, and Quiney's last recorded occupancy of the Cage is 1637.

Arden Street and Back Lane (now Grove Road) marked part of the twelfth-century boundary, and Henley Street, a departure from the grid system, followed the route to Henley-in-Arden. Windsor Street (meaning a 'pasture or meadow "at the edge"' of town (Bearman, 1988: 59)), at the top end of Henley Street, led into a meadow, a natural playground for the town's children. Evoking the smells of Stratford-upon-Avon at the time of Shakespeare, we might imagine that 'Tudor Stratford was an Augean stable, with the stench of animal excreta mingling with the refuse of trade and markets, exacerbated by badly-paved streets and open ditches' (Fogg, 2014: 22). There were at least five muck-heaps (Shakespeare Centre Library and Archive, MA, vi, 256), including one towards the top end of Henley Street. John Shakespeare was fined for having an illegal muck-heap outside his Henley Street house in 1552.

If you were to walk through the town to look at the buildings that survive from Shakespeare's time, then in many instances you would have to imagine away the later or modern frontages and think that you see half-timbered buildings. If you can do that, then in your mind's eye you will see some of what Shakespeare himself would have seen (Plate 12). Some of the original frontages survive, including, for example, 26 High Street, now known as Harvard House (built in 1596 by the prosperous butcher Thomas Rogers); the Falcon Hotel (dating from around 1500), which stands opposite New Place on Chapel Street and was, in Shakespeare's time, the home of the Walford family (a third storey was added to it between 1655 and 1661 when it became an inn (Bearman, 1988: 20)); and the splendid Shrieve's House at 40 Sheep Street, which dates from the early 1600s.

Figure 3.6 Shakespeare's corner of Stratford-upon-Avon showing the Guild Chapel and the Falcon (where his neighbours the Walfords lived and which had only two storeys in Shakespeare's time).

Religion, morality and theatre in Stratford-upon-Avon

From 1547, the first year of Edward VI's reign, images in churches all over the land had started to be defaced, removed or painted over, and all chantries and colleges were closed. They were seen as idolatrous expressions within a religion that was reforming itself in opposition to the influence of the Pope. The Guild Chapel, where, for more than 200 years, masses had regularly been said for members of the Guild – local tradesmen, their wives, children, gentry members from afar – and the College, founded in 1353, were no exception. The College could trace its beginnings back to John de Stratford, a local who became Archbishop of Canterbury (from 1333 to 1348). He left provision in his will for a chantry in Holy Trinity Church of five priests (including a warden and subwarden) to say masses for his soul. His nephew, Ralph de Stratford (Bishop of London from 1340 to 1354), built the College: a large, stone mansion, for them to live in. The Guild Chapel was probably 'simply locked up before being granted to the corporation, under its 1553 charter, as a piece of real estate – "all that former chapel … and all the lead on the same and bell tower and all the bells"' (Bearman, 2007: 97). We do not know how much dismantling took place; masses were said there from time to time during the five years that Mary I was restoring Roman Catholicism as the State religion (Bearman, 2007: 97). The bell survived and was repaired and rehung during Adrian Quiney's (Richard's father) time as bailiff in 1582. It would ring for funerals, to remind people to cover their fires at night (the curfew) and during times of fire. It was clearly much used, and was recast in 1591, repaired in 1615, and recast again in 1633 (Fripp, 1928: 46). Five bells were installed in Holy Trinity Church tower in 1558, probably to mark Elizabeth's accession to the throne. They, too, echoed with religious reform, having been recycled from Hailes Abbey (25 miles away). When thinking about what Holy Trinity Church looked like during Shakespeare's lifetime, it is important to imagine it without its distinctive spire, which was not added until 1763, replacing a shorter, wooden one.

Elizabeth I's religious settlement, especially the Act of Uniformity of Common Prayer and Service in the Church, and the Administration of the Sacraments of 1559 (for which none of her bishops voted, and which was passed by just three votes) required only outward conformity. A royal injunction, early in Elizabeth I's reign, also led to the destruction of images and iconography in parish churches. Stratford-upon-Avon's Roman Catholic pageant of St George, which had taken place every Ascension Day for centuries, was abolished in 1562 (Fogg, 2014: 20), and two years later, in January 1564, during his third term of office as chamberlain, John Shakespeare accounted a payment for the 'defasying [of] ymages in ye Chappell'. It cost the borough 2s for the lime pails and brushes. 'Defasying' seems to have meant 'covering', rather than 'scratching out the faces of'. By 10 January 1564, Shakespeare's father had supervised the whitewashing over of the images. Although it is not known which were covered over, it is most likely to have been all of them, which included, for example, St George and the dragon and the murder

Figure 3.7 The Collegiate Church of the Undivided Holy Trinity, by Joseph Greene, mid-eighteenth-century, showing the charnel house (far left), and the small, lead-covered, wooden spire that Shakespeare would have known. It was replaced by the current one, made from Warwick stone, in 1763.

of Thomas Becket on the west side of the nave, and the pictures of St Helen and the finding of the cross (after which the chapel and the Guild took their name) in the chancel area.

It has been suggested that the image of the Last Judgement on the chancel arch may not have been covered over in 1564, since such representations were only obliterated (or partly so) if they showed the intercession of saints (which was offensive to the puritans' spirituality (Lascelles, 1973: 74–5)). But the Last Judgement (or Doom) in the Guild Chapel did represent Mary as Queen of Heaven, as well as Mary and John at the foot of the cross, so was almost certainly covered over at the same time. Either the task overseen by Shakespeare's father was not done very thoroughly though, or else not all of the images were removed or hidden effectively, because in 1635 the puritan vicar, Thomas Wilson, seems to have been using at least part of the chapel as one of his own domestic spaces:

> he profaned the Chapple by sufferinge his children to playe at bale and other sports therein, and his servauntes to hange clothes to drye in it and his pigges and poultrie to lye and feed in it, and also his dogge to lye in it, and the pictures therein to be defaced, and the windowes broken. (Shakespeare Centre Library and Archive, ER1/1/97, fol. 124 (5 June 1635))

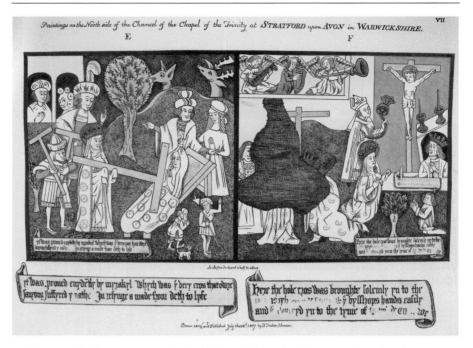

Figure 3.8 Wall-paintings in the Guild Chapel, drawn by Thomas Fisher when they were uncovered during restoration in 1804 (published in 1838). The Chapel of the Holy Cross took its name from the story of St Helen, depicted here. She was the mother of Emperor Constantine and located the site of Jesus's crucifixion in Jerusalem, where she found the true cross.

It seems likely that the chapel was divided up into different spaces and let out, which has led some scholars to speculate that the paintings in the chancel area were not all covered over at the same time (Giles and Clark, 2012: 159 and 166), hence this reference to their being defaced eighty years after John Shakespeare oversaw the initial whitewashing. The present state of the wall-paintings is mainly due to their deterioration since they were uncovered in the early nineteenth century.

The last mention of Mary and the saints in a Stratford-upon-Avon will was that of John Jeffreys in 1566 (Bearman, 2007: 105). 'High' altars were removed from churches (downgrading the visible, spiritual authority of the priest) and replaced with ordinary, communion 'tables' or 'boards'. Colourful vestments were destroyed or sold, in favour of plain, black cassocks or robes. All of these changes helped to de-emphasise the visual and ensured that the spoken word was central to people's experience of and engagement with the worship. Similar kinds of destruction occurred at Holy Trinity Church, though the medieval mercy-seats, known as misericords, added by the College from the early-to-mid-1400s, survived. The weirdness of their black oak carvings – including a Saracen's head; a sphinx; a camel; a mermaid and merman; an ape looking into a jar of urine; and a shrewish woman grabbing her husband by the

Figure 3.9 The Last Judgement, or Doom, in the Guild Chapel, drawn by Thomas Fisher. This and probably all of the paintings were whitewashed over under the direction of John Shakespeare in January 1564. This wall-painting has been uncovered since 1928 and has badly deteriorated.

beard, beating him with a frying pan, and kicking him in the balls – no doubt played their part in the young Shakespeare's surreal, domestic and religious imagination.

The church was the main arbitrator of moral and social behaviour, and had its own court, which became known as the Bawdy Court. This was presided over by the vicar, and the records for 1590 to 1616 and from 1622 to 1624 survive. The court's purpose is summarized by its proceedings' first editor, E. R. C. Brinkworth:

> Who was guilty of 'adultery, whoredom, incest, drunkenness, swearing, ribaldry, usury' and any other 'uncleannes and wickedness of life?' Who was guilty of absence from church on Sundays and holy days or from Holy Communion at Easter, of rude and disorderly behaviour in church, of brawling in church (or in the court), of breaking the Sabbath and holy days, of blasphemy, of scandalmongering, of not contributing to the church rate, of bigamy or irregular marriage, of not proving wills or taking out administrations? Was the church in good repair and was it provided with the necessary books and goods and were these in a respectable condition? Were all schoolmasters, physicians, surgeons and midwives duly licensed by the church authorities? (Brinkworth, 1972: 13)

Punishments often involved acts of public penance: for example, being required to dress in a white sheet in church on Sundays or at the High Cross on a Thursday (market day), and having to confess your misdemeanour in explicit detail before the congregation as part of the Sunday service. Bartholomew Hathaway, Anne's brother, was sworn in as churchwarden on 13 April 1608 and several of Shakespeare's family members are mentioned in the court records (Brinkworth, 1972: 110). Shakespeare himself is not mentioned and, whilst the church and all it stood for were inextricably interwoven with everyone's lives, it is worth remembering not only that the Bawdy Court records are incomplete, but that they only include known cases of misbehaviour.

The main service every Sunday was Matins. Sermons tended to last for around an hour or more, which only implies that the congregation were excellent listeners. The pulpit was placed centrally before the chancel partition, and New Place had its own pew close to this on the south side; the bailiff's and corporation's pew was next the pew owned by the College on the north side (Fripp, 1928: 68). It was the theology surrounding the sacrament of what became known (through the Church of England's Book of Common Prayer) as Holy Communion that was the most divisive. Roman Catholics continued to adhere to the doctrine of transubstantiation (which teaches that the consecrating prayer performs a miracle whereby the bread and wine become the body and blood of Jesus), whereas Protestant teachings promoted the belief in a spiritual 'real presence' of Jesus, or that the bread and wine are only a symbolic act of memorialisation and special intention. The rubric of the 1559 Book of Common Prayer allowed Holy Communion to take place at the discretion of the clergy, but everyone in the parish had to 'communicate at the least three times in the year, of which Easter to be one' (Booty, 2005: 268).

Elizabeth I's Act of Uniformity stated that all people had to attend church every Sunday, or pay a 12d fine (Booty, 2005: 9–10). The offence of refusing to attend church (as opposed to simple non-attendance) was known as recusancy, and was not very prevalent in the town's records. The 1592 list includes forty-two names, ten of whom were 'obstinate recusants', and of these four fled the town before the Court could catch up with them (Bearman, 2007: 106). 'Church papists' would attend church but not receive the sacrament. These 'existed in large numbers though it is impossible to estimate their strength with any exactitude. Under Elizabeth, if church papists could individually satisfy their consciences all was well with them: they attended the services and so avoided the fines' (Brinkworth, 1972: 44). Sometimes people stayed away from church because it was where business transactions might take place (in the porch). John Shakespeare and eight other townsmen appeared on a list for not attending church one Sunday in the spring of 1592, 'for fear of processes [for debt]' (Schoenbaum, 1987: 41).

Shakespeare was six years old when, in 1570, Elizabeth I was excommunicated by Pope Pius V. From then on, she was politically vulnerable to Roman Catholic assassination attempts, which meant the implementation of harsher anti-Catholic laws; meanwhile, puritanism was on the rise. One response – presumably to Elizabeth's excommunication – made itself felt in the town the following year when, on Midsummer's Day in 1571, the Guild Chapel's 'idolatrous' medieval, stained-glass windows were smashed. A glazier was paid 23s 8d to smash the windows and to replace them with plain glass (Shapiro, 2005: 164).

But in spite of religious reform, or perhaps because of it, a cultural innovation occurred during John Shakespeare's year in office as bailiff (1568–69). He hosted the leading theatrical troupe of the day, the Queen's Men, as well as the more regionally connected Earl of Worcester's Men. Shakespeare was five years old, and this is the first recorded occasion that any professional actors had ever performed in the town. Theatre combined word and spectacle in a way that church worship no longer did. The rise of professional acting troupes was relatively new, and it looks as though the recognition of companies' reputations and talents is reflected in their respective fees. John Shakespeare authorised a payment of 9s for the Queen's Men but only 12d for the Earl of Worcester's Men (Mulryne, 2012: 200), which has even been interpreted as their being 'damned with faint praise', it being 'the lowest reward on record in the annals of the borough' (Fripp, 1928: 10). They did not return again until 1574 (when they were paid the greater but still unhandsome sum of 5s 8d).

Any professional troupe had to perform before the bailiff on civic property in order to be given a licence to perform anywhere else in the town. John Shakespeare, in being the first bailiff to have overseen this process, was enabling the town to participate in a developing cultural trend. Robert Willis (born 1564) wrote the following in a religious memoir and treatise called *Mount Tabor*, published in 1639:

> In the city of Gloucester, the manner is (as I think it is in other like corporations) that when players of interludes come to town, they first attend the mayor, to inform him what nobleman's servants they are, and so to get licence for their playing; and if the mayor like the actors, or would show respect to their lord and master, he appoints them to play their first play before himself, and the aldermen and common council of the city; and that is called the mayor's play, where every one that will comes in without money, the mayor giving the players a reward as he thinks fit, to show respect unto them. At such a play my father took me with him, and made me stand between his legs, as he sat on one of the benches, where we saw and heard very well. (Chambers, 1923: Vol. I, 333)

This account, from nearby Gloucester (which already had the office of mayor), is just one example of the kinds of theatrical performances that were happening across the provinces (for example in Abingdon, Barnstaple, Coventry, Maldon, Shrewsbury and York), part of a growing civic pride in a contemporary and popular form of entertainment that was steadily becoming more and more associated with London itself and the new theatres being erected there. As son of the bailiff, the young Shakespeare would probably have shared his family's place of honour at the front, and heard his father present the players to the audience. Seven years later, what is regarded as the first major, purpose-built public playhouse opened in London: the Theatre in Shoreditch.

Shakespeare at school

Above the Guildhall, where these performances took place, was the main teaching room of the King's New School. For Shakespeare, the place of education was thus closely related to the costumed activities of civic authority and theatrical productions. A free place at the grammar school was available to all of the town's boys, and from around the age of seven; but in real terms this probably meant mainly sons of burgesses. Presumably their parents allowed them to attend for as many years as they could do without them around the home and workplace. Girls were educated, too, but only to a primary level at petty school. Duncan Salkeld has traced the unfortunate and colourful case of Elizabeth Evans in the papers of Bridewell, the House of Correction in London. Evans, who was the daughter of a Stratford-upon-Avon cutler, became a prostitute in London, and was executed for forgery. One of the witnesses at her trial was Joyce Cowden, who said she had gone to school with her in Stratford-upon-Avon and had known her father (Salkeld, 2003: 60–1).

For the town's boys, there was on offer the demanding and disciplined Humanist, grammar-school curriculum, which drilled them mainly in Latin. Greek was studied through the New Testament. Like most schools of the time, its records do not survive, but based on evidence surviving from other schools, the days started from around 6.00 a.m. in summer, 7.00 a.m. in winter, and ended at dusk. The boys went home for the main family meal of the day (dinner), which was served early from around 11.00 a.m. It is probable that they had Thursdays and Saturday afternoons off. There were no formal school holidays, except for some of the religious festivals. The main textbook was William Lyly's *Short Introduction of Grammar* (1540) through which the boys were taught how to shape language for powerful effects by using a wide range of rhetorical devices, writ large across Shakespeare's works.

Figure 3.10 The fifteenth- or sixteenth-century school desk from the Stratford-upon-Avon borough collection from which the master in Shakespeare's time would have conducted his lessons. The boys themselves would have sat on forms (benches) in front of him. The desk is made mainly from elm wood, presumably sourced locally.

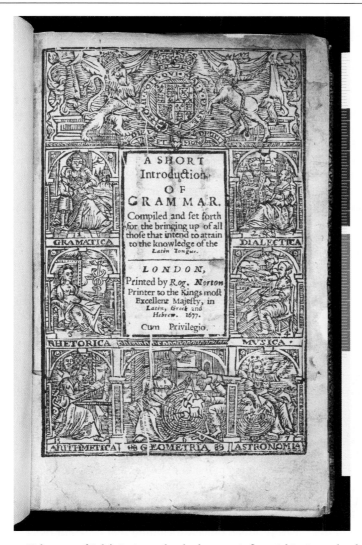

Figure 3.11 Title-page of Lyly's Latin textbook, the most influential Latin textbook during Shakespeare's time, with which he was intimately acquainted.

Other key writers included the Roman playwrights Terence and Plautus (whose play the *Menaechmi*, for example, Shakespeare was intimately acquainted with and used as a source for *The Comedy of Errors*, performed at Gray's Inn in 1594). Pupils were expected to speak in Latin while they were at school, in the playground and even at home. The curriculum encouraged them to perform extracts of classical works in their original languages. Education of this kind was part of the State's machinery to make sure, as one charter has it, that 'good literature and discipline might be diffused and propagated throughout all parts of our Kingdom, as wherein the best government and administration of affairs consists' (Bate, 2008: 81). The teaching of morality and the acquisition of linguistic power through pagan writers was not thought to conflict in any way with the established, State religion. The vicar John Bretchgirdle, who died in the year Shakespeare was born, bequeathed several classical texts to the school, 'including a Sallust, a Justin, Tully's Offices, a Horace, a Virgil, and copies of a favourite and characteristic volume, Tye's *Acts of the Apostles in English Metre for the Lute*' (Fripp, 1928: 34).

The young Shakespeare probably had two (or perhaps three) schoolmasters. The first was the Oxford graduate Simon Hunt (1571–75), who may have been the Simon Hunt who became a Jesuit priest and died in Rome in 1585, or (far more likely) 'the Simon Hunt of Stratford who died in or before 1598' (Eccles, 1961: 56). Another Oxford graduate, Thomas Jenkins, was schoolmaster from 1575 to 1579. From 1566 to 1572 he was a fellow of St John's College and had owned a lease on Chaucer's house in Woodstock. John Cottom followed him briefly (1579–81), and Shakespeare was fifteen when he arrived. After just two years, Cottam was asked to leave, or resigned: he was a Roman Catholic. His Jesuit brother, Thomas, was tortured on the rack and hanged, drawn and quartered with Edmund Campion in 1582.

Although not his exact contemporaries, Shakespeare's schoolfellows who became his lasting friends probably included John Combe (before 1561–1614); Richard Field (1561–1624); Richard Quiney (before 1577–1602); Hamnet Sadler (died 1624); July, Julius or Julyns Shaw (1571–1629); and Richard Tyler (1566–1636). Children were traditionally named after their godparents, a very important neighbourly and spiritual bond, and Hamnet Sadler and his wife Judith (died 1614) were very probably the godparents to Shakespeare's twins Hamnet (1585–96) and Judith (1585–1662), while the Shakespeares probably stood as godparents to Richard Quiney's son William (born 1590) and his daughter Anne (born 1592). July Shaw lived two doors away from New Place and would be one of the witnesses of Shakespeare's will, in which he bequeathed his friend John Combe's nephew, Thomas, his sword (Shakespeare himself having inherited £5 from John, who had died two years earlier). Richard Tyler, the son of a butcher, is mentioned in the first draft of Shakespeare's will, but his name was struck out when the document was being redrafted.

The Quiney family were friendly with the Shakespeares for four generations (Fripp, 1924: 13–14). While representing the town's affairs in London, Richard Quiney (who held several public offices, including that of bailiff twice in 1592–93 and 1601–02) wrote to his wife in a combination of English and Latin, apparently read to her by their friend Abraham Sturley, who also wrote her replies (Orlin, 2014: 431 and 440); even the most prominent women of the town were unable to write fluently, though they were highly literate in thought. Quiney's son Richard, 'aged around eleven, wrote in Latin a touching letter asking his father to bring back from London books of blank paper for himself and his brother' (Wells, 2002: 12). George, son of Richard Quiney the younger, died aged twenty-four in April 1624, and is mentioned by Shakespeare's son-in-law, the physician John Hall, in his casebook as being 'of good understanding, skilled in languages and for a young man widely learned' (Brinkworth, 1972: 28): a fine tribute to another Stratford-upon-Avon grammar-school boy, no doubt.

No years lost: occupation, marriage and family life

We do not know how old Shakespeare was when he left school, but apprenticeships usually started at the age of fourteen. There are sixty-nine different occupations listed in the town (Jones, 1996: 21–2); the most popular trades were tailors (twenty-four), glovers (twenty-three, including Shakespeare's father, John) and butchers (also twenty-three). Then follow weavers (twenty), shoemakers (sixteen), bakers (fifteen), carpenters (fifteen), smiths (twelve), skinners (seven), fullers (seven) and tanners (six). That John Shakespeare removed his eldest son from the school to learn the family trade of glove-making (by apprenticing him either to himself, or to another of the town's glovers) seems highly likely, and was mentioned by Nicholas Rowe (1674–1718) in the earliest, formal biographical account of Shakespeare.

Figure 3.12 Eighteenth-century portrait of Nicholas Rowe (1674–1718), School of Godfrey Kneller, oil on canvas, 875 × 690 mm (34½ × 27½ in). Rowe published a six-volume edition of Shakespeare's plays in 1709. He included *Some Account of the Life, &c. of Mr William Shakespear*, which is regarded as the first Shakespearian biography. Rowe recorded oral traditions about Shakespeare's life that might otherwise have been lost.

Based on anecdotal evidence and local, oral history (which Rowe gathered by sending Thomas Betterton, a leading actor of the day, to talk to the townsfolk), Rowe suggests that 'upon leaving his school, he seems to have given entirely into that way of living which his father proposed to him' (Rowe, 1709: II). Or, perhaps Shakespeare was apprenticed to a local butcher, as stated in John Aubrey's (1626–97) brief life of Shakespeare, written around 1681 ('when he kill'd a Calfe, he would doe it in a high style, and make a Speech' (Aubrey, 1958: 275)). Lena Orlin adds further support to the idea that Shakespeare was apprenticed to a butcher:

> in 1693 an octogenarian Stratford clerk told John Dowdall that Shakespeare 'was formerly in this town apprentice to a butcher, but that he run from his master to London'. Glovers like John Shakespeare trafficked with butchers, for whom leather hides were by-products, and it is plausible that John Shakespeare arranged his son's apprenticeship with one of his butcher-partners. The Stratford leatherworker William Trowte did the same for his son, who was born just two years later than Shakespeare in 1566. (Orlin, 2014: 422)

Certainly, everything changed when Shakespeare was eighteen. He married Anne Hathaway of Shottery in November 1582 because she was already pregnant by him. Between 1570 and 1630, the average age for the townsmen to marry was twenty-six, and only three married under the age of twenty: George David (at seventeen), William Baylis (eighteen) and Shakespeare (eighteen). Of those three men, Shakespeare was the only one whose wife was already pregnant. Anne Hathaway (?1556–1623) was probably twenty-six years old: 'although pre-nuptial conception was not uncommon in Stratford, the youth of the bridegroom, particularly when compared with the age of his bride, made Shakespeare's marriage an unusual event which was doubtless a subject of comment among the townsfolk' (Jones, 1996: 90). Out of 393 marriages, fifty-four included premarital pregnancy (Jones, 1996: 86). All marriages by licence (as opposed to the reading of banns) required proof of financial security, which took the form of a bond (as insurance against there being any impediment to the marriage). In the Shakespeares' case, this was for the enormous sum of £40 from Fulk Sandells and John Richardson, two of Hathaway's friends. They had to be able to raise the money if any obstacle prevented the marriage. But, unlike the people he had gone to school with, making a living through a trade was not possible for Shakespeare because apprentices were not allowed to marry until they had finished their seven-year term (usually around the age of twenty-one). So, if he had undertaken a placement as an apprentice glover, or butcher, his chances of completing his apprenticeship were, from the age of eighteen, legally ruined.

After his marriage to Anne Hathaway in 1582, it would have been normal for them to settle away from the family home, if they could afford it. Or perhaps they had to remain in the Henley Street house and raise their children (Susanna, born in 1583, and the twins Hamnet and Judith, born in 1585) among Shakespeare's own surviving siblings. Mark Eccles points out that 'Henley Street was full of children, for John Ainge, baker, had seven children, including two sets of twins, and George

Ainge, mercer, had fourteen children including two sets of twins. George Ainge the younger, born in 1569, became a citizen and skinner in London' (Eccles, 1961: 41). The Shakespeares' next-door neighbour, George Badger, had sixteen children, 'fifteen of whom lived to adulthood – quite a record!' (Jones, 1996: 91).

In the same year that Shakespeare married, Alexander Aspinall was appointed as the schoolmaster and continued teaching until his death in 1624. He became a burgess in 1596, an alderman in 1602, and chamberlain and head of the Chapel Street ward in 1603 (Eccles, 1961: 58). Shakespeare's own son, Hamnet, would also have attended the school and been taught by Aspinall, Shakespeare no doubt reinforcing his only son's learning to make sure he got ahead.

Some Shakespearian biographies like to identify 1585–92 as 'lost years' because there is little documentary evidence that relates directly to his life. But gaps in the record are unremarkable in the lives of early modern people. In any case, Shakespeare was mentioned in an unsuccessful lawsuit against John Lambert for the return of some of his mother's land in Wilmcote in 1587 (Chambers, 1930, Vol. II: 37).

From the time of his marriage onwards, it is most likely that Shakespeare was living in the Henley Street home, raising his family, helping out with his father's glove-making business and considerable wool-dealing, and no doubt reading and writing whenever he could. Aubrey's biographical sketch also records that Shakespeare was 'in his younger yeares a school master in the countrey' (Aubrey, 1958: 276), which could refer to Stratford-upon-Avon because Aubrey was writing as a Londoner. If so, then perhaps Shakespeare helped out from time to time at the grammar school as well (monies were allocated each year for an usher's salary and school repairs). The first recorded usher, William Gilbard, was paid by John Shakespeare during the latter's first year as chamberlain. Gilbard became an important figure in the town and was curate there for fifty years. There are no details of any more ushers from 1565 until 1597, when we learn that Abraham Sturley's twenty-year-old son Henry, a graduate from Oxford, was about to assist Aspinall with the teaching (Eccles, 1961: 54–5). There is evidence for a notable connection between Aspinall and Shakespeare. Well into the seventeenth century, Sir Francis Fane (1611–80) wrote in his commonplace book:

> The gift is small
> The will is all:
> A shey ander Asbenall.
> Shaxpaire upon a paire of gloves that mas[t]er sent to his mistris.
> (Eccles, 1961: 57)

There is no reason to suppose that these lines are not by Shakespeare ('the will is all' puns on his first name, as happens in Sonnets 134, 135, 136 and 143). They suggest a neighbourliness and friendship (Aspinall lived across the road from New Place), which may have started as early as 1582 with Aspinall's arrival at the school and his first meeting with Shakespeare.

Seeing plays in Stratford-upon-Avon

From Shakespeare's childhood until into his thirties (from 1569 to 1597), Stratford-upon-Avon continued to host theatrical performances. Sometimes these were mounted by the locals themselves. In 1583 13s 4d was paid 'to Davi Jones and companye for his pastime at Whitsontyde' (Jones happened to be related to the Hathaway family by marriage (Schoenbaum, 1987: 112)). Thirty-one visiting troupes of players were formally welcomed by the bailiff to perform in the Guildhall. And there were other performance venues dotted around the town. The inns, especially the larger ones like the Swan and the Bear on Bridge Street, could host visiting performances 'other than those presented by the bailiff' (Mulryne, 2012: 172). Stratford-upon-Avon provided just enough opportunities for the young Shakespeare's developing awareness of professional theatre to be encouraged and could easily have led him to develop some early, significant contacts. J. R. Mulryne suggests:

> that Edward Alleyn, the most celebrated actor of his day, came to Stratford with Worcester's Men in 1583–4, although this was at the age of 17 or 18, before the triumphs of his later career. James Burbage, theatrical entrepreneur, actor and irascible leader of men was, we know, one of the Earl of Leicester's company in 1572–3, the year of one of their two Stratford visits, and may have come with them in 1576–7 also. (Mulryne, 2012: 185)

John Ward (1629–81), a later vicar of Stratford-upon-Avon, would record in his notebook for 1661–63: 'I have heard that Mr Shakespeare was a natural wit, without any art at all; he frequented plays all his younger time' (Chambers, 1930, Vol. II: 249). It is often assumed since Ward writes, towards the end of his notes about Shakespeare, 'to see Mrs Queeny [Judith Quiney]' (Chambers, 1930, Vol. II: 250) that Ward was about to see her to ask her about her father, and that she died before he was able to do so. But supposing he had managed to see Judith already (an old woman in her early seventies) and recorded what she had told him about her father, and that Ward's note 'to see' her is actually a reminder to himself to visit her again for more information: that would mean his records about Shakespeare were based on what the poet's own daughter had told him ('I have heard', writes Ward), and very likely true. Ward's notebooks should probably be taken quite seriously as providing reliable evidence about Shakespeare.

The Queen's Men returned almost eighteen years after their first visit, when Shakespeare was twenty-three: 'an entry in the 1587 *Minutes and Accounts* recording payment "for mendinge of a forme that was broken by the queens players xvj d.", is a token of the risk to civic property that hosting theatre entailed, even in the case of official performances' (Mulryne, 2012: 186). The players themselves may or may not have been responsible for the damage done to civic property. They returned in 1592 and 1597. We cannot be sure what plays they performed on these occasions, but their repertoire included the popular plays of *The Famous Victories of Henry V*, *The*

True Chronicle History of King Leir, The Troublesome Reign of King John and *The True Tragedy of Richard III*, all of which informed Shakespeare's own dramatic adaptations of these stories.

Until the Spanish Armada of 1588, the plays that had been presented were, on the whole, didactic and anti-Catholic in flavour. As far as the borough authorities were concerned (called on as they were to implement the incremental changes in Church and civic administration) the performances of such plays and interludes were, for a time, in their best interests and helped to form and maintain the status quo. After the death of Mary Queen of Scots in 1587 and the defeat of the Armada in 1588 (Stratford-upon-Avon had sent eight recruits to help with the nation's defence effort), the subjects of plays started to change. They began to be more secular in their orientation at around the same time that Shakespeare was beginning to write for the professional theatre. This development in the drama, coupled with the long-established, anti-theatrical rhetoric of the puritans, eventually led to Stratford-upon-Avon's civic authorities banning all theatrical performances from taking place on civic premises.

Stratford-upon-Avon, Shakespeare and London

In 1592, Shakespeare's work as a freelance writer was being noticed in London by the author of *Greene's Groatsworth of Wit Bought with a Million of Repentance* (the attribution of the work to Robert Greene is disputed). Shakespeare is there jealously mocked as being a jack-of-all-trades, 'an upstart crow', and of having too high an opinion of himself, 'the only Shake-scene in a country'. Shakespearian biographies have to send Shakespeare to London at some point or other, and explain why he went there. This is tricky, because the precise reason and circumstances are unknown. Myth and romance have long ingratiated themselves into this awkward historical gap, and the kind of biographical narrative we construct to fill it will colour and affect the way we understand the trajectory of Shakespeare's career.

From Edmond Malone in the eighteenth century onwards, biographers have had Shakespeare joining an acting troupe and going to London, star-struck. In 1961, Mark Eccles was able to support A. W. Pollard's conjecture that Shakespeare joined the Queen's Men in 1587 (when the troupe performed in Stratford-upon-Avon) because Eccles discovered that a member of their company, William Knell, had been murdered in a fight in Thame. Shakespeare, it was supposed, filled the gap Knell had left behind. In fact, we do not know whether the company performed in Stratford-upon-Avon before or after the murder. Schoenbaum takes a characteristically cool view, emphasising that 'no evidence exists of any Elizabethan troupe ever having recruited while on the road' (Schoenbaum. 1991: 541). Shakespeare running away, as it were, to join the circus, and leaving behind his wife, family, his economic and his personal responsibilities smacks of a Dick Whittington narrative that has etched itself into the way his life has come to be thought about.

A similar kind of tone (though one more evocative of Robin Hood) can be detected in Rowe's account of why Shakespeare went to London, because he fell:

> into ill company: and amongst them, some that made a frequent practice of deer-stealing, engaged him with them more than once in robbing a park that belonged to Sir Thomas Lucy of Charlecote, near Stratford. For this he was prosecuted by the gentleman, as he thought, too severely; and in order to revenge that ill usage, he made a ballad upon him. And though this, probably the first essay of his poetry be lost, yet it is said to have been very bitter, that it redoubled the prosecution against him to that degree, that he was obliged to leave his business and family in Warwickshire, for some time, and shelter himself in London. (Rowe, 1709: III)

The deer-poaching story was first recorded in 1688 (within the life-time of Shakespeare's great-nephews and -nieces) by Richard Davies, chaplain of Corpus Christi College, Oxford, who included the detail that Sir Thomas Lucy 'oft [had Shakespeare] whipped and sometimes imprisoned and at last made him fly his native county to his great advancement' (Schoenbaum, 1987: 98). The main problem with these accounts (apart from there having been no formal deer park at Charlecote at the time) is that the punishment here does not seem to fit the crime: a man was hanged for stealing a sheep as late as 1830. The biographical ramifications of the deer-poaching story lead to a portrayal of Shakespeare who escapes into the world of the theatre, somehow remains hidden there and leaves his life in Stratford-upon-Avon behind him. This does not ring true. Robert Bearman (in an unpublished talk that he has kindly allowed me to read) convincingly argues that the story is likely to have been based on folk ballads about Shakespeare in circulation in the seventeenth century and that these, far from being based on fact, were probably based on an early biographical reading of the first few lines of *The Merry Wives of Windsor*, in which Shakespeare puns on Sir Thomas Lucy's name in a scene partly about deer-poaching. Margreta de Grazia notes that 'the anecdotes are less a form of biography than of literary criticism: they record not the life Shakespeare lived between 1564 and 1616 but the impression his works made after his death' (De Grazia, 2015: 14).

Far more likely is that Shakespeare started going to London on his father's business, or even to get a taste of the capital with which his hometown had such strong links. Stratford-upon-Avon was very permeable as far as London was concerned. William Greenaway, the carrier, travelled back and forth to London with pack-horses. He would regularly ride 30 miles each day via either Banbury, Oxford, or Chipping Norton, accompanied by other travellers for safety. Greenaway's large house stood almost opposite the Shakespeares' on Henley Street. John Shakespeare and his neighbour Adrian Quiney travelled to London on town business, for example in 1572. Stratford girls sometimes went into service in London: Elizabeth Trowte, for instance, in 1594, the sister of a local butcher (Fogg, 2014: 41).

In light of his work on John Shakespeare's finances, David Fallow has proposed a new, economically based theory about why Shakespeare started spending time in London. He builds a factually supported case for John Shakespeare's quasi-legal wool-dealing ('broking' or 'brogging') business forging links with other dealers in the capital. Through the efforts of professional informers (seeking a part of any fine),

John Shakespeare was convicted for illegal wool-dealing in the London courts in 1570 (evidence for which only came to light in 1984). Fallow holds that informers would not have bothered with a case involving a small-scale dealer and that the cases show that large amounts of wool and money were involved – amounts comparable to those handled by the largest wool traders of the day (Fallow, 2015: 33). We know, for example, that John Shakespeare bought £210 worth of wool in 1572. Fallow's revisionist study permits at least four compelling conclusions. First, it unsettles the traditional view that John Shakespeare suffered a period of financial ruin from the mid-1570s to the late 1590s. Significantly, the last meeting of the corporation that Alderman Shakespeare routinely attended (in 1576) coincides with an attempt by decree to drive broggers, such as Shakespeare, out of business. His subsequent disposals of property into family and 'friendly' hands at discounted prices (the mortgaging of his 142 acres of land at Wilmcote in 1578 and selling-off of his shares in a property at Snitterfield in 1579, for example) can therefore be reinterpreted as John Shakespeare shielding his assets from the State's drive to regulate the wool market and fine those operating on the fringes of the law. Second, Fallow's theory proposes that Shakespeare's arrival in London, some time in the late 1580s or early 1590s, was first and foremost to represent his father's business affairs in the wool trade: 'given John Shakespeare's relative market position in the English wool broking scene, the probability is that William first went to London as a businessman rather than as an impoverished poet' (Fallow, 2015: 38). Third, it explains how Shakespeare himself learned how to become an astute businessman and entrepreneur. Fourth, Fallow's theory offers an explanation as to how Shakespeare could afford to co-found and buy shares in the Lord Chamberlain's Men theatre company in 1594 long before his theatrical income could have delivered the necessary cash: the funding came from the family business. In fact, two years later, on John Shakespeare's grant from the College of Heralds for a coat of arms, he was listed as being worth £500, in addition to his land and tenements. So, a plausible sequence of events is: Shakespeare, working in London on behalf of his father's wool business, starts freelance playwrighting and becomes knowledgeable about the opportunities in the unregulated professional theatre business. Consequently, his father agrees to support him financially, becoming, as it were, his son's first patron.

Another important link with London for Shakespeare came through his Stratford-upon-Avon neighbour, Richard Field. Although the stationers' trade was absent from the town, and printing and publishing arrived there later, at least two young men took up apprenticeships with London stationers, possibly introduced to the profession by encouraging grammar-school teachers. George Badger's son, Richard, one of his sixteen children who lived next door to the Shakespeares on Henley Street, was apprenticed to London-based Peter Short (Eccles, 1961: 47). Another stationer's apprentice was Shakespeare's schoolfellow Richard Field (baptised 16 November 1561), son of Henry, a tanner on Back Bridge Street. Their fathers would have known each other, too; John needed tanned skins from which to make gloves. Around 1575, when he was fourteen, Richard Field left Stratford-upon-Avon for London to start his apprenticeship with George Bishop, and served his first six years out of seven with Thomas Vautrollier, a Huguenot printer. Henry Field, Richard's father, died in 1592, and his neighbour John Shakespeare appraised and made an inventory of his goods

(Eccles, 1961: 59). If John Shakespeare's wool-dealing associates did not help to find Shakespeare somewhere to stay in London during his increasingly extended visits, then the chances are that Richard Field helped him to do so. Field may have introduced Shakespeare to the Huguenot Mountjoy family (Kathman, 2015: 177) with whom he was to lodge on Silver Street, possibly from around 1602 (and definitely by 1604).

The year 1592 saw the closure of the London public playhouses for about two years because of a severe outbreak of the plague. Ten thousand people died in 1593. While the theatres were closed Shakespeare probably began work on his first long poem, *Venus and Adonis*. Richard Field, who had finished his apprenticeship in 1587, printed the poem in the following spring, entering it into the Stationers' Register on 18 April 1593 (a few days before Shakespeare's twenty-ninth birthday). Field's work with Vautrollier had included an edition of one of Shakespeare's favourite books, Ovid's *Metamorphoses* (1589) and an augmented version of Holinshed's *Chronicles of England* (1587 (Rutter, 2015: 168)), the source for many of Shakespeare's history plays. *Venus and Adonis* represents nothing less than a truly Stratford-upon-Avon collaboration of two school friends, Field helping Shakespeare make his way in the capital. For Shakespeare, who never completed an apprenticeship, *Venus and Adonis* is really his first 'masterpiece', the moment when his name first appeared in print. In the dedication, Shakespeare himself refers to the work as 'the first heir of my invention', so the poem even has a claim to be Shakespeare's first ever literary endeavour. It attracted the patronage of the extremely wealthy and high-profile aristocrat Henry Wriothesley, Earl of Southampton, the poem's dedicatee, and Shakespeare would see *Venus and Adonis* become his most popular printed work. He may have received as much as £5 or £6 from Wriothesley (Nelson, 2015: 277–8), who was to remain Shakespeare's only major literary patron. In Shakespeare's dedication to him the poem is presented as an offspring, the 'first heir' for whom Wriothesley has agreed to stand as godparent. Shakespeare also promises another, 'graver labour', *Lucrece*, which appeared the following year, printed by Field and again dedicated to Wriothesley, but this time in terms unusually intimate for a poet to use when addressing his patron: 'the love I dedicate to your lordship is without end … what I have done is yours; what I have to do is yours, being part in all I have, devoted yours'.

Although Stratford-upon-Avon had no printing or publishing industry, it did have books in circulation and for sale, and it may be that Shakespeare himself was around and about the town buying a book on 25 August 1595. A widow named Perrott had obtained some goods from another widow called Young. The circumstances by which Perrott had acquired them were dubious and Young sued her, but not until after some or all of the goods had been sold. Perrott had to pay the damages and the memoranda of the case mention among the purchases 'mr Shaxpere one boke', which, Fripp adds, 'apparently was not a prayer-book' (Fripp, 1924: 94–5). Three prayerbooks are mentioned as a separate item valued at 10s, and, in the same memorandum as 'mr Shaxpere' is mentioned, a 'mr barber' buys '3 bokes' (Shakespeare Centre Library and Archive, BRU 15/6, no. 170b; and BRU 15/7, no. 246). Of course, the purchaser may have been John, Gilbert, Richard or Edmund Shakespeare. But William is the member of the family most likely to have been out and about buying books. The purchase suggests that 'mr Shaxpere' might have had some interest in the court case, too.

Figure 3.13 Shakespeare's first literary patron, Henry Wriothesley (1573–1624), the third Earl of Southampton and Baron of Titchfield, and the only person to whom Shakespeare dedicated a work. Attributed to John de Critz the Elder (1551/52–1642), *c.* 1593, oil on panel, 610 × 438 mm (24 × 17¾ in). This painting is thought to represent the Earl around his coming of age, the time when Shakespeare dedicated *Venus and Adonis* and *Lucrece* to him. Until 2002, the sitter was thought to be a distant, female descendant of the Earl, Lady Norton. But the attire is male, and the Earl was proud of his very long hair (which can be seen in his other portraits).

Financial and social investments

Stratford-upon-Avon's economy was greatly damaged by the two devastating fires of 1594 and 1595, which, it is estimated, destroyed around 200 buildings, caused £20,000 worth of damage and put 400 townsfolk on the poor-relief lists, a number that rose to 700 by 1601 (Bearman, 1994: 23). The leather fire buckets, fire-hook and a ladder that hung from the sides of the clock-tower at High Cross were of little use. Houses and livelihoods were ruined on Henley Street, Bridge Street, Wood Street ('the south side seems to have been burnt from end to end' (Fripp, 1924: 102)), High Street, Sheep Street and Chapel Street (on the side opposite New Place). The houses of Adrian Quiney, Abraham Sturley, William Parsons, Hamnet Sadler and Thomas Rogers (bailiff in 1595) 'were partially or totally destroyed' (Fripp, 1924: 102). The fires were obviously disastrous for the town – for people whom the Shakespeares knew and cared about – and provide a crucial context in which to assess the Shakespeares' finances.

If John Shakespeare's finances did not help provide Shakespeare with the money to buy shares in the Lord Chamberlain's Men (which Andrew Gurr estimates cost Shakespeare between £50 and £80 (Gurr, 2004: 89 and 108)), then perhaps the Earl of Southampton himself helped Shakespeare out financially.

The poet and playwright William Davenant (1606–68) is cited by Nicholas Rowe as saying that Southampton gave Shakespeare £1,000 'to enable him to go through with a purchase which he heard he had a mind to' (Rowe, 1709: X). Davenant, who was born in the Crown Inn in Oxford, where Shakespeare may often have stayed whilst commuting from Stratford-upon-Avon to London, liked to say he was Shakespeare's illegitimate son. Davenant's first play was staged by the King's Men at the Blackfriars in 1627. Some of Shakespeare's closest friends and colleagues, for example John Heminges and Henry Condell, were still alive. Their folio of Shakespeare's works had been published four years earlier, and it is likely that Davenant, who was eager to find out more about Shakespeare, asked them about their late and famous friend. Davenant succeeded Ben Jonson as the leading poet at Court (effectively the Poet Laureate). A version of the £1,000 story also circulated around Stratford-upon-Avon, possibly independently of Davenant's account. The late-eighteenth–early-nineteenth-century local historian and antiquarian Robert Bell Wheler describes the Earl's giving Shakespeare £1,000 as being a 'unanimous tradition' and one that explains how Shakespeare was able to 'purchase houses and land in Stratford' (Wheler, 1806: 73). The income from Southampton's estate has been calculated at £3,000 in 1594 (Akrigg, 1968: 38). Lord Burghley apparently fined Wriothesley £5,000 for refusing to marry his eldest granddaughter, Elizabeth Vere (daughter of Anne Cecil and Edward de Vere, the Earl of Oxford), which indicates that Shakespeare's patron was clearly very rich by anyone's standards, and extravagant: the Earl's steward, Arthur Bromfield, gave £1,000 as a dowry for his daughter (Wells, 2011: 50).

The sum involved is often dismissed as being impossibly large, but the vicar John Ward provides corroborative evidence when recording, in his 1661–63 notebook, that Shakespeare had an 'allowance so large that he spent at the rate of £1,000 a year' (Chambers, 1930: 249). Ward has recalled the impressive amount and confused this with Shakespeare's annual spending. Or perhaps Shakespeare's allowance and his spending were enormous, too. Certainly, Rowe gets his equivalent figures right. He compares £1,000 as being 'almost equal to that profuse generosity the present age has shown to French dancers and Italian Eunuchs' (Rowe, 1709: X). De Grazia notes that 'in 1710, Senesino, a celebrated castrato from Sienna (for whom Handel wrote arias) was offered a vast sum of £2,000 a year to perform in London'. She adds:

This adds peculiar interest to Southampton's generosity: the sum he has given Shakespeare in exchange for his services to literature approximates what theatre impresarios of Rowe's day were willing to pay out to French dancers, known for their sexual availability and technique, and to Italian castrati, whose sexual ambiguity piqued prurient curiosity. (De Grazia, 2015: 8)

None of the accounts makes it clear when Southampton allegedly gave Shakespeare £1,000. Wheler's comment, which refers to 'houses and land in Stratford', may suggest it was after Shakespeare had bought the company shares in 1594. Wriothesley was in the Tower from 1601 to 1603 because of his involvement with the Earl of Essex's attempted coup, so perhaps if the Earl did give Shakespeare any money, it was between the Earl's coming of age in 1594 and 1597 (£1,000 over three years perhaps), enabling Shakespeare to buy shares in the company, the family's coat of arms and New Place. Even if the sum is disputed, it seems likely that Wriothesley gave Shakespeare a large amount of money.

The going rate for a coat of arms, for someone with property and land over £100, would be £6 13s 4d (10 marks). This had been decided between 1524 and 1533, and was transcribed as a standard procedure by the College of Heralds in 1591. The rate was set at £10 for craftsmen and higher clergy (Cheesman, 2014: 77). How much might the Shakespeares have paid for theirs? By the time the Heralds had been paid – possibly as much as £20 (Duncan-Jones, 2001: 86) – and Shakespeare had implemented the use of his new coat of arms on his father's 'moveables and immoveables, such as trunks, furniture, bed canopies, book-bindings, glass windows, seal-rings, as well as carved and painted above the entrance to his gentlemen's residence', bought at least one new suit of silk (a material he and his father were now entitled to wear) and bought New Place, '£100 seems entirely plausible' (Duncan-Jones, 2001: 86). If the shares in the Lord Chamberlain's Men cost between £50 and £80, and New Place around £120 (Bearman, 1994: 18), then it seems that between 1594 and 1597 Shakespeare spent at least £250 on investments.

When John Shakespeare died, in September 1601, Shakespeare could formally display the coat of arms and officially call himself a gentleman, though he would have started assuming that status from 1596. There were forty-five gentlemen in Stratford-upon-Avon between 1570 and 1630. Twenty-eight were born into the title (the Nashes, Reynolds, the Tylers and the Combes, who purchased and moved into the College in 1596). The other seventeen 'gentlemen' were individuals from different families, and had a trade. Like Shakespeare, they had successfully applied for their coat of arms (Jones, 1996: 36). Adrian Quiney was styled a gentleman in 1574. Nine men are known to have carried a sword, rapier and dagger, four of whom were gentlemen (Jones, 1996: 64). Shakespeare may have been among those who liked carrying a sword around the town – an important and intimate possession.

Gentlemen's coats of arms are all very well, but the main patriarch of the Shakespeares, John, acquired his after his only grandson (who was expected to carry on the family name) died, almost certainly in the Henley Street house, in the second

Figure 3.14 The Shakespeares' coat of arms, awarded by the College of Heralds to John Shakespeare in 1596, and no doubt proudly displayed above the front door of New Place.

week of August 1596. Hamnet Shakespeare was only eleven years old. He was buried on 11 August; the draft for the Shakespeares' coat of arms was drawn up on 20 October. Anne and William were unlikely to have any more children (she had just turned forty). The boy's death marked the end of an era, and the family's coat of arms probably felt as much like a memorial for Hamnet as a sign of social status.

References

Akrigg, G. P. V. (1968). *Shakespeare and the Earl of Southampton* (London: Hamish Hamilton).

Aubrey, John ([1949] 1958). *Aubrey's Brief Lives*, ed. Oliver Lawson Dick, 3rd edn (London: Secker and Warburg).

Bate, J. (2008). *Soul of the Age: The Life, Mind, and World of William Shakespeare* (London: Viking).

Bearman, R. (1988). *Stratford-upon-Avon: A History of Its Streets and Buildings* (Nelson: Hendon Mill Publishing).

—— (1994). *Shakespeare in the Stratford Records* (Stroud: Alan Sutton and the Shakespeare Birthplace Trust).

—— (2007). 'The Early Reformation Experience in a Warwickshire Market Town: Stratford-upon-Avon, 1530–1580', *Midland History*, 32: 68–109.

Booty, J. E. ([1976] 2005). *The Book of Common Prayer 1559* (Charlottesville and London: Folger Shakespeare Library and University of Virginia Press).

Brinkworth, E. R. C. (1972). *Shakespeare and the Bawdy Court* (London: Phillimore).

Chambers, E. K. (1930). *William Shakespeare: A Study in Facts and Problems*, 2 vols (Oxford: Clarendon Press).

—— ([1923] 2009). *The Elizabethan Stage*, 4 vols (Oxford: Clarendon Press).

Cheesman, C. (2014). 'Grants and Confirmations of Arms', in N. Ramsey (ed.), *Heralds and Heraldry in Shakespeare's England* (Donington: Shaun Tyas), 68–104.

Cooper, H. (2010). *Shakespeare and the Medieval World* (London: A & C Black).

De Grazia, M. (2015). 'Shakespeare's Anecdotal Character', in P. Holland (ed.), *Shakespeare Survey 67* (Cambridge: Cambridge University Press), 1–14.

Duncan-Jones, K. (2001). *Ungentle Shakespeare: Scenes from His Life* (London: Thomson Learning).

Eccles, M. (1961). *Shakespeare in Warwickshire* (Madison: University of Wisconsin Press).

Fallow, D. (2015). 'His Father, John Shakespeare', in P. Edmondson and S. Wells (eds), *The Shakespeare Circle: An Alternative Biography* (Cambridge: Cambridge University Press), 26–39.

Fogg, N. (2014). *Stratford-upon-Avon: The Biography* (Stroud: Amberley Publishing).

Fripp, E. I. (1924). *Master Richard Quyny: Bailiff of Stratford-upon-Avon and Friend of William Shakespeare* (London: Humphrey Milford for Oxford University Press).

—— (1928). *Shakespeare's Stratford* (London: Oxford University Press).

—— (1929). *Shakespeare's Haunts near Stratford* (London: Humphrey Milford for Oxford University Press).

Giles, K. and J. Clark (2012). 'The Archaeology of the Guild Buildings of Shakespeare's Stratford-upon-Avon', in J. R. Mulryne (ed.), *The Guild and the Guild Buildings of Shakespeare's Stratford: Society, Religion, School and Stage* (Farnham: Ashgate), 135–69.

Gurr, A. (2004). *The Shakespeare Company 1594–1642* (Cambridge: Cambridge University Press).

Hotson, J. L. (1937). *I, William Shakespeare Do Appoint Thomas Russell, Esquire* (London: Jonathan Cape).

Jones, J. (1996). *Family Life in Shakespeare's England: Stratford-upon-Avon 1570–1630* (Stroud: Sutton Publishing and the Shakespeare Birthplace Trust).

Kathman, D. (2015). 'Living with the Mountjoys', in P. Edmondson and S. Wells (eds), *The Shakespeare Circle: An Alternative Biography* (Cambridge: Cambridge University Press), 174–85.

Lascelles, M. (1973). '*King Lear* and Doomsday', in K. Muir (ed.), *Shakespeare Survey 26* (Cambridge: Cambridge University Press), 69–79.

Mulryne, J. R., ed. (2012). *The Guild and the Guild Buildings of Shakespeare's Stratford: Society, Religion, School and Stage* (Farnham: Ashgate).

Nelson, A. H. (2015). 'His Literary Patrons', in P. Edmondson and S. Wells (eds), *The Shakespeare Circle: An Alternative Biography* (Cambridge: Cambridge University Press), 275–88.

Orlin, L. C. (2014). 'Anne by Indirection', *Shakespeare Quarterly*, 65.4: 420–54.

Rowe, N. (1709). *Some Account of the Life of Mr. William Shakespeare* (London: Jacob Tonson).

Rutter, C. C. (2015). 'Schoolfriend, Publisher and Printer Richard Field', in P. Edmondson and S. Wells (eds), *The Shakespeare Circle: An Alternative Biography* (Cambridge: Cambridge University Press), 161–73.

Salkeld, D. (2003). 'The Case of Elizabeth Evans', *Notes and Queries*, 50.1: 60–1.

Schoenbaum, S. ([1977] 1987). *William Shakespeare: A Documentary Life* (Oxford: Oxford University Press).

—— (1991). *Shakespeare's Lives* (Oxford: Clarendon Press).

Shapiro, J. (2005). *1599: A Year in the Life of William Shakespeare* (London: Faber and Faber).

Weis, R. (2007). *Shakespeare Revealed: A Biography* (London: John Murray).

Wells, S. (2002). *Shakespeare for All Time* (London: Macmillan).

Wells, S., ed. (2011). *Shakespeare Found! A Life Portrait at Last: Portraits, Poet, Patron, Poems*, 2nd edn (Bookham: The Cobbe Foundation and the Shakespeare Birthplace Trust).

Wheler, R. B. (1806). *History and Antiquities of Stratford-upon-Avon* (London: J. Ward).

4

Shakespeare and New Place, 1597–1616, and later occupants to 1677

Paul Edmondson

Shakespeare began to take legal possession of New Place, the largest house in the borough, in May 1597. It was a significant personal and professional investment in both monetary and social terms. Stratford-upon-Avon was still reeling from the effects of the two devastating fires of 1594 and 1595, and the cruel winter of 1596–97 had witnessed a high rate of deaths. The poverty of townsfolk whose livelihoods and dwellings had been destroyed was compounded by the national shortage of grain that summer. There were 400 people on poor relief, and the death-rate rose. There would be 313 burials over the next three years (Jones, 1996: xix), and 700 registered poor, a third of the town's population, by 1601 (Bearman, 1994: 23). On 25 March 1597, a royal proclamation had placed a ban on all malt-making until Michaelmas (29 September), a measure that would further damage the failing economy of the town: malting was a major industry on which many depended for their livelihoods.

On the corporation, the predominantly puritan faction held increasing influence. In July 1597, the Queen's Men played for a licence at the Guildhall, the last time a professional company was formally permitted to perform in Stratford-upon-Avon for twenty-one years (Mulryne, 2012: 201). In December 1602, the corporation decreed that there should be no plays or interludes on corporation property, which effectively meant no visiting troupe could obtain a licence (since they would not be able to perform before the bailiff), subject to a fine of 10s (which was increased to a crippling £10 in 1612). At least for the time being, the Stratford-upon-Avon authorities wanted nothing more to do with players or playing. There are two records of payments to players in 1618 and one in 1620 (Mulryne, 2012: 201). In 1622, friends and colleagues of Shakespeare's in the King's Men, who were touring Warwickshire, and who visited Stratford-upon-Avon in part presumably to see Shakespeare's memorial bust and grave, seem to have been made to feel formally and emphatically unwelcome. The corporation actually paid them 6d for not performing in the Guildhall – a performance that might even have been given in Shakespeare's memory. It can be hoped that John and Susanna Hall and Anne Shakespeare offered them generous hospitality at New Place instead. The King's Men certainly had their work on the Folio edition of *Master William Shakespeare's Comedies, Histories, and Tragedies* to discuss with Shakespeare's family; the ambitious volume, at least seven years in the making, would appear at the end of the following year.

Jeanne Jones comments that 'this hostility of the ruling oligarchy to the means by which Shakespeare earned his living must have caused a certain amount of mistrust between the council and the playwright, and surely accounted in part for his non-participation in civic affairs when he was in Stratford' (Jones, 1996: 111). Equally, Shakespeare could not easily take up civic offices as his father had done because of his intermittent work in London, and one suspects he is likely to have been only too pleased to have had the constant excuse not to have to join a committee of puritans. Meanwhile, New Place was virtually next door to the headquarters of the corporation, the Guildhall, 'a symbol of the ascendancy of the leading townsmen. By February 1606 there is even reference to it as the town hall as opposed to the Guildhall' (Bearman, 2012a: 106).

It is precisely this context that makes Shakespeare's purchase of New Place in 1597 seem socially and culturally audacious. By the age of thirty-three, and in spite of the ongoing prejudice against his theatre profession, Shakespeare had established himself and his family in the most prominent of the town's dwellings. His friends, the Combe family, had taken possession of the College the year before. Although their new home was bigger than New Place, it was technically outside the town and jurisdiction of the borough, and befitted the Combes' even more substantial wealth. Shakespeare's acquisition of New Place was socially symbolic. He did not choose a cottage or a small town house with one or two gables, neither did he have such a dwelling built or renovated (as Thomas Rogers the butcher did in 1596, at 26 High Street, now known as Harvard House). And, while he was no doubt aware of Rogers having entertained, on behalf of the corporation, Sir Thomas Lucy (knighted by Queen Elizabeth during her visit to nearby Charlecote house) in his new town house on Thursday 20 January 1597 (Fripp, 1938: 463), Shakespeare's social ascendancy to New Place would be far more impressive.

His moving into New Place with his wife and two surviving children was no doubt a cause of family pride among the Shakespeares and the Hathaways. It is perfectly plausible to suppose that John and William Shakespeare's whole families lived at New Place. A house of its size and status would have been regarded as a resource for all the Shakespeares, and meant that they would always have a roof over their heads. None of William's three brothers would marry and, perhaps because of New Place, they did not need to set up homes of their own. William had achieved domestic security and was laying down significant roots in his hometown. As far as John and Mary Shakespeare were concerned, New Place would be the perfect residence for John, whose newly acquired status as a gentleman meant that the family's coat of arms could be displayed above the front door, signifying both the father's status, and that

Figure 4.1 The College, built in 1351 by Ralph de Stratford as a dwelling for five priests, closed by Edward VI from 1547, and later converted into a large family residence. It was a grand house, built of stone, and the largest in the vicinity, with fifteen hearths recorded in 1670. Shakespeare's friends, the Combes, lived there. This engraving, published in 1806, was made before the College's demolition in 1799.

of the son who would eventually inherit it. The hearth tax returns for 1663 and 1670 list one house on Chapel Street with ten hearths (Chambers, 1930, Vol. II: 99; Arkell and Alcock, 2010: 217). We can deduce that these records refer to New Place because it was the largest dwelling on that street. Ten hearths means it could have had up to thirty rooms, since comparison of the numbers of hearths with the numbers of rooms given in probate inventories suggests that ratios of at least two rooms per hearth are typical (Arkell and Alcock, 2010: 110–16). That means New Place could easily and comfortably have accommodated all of the Shakespeares: John and Mary; William and Anne; Susanna and Judith; Shakespeare's brothers Gilbert, Richard and Edmund; and his sister Joan – ten people, some of whom would have probably shared rooms. But New Place was a shrewd financial investment, too. Being able to afford New Place significantly increased Shakespeare's family's social standing and prospects. The fact that he bought New Place at all also raises important questions about how it would relate to his career in London.

This chapter argues that Shakespearian biography in relation to New Place needs thorough revision and a greater level of nuance in order to increase understanding of Shakespeare's relationship to Stratford-upon-Avon. Indeed, there is every reason to suggest that, given the archaeological evidence and what we know about Shakespeare's family home, he would have been unlikely to buy it in 1597 if he had not intended to spend as much time there as possible. Certainly, he occupied lodgings in more than one location in London (from 1597), and we know he acted in at least two plays (Ben

Figure 4.2 Thomas Rogers's one-gabled house on High Street (now known as Harvard House).

Jonson's *Every Man in His Humour* from 1598 and *Sejanus* in 1603/04), but he was, from 1594, the leading writer for the Lord Chamberlain's Men. He needed space and time and a concentrated focus and energy in order to compose his (on average) two plays a year.

Rehearsals and touring and performing are physically demanding and time-consuming activities that require a lot of emotional and mental energy. The more Shakespeare acted, the less time he would have had to write, and, in the meantime, his company still needed fresh material. As James Shapiro notes, Shakespeare is not listed as an actor at the Globe after 1603, 'and the omission of his name from a 1607 fee list of "players of interludes" that identifies the other leading members of his company further suggests that by 1606 he was no longer acting on a daily basis' (Shapiro, 2015: 7–8). Certainly, 1603 and 1604 were terrible years for the plague in London (from 20 deaths a week in February 1603 to 3,000 deaths a week in August

1604 (Shapiro, 2015: 26–7)). The theatres opened briefly in April 1604, but the plague returned and they remained closed until September 1604. From 1603 to 1605, the King's Men toured, and surviving records list performances in Shrewsbury, Ipswich, Coventry, Bridgnorth, Oxford, Bath, Barnstaple, Fordwich, Faversham, Maidstone and Saffron Walden (Gurr, 1996: 304). It is likely that Shakespeare sought escape from both the plague and the exhausting demands of touring, and retreated to Stratford-upon-Avon. In describing the 'contours of Shakespeare's career', Jonathan Bate provides the following summation:

> during the first six and a half years of James's English reign, the public theatres were closed for over four years, open for under two … He no longer needed to endure the discomfort of touring. In all probability, he spent the greater proportion of these long plague years at home. Only one foot remained in London. The other was planted ever more firmly back in Stratford, despite that lack of desire to play a part in local government or the civic life of the community. (Bate, 2008: 355)

Furthermore, the constant distractions of rehearsals and performances in London, or on tour, would never provide the opportunities required by a writer. New Place would, and in abundance. When set alongside all that New Place represented to Shakespeare and his family, his commitments in London seem at best intermittent, and at worst a distraction from his main professional duties of writing. Temporary lodgings in London were all he needed to fulfil any demands the company might make on his time.

In the Christmas seasons, it is likely that he joined the company for their appearances at Court. We do not know who exactly acted in the plays there, but the company's chief playwright would have been a highly desirable presence, if not a prerequisite. From May 1603, when the company was renamed the King's Men, nine of them (including Shakespeare) were listed in the patent that made them Grooms of the Chamber (members of the royal household (Schoenbaum, 1987: 250–1)). Those nine were granted 4½ yards of scarlet cloth for their liveries and formed part of James I's triumphal procession through London on 15 March 1604 (the coronation itself had taken place in July 1603, but the public processions had to be deferred because of a plague epidemic). Grooms of the Chamber were sometimes called on to attend special State occasions and visits. From 9 to 27 August 1604, for example, there was the visit to Somerset House of Don Juan Fernández de Velasco, Duke of Frías, Earl of Haro, Great Chamberlain to Philip III of Spain and Constable of Castile (to name but a few of his eminent titles), and 234 gentlemen, for signing the Spanish peace treaty. On that occasion, twelve of the King's Men (of whom only John Heminges and Augustine Phillips are named) were paid £21 12s, and a per diem of 2s (that was the same as the going rate for an ordinary Yeoman of the Guard (Honan, 1998: 312)).

Shakespeare's professional commitments in London, as well as the many distractions that the capital offered, need to be seen in the context of the considerable financial investment he had made in a Stratford-upon-Avon family home. What precisely did Shakespeare buy in 1597?

Some residents of New Place before Shakespeare

New Place remained in the Clopton family until well into the sixteenth century. Then, in 1543, William Clopton (the great-nephew of Hugh) let New Place (until 1549) to Dr Thomas Bentley, a physician to Henry VIII, and a president of the Royal College of Physicians. On Bentley's decease in 1549, there was a lawsuit because of a complaint from the Cloptons that 'he left the said manor place in great ruin and decay and unrepaired' (Schoenbaum, 1987: 232). Clopton, who was short of money, sold New Place to William Bott, who took up residence from 1563.

Bott comes across as truly villainous in all the contemporary accounts. In the words of his son-in-law, John Harper of Henley in Arden, Bott was 'void of all honesty and fidelity or fear of God, and openly detected of divers great and notorious crimes, as namely felony, adultery, whoredom, falsehood, and forgery' (Schoenbaum, 1987: 233). Shortly after moving into New Place, in April 1563, Bott allegedly tricked his then under-age son-in-law, John, into leaving his estate to him if Bott's own daughter (Isabella, John's wife) died without producing an heir. In May, Bott apparently plotted the murder of Isabella by organising for his wife unwittingly to administer poison (trioxide of arsenic, or 'ratsbane') to her while she was recovering from an illness. Bott's man, Roland Wheler, was a witness to the event, which can be interpreted as either murder, or accidental death:

> The said Bott having in this wise forged the said deed and so conveyed the said lands, the said Bott's daughter, wife of the said John Harper, did die suddenly and was poisoned with ratsbane, and therewith swelled to death. And this deponent knoweth the same to be true, for that he did see the wife of the said Bott in the presence of the same Bott deliver to the said Harper's wife in a spoon mixed with drink the said poison of ratsbane to drink, which poison she did drink in this deponent's presence, the same William Bott by and at that time leaning to the bed's feet. And this deponent saith that the said William Bott did see this when it was done. And this deponent saith that after the wife of the said William Bott had so given the said drink to the said Harper's wife, the said Harper and this deponent did see her lay a thing under the green carpet. (Schoenbaum, 1987: 233)

Schoenbaum continues the account: 'this "thing" Harper offered to taste, thinking it brimstone, "but by the persuasion of this deponent, who suspected it to be ratsbane, he did forbear"' (Schoenbaum, 1987: 234). The tragedy almost certainly occurred in New Place itself. If there had been a murder (Wheler's allegations were made eight years later), then neither Bott nor his wife was ever brought to justice. A year after the death of his daughter, Bott was elected to be a Stratford-upon-Avon alderman, but lost his office in 1565 for remarking 'that there was never an honest man of council or the body of the corporation of Stratford' (Schoenbaum, 1987: 233). It was John Shakespeare who replaced Bott as alderman (Schoenbaum, 1987: 35).

In 1567, William Underhill of the Inner Temple (a clerk of law in Warwick and significant property- and landowner), purchased New Place from Bott. Underhill died just three years later. His son, also called William, succeeded him in 1570, aged only fourteen. He had strong Roman Catholic connections and was to become a 'stubborn' recusant (Fripp, 1938: 195). Underhill, who was only eight years older than Shakespeare, was the owner of New Place when Shakespeare would have walked past it on his way to the King's New School. I am indebted to Robert Bearman's research into Shakespeare's purchase of New Place, which includes rich detail about the second William Underhill's family life, Roman Catholic connections and finances. His first child, Fulke Underhill, was baptised in Idlicote in 1579, but his next four children were baptised (and one buried) at Holy Trinity Church, so it looks as though his family was residing in New Place from 1580 to 1588. A sixth child was baptised in Idlicote the following year (Bearman, 2012b: 478). Hugh Hall, a Roman Catholic priest associated with John Somerville's notorious plot to assassinate Elizabeth I in 1583, fled to Underhill's Idlicote residence, was arrested there, tried in London and convicted. From the early to the mid-1590s, Underhill's recusancy was exacerbated by debts owed to him and his inability to raise enough cash. He left £1,600 to his children in his will, but claimed he was owed £2,070. Most importantly, Underhill was in debt to the Stratford-upon-Avon corporation for the rent on all the annual tithes of Little Wilmcote, and, by Easter term 1596, owed them £16 13s 4d (Bearman, 2012b: 479). It was time for Underhill to raise some cash, so he decided to sell New Place.

Bearman speculates that Richard Quiney, during his visits to London, spoke to Shakespeare about Underhill's seeking to sell New Place, which would bring money to the corporation by allowing his debt to be settled, and that 'perhaps the transaction needed to be done in haste' (Bearman, 2012b: 482). Hastiness is a possible explanation for why we do not have a deed of conveyance signed by the vendor and given to the buyer. Such a deed would normally be expected in this period for the sale of a house like New Place (Bearman, 2012b: 467). Or, the deed could have been lost. Instead, we have an exemplification of the transfer of the title by fine, still possible in English law at the time.

Underhill's and Shakespeare's copies of final concord have disappeared, but the court records survive in The National Archives. Shakespeare, however, had a grander document drawn up, too, formally certifying the whole process and carrying the seal of the court. It is this document that survives in the Shakespeare Centre Library and Archive. The process of transferring a title by fine effectively meant that the purchaser had to sue the vendor of the right to own the property. Using this process to convey a property was complicated because the buyer's right to the title could be challenged within five years of the coming of age of an heir of the original title-holder.

Only a few weeks after having agreed to settle the title of New Place on Shakespeare, William Underhill was poisoned by his eldest son, Fulke, and died on 7 July 1597 in another of his houses at Fillongley, in Warwickshire (about 25 miles from Stratford-upon-Avon). Two years later, Fulke Underhill, aged twenty, was tried and hanged at Warwick, and the next in line to inherit his father's estate was Hercules Underhill, still a minor. By documenting the legal process of exemplification of title by fine as definitely as he did, Shakespeare could impressively produce the legal evidence if Underhill's second son tried to sue Shakespeare for the title when he turned twenty-one in 1602. In fact, Shakespeare seems to have

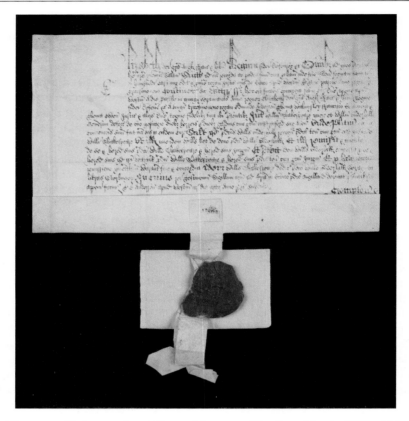

Figure 4.3 Shakespeare's certificate of the exemplification of fine in 1597, which confirmed his legal possession of the title to New Place. He would have been proud of this document, but not quite proud enough to have commissioned a scribe to produce its initial, flourishing letter. Or perhaps it was one of those jobs Shakespeare never quite got round to.

been waiting for the date to arrive and to have drawn up another fine as soon as the courts reconvened that Michaelmas to ensure that Hercules Underhill agreed to forfeit any claim he might have on New Place. The vendor's and the purchaser's copies of the final concord by fine of 1602 are in the Folger Shakespeare Library, Washington, DC.

Freeholders during this period were in the minority; most people rented property to live in, so the evidence for the cost of comparable real estate in Stratford-upon-Avon is thin. A difficult issue to resolve is how much Shakespeare is likely to have paid for New Place. The exemplification of fine in 1597 mentions £60 in silver, which Schoenbaum suggests was the customary 'legal fiction' for exemplifications of fine (Schoenbaum, 1987: 234). What mattered most was the legal process of transfer, not how much money was mentioned in the deed of fine. If all Shakespeare paid was £60, then New Place, irrespective of its condition, was a bargain. Given the amounts of money in which the Underhill family were used to dealing, and Underhill's own, immediately pressing debts, £60 seems too little. A house with a hall, two parlours, a kitchen and a loft, on half a burgage in Middle Row, sold for £19 in 1582, and again in 1609 for £30 (Jones, 1996: 9). In 1602 Elizabeth Quiney (widow of Richard) sold a Henley Street house to Thomas Allen the baker for £60, and in 1611 she and her son Adrian sold a house in Wood Street for £131 (Jones, 1996: 9–10). Bott had paid £140 for New Place in 1563, and Underhill £110 in 1567, and the amount named in fines was often half the amount eventually paid (Bearman, 1994: 18). So, it seems that Shakespeare probably paid £120 for New Place.

The extent of Shakespeare's purchase is named in the fine as comprising the house, two barns and two gardens. The burgage plot on which New Place was built had a peppercorn rent worth 12d a year, which was payable to the Lord of the Manor (incidentally the same peppercorn amount that Shakespeare would charge his sister's family each year for living in part of the Henley Street house in his will). There was land stretching as far as 54.86 m (180 ft) at the back of New Place, alongside Walkers Street (now Chapel Lane). This was divided into portions and owned by the Ettington chantry, Pinley Priory (Rowington), the parish of Clifford Chambers and Reading

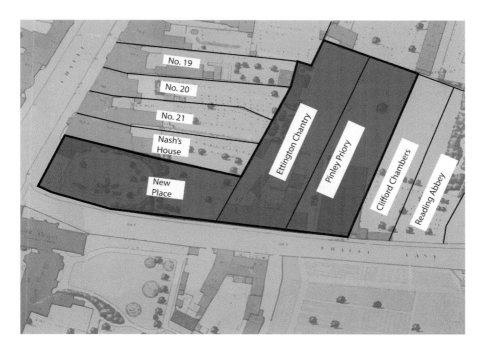

Figure 4.4 A plan showing the extent of Shakespeare's land ownership (the darker grey area), superimposed over a version of the Board of Health map from 1851, and based on a map produced by Robert Bearman for Colls and Mitchell (2012).

Abbey. Together they covered what has come to be known as the Great Garden of New Place. The amount Shakespeare owned (and indeed the extent of the New Place estate until 1758) included the portions formerly owned by Ettington chantry and Pinley Priory, which seem to have been 27.43 m (90 ft) wide (abutting on to the street) and 54.86m (180 ft) long (Bearman, 1994: 18–19), making up about half of the current Great Garden. Walkers Street whilst not on the edge of town, went through what must have looked a little like a farmyard (especially with the stream running down it in a ditch and Fulling Mill at the end, close to the river): 'in Shakespeare's time, and for long afterwards, Chapel Lane ran almost exclusively through gardens and barns, these barns being the storehouses for corn so numerous in Stratford before the various enclosures of the common lands in the neighbourhood' (Halliwell, 1864: 37). In fact, no fewer than ten barns were listed on Walkers Lane in a survey undertaken on the death of the Earl of Warwick (the Lord of the Manor) in 1590 (Shakespeare Centre Library and Archive, MA, iv, 106–7). Shakespeare's own malt barn was among them (Halliwell, 1864: 37–8). The Shakespeares would have been very aware of the sound of livestock – chickens, cows, sheep, goats, pigs – which would have been among their closest neighbours in this part of town.

New Place in Shakespearian biography

Nicholas Rowe was the first to present Stratford-upon-Avon and New Place as Shakespeare's retirement home: 'the latter part of his life was spent, as all men of good sense will wish theirs may be, in ease, retirement and the conversation of his friends [… he] is said to have spent some years before his death at his native Stratford' (Rowe, 1709: XXXV). Rowe's suggestion exudes a sense of bucolic relaxation. In Aubrey's brief life of Shakespeare, written around twenty years earlier (though not published until the early nineteenth century), comes the report that Shakespeare 'was wont to goe to his native Countrey once a yeare' (Aubrey, 1958: 275). Aubrey does not say when in the year, nor for how long, nor for how many years Shakespeare is supposed to have visited at this interval. But together, Aubrey's and Rowe's accounts have taken root over time, and have been compounded with the fact that, since the demolition of the second Cloptons' New Place in 1759, there has been no sense of any home or residency on the site. The large gap on the corner of Chapel Street and Chapel Lane – at least the size of the burgage plot – has led to a New Place-shaped lacuna in Shakespearian biography. In fact, the predominant narrative across most accounts of Shakespeare's life – exemplified perfectly by the title of Schoenbaum's final chapter, 'Stratford Again', in his *William Shakespeare: A Documentary Life* – is that Shakespeare left his wife, family and friends behind him in around 1587, went away to London, hardly returned, and then 'retired back to Stratford' from around 1611. The major Shakespeare biographies into the twenty-first century bear witness to the still-popular trope of Shakespeare's retirement.

There was something of a landmark shift in Stanley Wells's *Shakespeare for All Time* (2002). What follows might be regarded as the beginning of a new point of departure for New Place in Shakespearian biography:

> Shakespeare was a rich man, a householder and a landowner, possessed of a grand mansion with barns and extensive gardens, the smaller but still substantial house in which he had been born, at least one cottage with a garden, a large area of land which he leased for farming, and a major investment in tithes. All this centred on Stratford, the accumulated product of years of careful husbandry on income earned from the theatre … I find it hard to accept the common view that for twenty years he virtually abandoned the town where he owned a grand establishment and extensive property, where his mother and father, his wife and children and at least some of his brothers and sisters lived … He also needed books … And some of them were massive folios, bigger and heavier than a modern encyclopaedia, not the sort of book he could slip into his back pocket while travelling on foot or horseback from one guildhall to another. Can we really imagine that, having these needs, a writer who owned a splendid house in a small and relatively peaceful town in Warwickshire would not make every possible opportunity to spend time there? And is it not likely that his fellows, who relied on his literary productivity for their great financial success, encouraged him to do so? And if so, does not this modify the traditional picture of Shakespeare as a man who abandoned his family for the greater part of every year, and only resumed spending much time with them when, in the rather anachronistic term, he 'retired' to Stratford …? Shakespeare was, I suspect, our first great literary commuter. All of his contemporaries who wrote for the theatre based themselves in London. Only he had the good sense to maintain a household miles away. We know little about the contents of New Place, but my guess is that it contained a comfortable, book-lined study situated in the quietest part of the house to which Shakespeare retreated from London at every possible opportunity, and which members of the household approached at their peril when the master was at work. (Wells, 2002: 36–8)

Wells's account contradicts any presumed 'retirement' on Shakespeare's part; it counters the popular image of the inky-fingered Shakespeare of Joseph Fiennes in the 1998 film *Shakespeare in Love* – dashing off plays between pints of ale in the green room – by reiterating the quintessential literariness of Shakespeare's output, and signals the importance of Stratford-upon-Avon in Shakespeare's life. Wells's Shakespeare is a professional writer and reader who enjoys a reasonably high social status in his home town, quite different from the Shakespeare presented in most other biographies.

In contrast to Wells, most Shakespearian biographies perpetuate the retirement-back-to-Stratford-upon-Avon trope. Katherine Duncan-Jones has Shakespeare begrudgingly returning to Stratford-upon-Avon (to his closest, familial ties): 'the six months or so that he spent there when he was dying were of necessity rather than choice' (Duncan-Jones, 2001: 25). Stephen Greenblatt imagines that 'sometime around 1610, Shakespeare, a wealthy man with many investments, retired from London and returned to Stratford, to his neglected wife in New Place' (Greenblatt, 2004: 144). Germaine Greer takes up that image of a long-suffering Anne Shakespeare and appropriates it in order to disparage Shakespeare as much as possible in *Shakespeare's Wife* (2007). Greer appears not to want to allow Shakespeare to enjoy 'the leafy lanes of Warwickshire', since 'there were woods and green fields aplenty within a few hundred yards of the theatres on the Bankside' (Greer, 2007: 213), but, at the same time, self-contradictorily admits that 'scholars cannot agree on why or when Shakespeare returned to Stratford', and that 'it is possible that Shakespeare never really left Stratford' (Greer, 2007: 278). Eventually, Greer pursues the retirement line (leaving her main subject of interest, Anne, inviolable, isolated and hard-done-by for the greater part of two decades).

René Weis, however, is able to imagine Shakespeare returning home each year during Lent (when the theatres were closed):

> There were plays to be written in preparation for the new season, background reading to be done and perhaps his father and siblings to be helped in their glovers' business. In New Place Shakespeare would be comfortable, warm in front of his many large fires, with time enough despite the calls on it to play with his daughters, go for walks, and generally enjoy the life of a country gentleman. (Weis, 2007: 261)

Weis's Shakespeare is a boy from rural Warwickshire who makes himself into a country gentleman, and who needed the city as well as the peace and quiet of a market-town retreat. Jonathan Bate actually questions 'the myth of Shakespeare's retirement' (Bate, 2008: 358). Rather, we should consider carefully how and why Stratford-upon-Avon remained an important centre of his life.

A retired Shakespeare features, however, in the biographies of Lois Potter and Nicholas Fogg. Potter casts Shakespeare's brother Gilbert as 'the unofficial manager' of New Place from 1602 (Potter, 2012: 217), the year of the second 'fine', which settled the title of New Place, and the same year that Gilbert would represent Shakespeare in the purchase of 107 acres of land from the Combe family ('and also all the Common pasture for Sheepe horse kyne or other Cattle in the feildes of Olde Stretford' (Eccles, 1963: 101)). 'Stratford may not have been the quiet retreat that is sometimes imagined', Potter writes (2012: 403), even though her Shakespeare eventually decides to retire there. Nicholas Fogg's *Hidden Shakespeare* also presumes that Shakespeare retired back to Stratford-upon-Avon, even though he had to commute to London on several occasions – for example for the Belott–Mountjoy lawsuit in May 1612 (Fogg, 2012: 274), when he is described as 'of Stratford-upon-Avon' (Chambers, 1930, Vol. II: 91).

Interestingly, the first person to ask the stark and toughly realistic question – 'did Shakespeare purchase New Place as a residence for himself?'– was none other than the man who instigated and undertook the first archaeological dig there in the 1860s: James Orchard Halliwell (later Halliwell-Phillipps (Halliwell, 1864: 22)). By, as it were, inhabiting the site, with his feet in its soil, unearthing some of its surviving foundations and getting a sense of the size of dwelling that stood there in Shakespeare's time, Halliwell starts to appreciate what New Place would have meant to Shakespeare symbolically as well as financially. With this in mind, New Place – its size, its location, its cost (both personally and financially) – requires that Shakespearian biography offer a much more complex understanding of how and where Shakespeare spent his time.

The mistress of New Place: Anne Shakespeare

Anne's husband was only ever a lodger in London, so he did not leave either his home or his marriage permanently. The earliest mention of a place of residence for Shakespeare in London is in the St Helen's, Bishopgate ward where, in 1597 and 1598, he is listed among those who have not paid their taxes. Rather than leaping to moral conclusions about whether he was deliberately evading paying his taxes or not, the most likely explanation is that he was not there. In fact, he may not have been around in Bishopgate very much, and instead may have been spending more time in Stratford-upon-Avon. He was just settling into New Place, and was probably overseeing the desired (but costly) renovations and structural changes to its frontage (see Chapter 5).

However much (or however little) Shakespeare commuted back and forth between Stratford-upon-Avon and London, his wife Anne was his constant point of contact. The journey taken comfortably took four days (25 miles a day; the carrier, Greenaway, travelled 30 miles a day), but it could be undertaken in three, or even two days. It was Anne who ran the household whether her husband was there or not, Anne who looked after the children, Anne who organised the work that took place on the site. Germaine Greer's presentation of her in *Shakespeare's Wife* (2007) is important, but should be treated with caution. Her biography places Shakespeare's silent wife firmly into our historical and biographical perspectives, especially by emphasising the kinds of work and industry that she would probably have been involved with during her life at New Place, all of which is borne out by the archaeological evidence for cottage industries. Greer has Anne knitting stockings (Greer, 2007: 172), making and selling 'butter, cheese, and cream, her eggs, honey and pies' (167), and (most certainly) making malt (229). Malt, which requires specialist equipment, time, attention and space, was made like this:

> barley, or mixed oats and barley called maslen, was soaked in water in a 'yealing vat' and spread on the floor of a 'couch house' to begin the germination process that converts the starches in the grain to sugar or maltose. For this process space was needed … As soon as rootlets began to emerge from the grain, the malt was swept up and put on a 'kill' or 'keele', a wooden frame supporting a 'hair cloth' made of woven horse hair, which was set over a fire of straw. Straw was chosen because it does not create the kind of thick smoke that would taint the malt, which was meant to assume a golden colour. The process was dangerous, especially when carried out in a confined, poorly ventilated space. All of the fires that devastated Stratford probably involved the mismanagement of some stage of the malting or brewing process. It was essential to dry the malt thoroughly, if it was not to spoil. (Greer, 2007: 218)

Anne Shakespeare, and her lucrative, working-day world as manager of New Place, are now an important part of Shakespearian biography. She has emerged from centuries of silence as the female equivalent of what the writer of *Greene's Groatsworth of Wit* called her husband in 1592: a 'Johanna' (rather than a 'Johannes') Factotum, even 'probably singing ballads as she worked' (Greer, 2007: 55). Importantly, Anne was financially able, too. She was named in the will of Thomas Whittington, a husbandman in Shottery (who died in 1601): 'Item I geve and bequeth unto the poore people of Stratford 40s. that is in the hand of Anne Shaxspere, wyf unto Mr Wyllyam Shaxspere, and is due debt unto me, being payd to myne Executor by the sayd Wyllyam Shaxpere or his assigns' (Chambers, 1930, Vol. II: 42). Whittington knew Anne Shakespeare could be relied on to distribute the large sum of 40s to the poor of Stratford-upon-Avon; she was financially capable. But Greer overstates Anne's role as a hard-working heroine by over-emphasising Shakespeare's absence from Stratford-upon-Avon, and by portraying an indifference on his part to his wife and family.

Lena Cowen Orlin's important article 'Anne by Indirection' employs a not dissimilar methodology to Greer's by making analogous biographical connections. But Orlin focuses only on one: Elizabeth, wife of Richard Quiney. By looking at Elizabeth Quiney's well-documented life, Orlin is able to deduce the following about Anne Shakespeare: both women ran households and were therefore property managers; both took lodgers; made malt; offered civic hospitality (Anne and William entertained a visiting preacher on behalf of the corporation in New Place in the spring of 1614 (Schoenbaum, 1987: 280)); and both women borrowed and lent money, so were financially competent (Orlin, 2014: 446–8). Orlin also presents New Place as not only a status symbol, but also an income generator: 'How could [Shakespeare] have afforded shares in the Globe? Purchased New Place and other properties in Stratford? The tithes? The Blackfriars gatehouse? Perhaps the answer lies with Anne, his partner in a two-earner marriage' (Orlin, 2014: 448). To Anne's hard work and home-management must be added her ability to keep secure the family plate, much of which would have been made from silver (or perhaps gold) with the expectation it would be ready to be turned into cash if needed. When Shakespeare was away from home, there were servants around to help Anne feel secure, and very probably at least one of Shakespeare's three brothers. From 1597 until 1601, John Shakespeare was probably living in New Place, too, and then there were the Shakespeares' lodgers who lived there for eight years from 1603 (Bearman, 2012c: 295): Thomas and Lettice Greene and their two children (almost certainly the Shakespeares' godchildren), Anne (born 1604) and William (born 1608).

It was Anne Shakespeare, rather than her husband, who would have been in charge of the malt supplies when Richard Quiney's note of corn and malt listed Shakespeare as a householder in the Chapel Street ward and noted that he was holding 10 quarters, or 80 bushels, on 4 February 1598 (Schoenbaum, 1987: 236). There are 60 lb in 1 bushel (27.22 kg), so that makes 4,800 lb of malt being stored at New Place (2,177 kg: just over two tonnes). Malt was worth 50s a quarter in 1597 (Bearman, 1994: 27), so the Shakespeares' stock was worth around £25. There was nothing unusual about storing malt in Stratford-upon-Avon. In fact, Alexander Aspinall, the schoolmaster across the road, was storing 8 bushels more of malt than the Shakespeares when the 1598 list was drawn up (Eccles, 1961: 57–8). To put those quantities into perspective (80 bushels for the Shakespeares and 88 for Aspinall), it is worth looking back to 1595 and a household survey that lists Richard Quiney with 32 quarters of malt (256 bushels (Orlin, 2014: 432)). At that time, sixty-seven of the

Plate 1 Photograph of two fragments of prehistoric pottery recovered from the excavations at New Place in 2011.

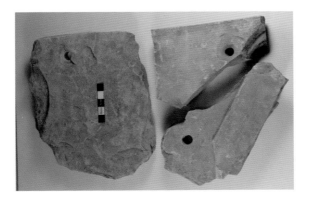

Plate 2 Stone roof tiles recovered from pits dating to the late sixteenth century.

Plate 3 A near-complete Brill-Borstall ware vessel dating to the thirteenth century.

Plate 4 Examples of thirteenth- and fourteenth-century North Warwickshire ware pottery recovered from the site.

Plate 5 Close-up image of one fragment of thirteenth–fourteenth-century North Warwickshire ware recovered from the site.

Plate 6 Similar to the hall at New Place: an 1839 watercolour by H. H. Lines of the Commandery, Worcester, and today showing the screens passage and beamed ceiling.

Plate 7 The area of the buttery and pantry at New Place. The oven is visible at the top of the photograph, with the sunken stone tank to the bottom right. The brick wall to the left of the photograph represents repairs completed during Shakespeare's ownership.

Plate 8 An example of the olive green-glazed decorative ridge tiles found during the excavation. These would have given the New Place roof a very distinctive appearance at its apex.

Plate 9 Coxcomb-crested roof tiles such as this would also have given the roof a distinct appearance at the time of Hugh Clopton and William Shakespeare.

Plate 10 The pottery from Hugh Clopton's New Place indicates high-status occupation, for example specialised tablewares and cooking implements such as this chafing dish.

Plate 11 A bone die recovered from the site. Examples such as this date to between the thirteenth and fifteenth centuries.

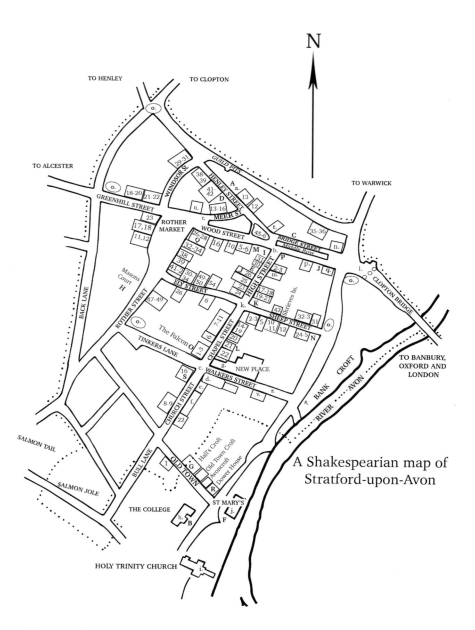

Plate 12 A Shakespearian map of Stratford-upon-Avon showing some of the surviving buildings Shakespeare knew, landmarks, and where some of his neighbours and friends lived.

Key to Shakespearian map of Stratford-upon-Avon

Some of the buildings that Shakespeare knew and which still survive today

Chapel Street
Nos. 1-3 (now The Falcon from around 1661); 6; 7-11; 14-19; 20 and 21; part of the buildings now known as the Shakespeare (hotel); No 22 (now Nash's House)

Church Street
Nos 8-9; 16; No 22 (now The Windmill)

Ely Street
No. 6 (now The Cross Keys); 26; 30-34; 49-50; 54 (now The Queen's Head)

Greenhill Street
Nos.18-20; 21-22; 23 (now The Old Thatch)

Guild Pits (now Guild Street)
Nos 35-36

Henley Street
No.12 (now the Public Library); 13 (now Hornby Cottage); 29-31; 38-39; 41-42

High Street
Nos. 2-3; 17-18; 19-21; 23-24; 25 (now The Garrick); 26 (now Harvard House); 30-31

Meer Street
Nos. 13-14; 15-16

Old Town
No.1; Old Town Croft; The Dower House; Avoncroft; Hall's Croft

Rother Street
Nos.11-12; 17-18; 34; 38-39; 40-41 (now the Lamplighter); 47-49; Masons Court

Sheep Street
Shrieve's House; Nos. 2-3; 5; 10-12; 24-25; 31-33; 42

Wood Street
Nos. 5-6; 10; 16; 26-28; 45-46

Location of some of Shakespeare's neighbours at different times of his life

A. George Badger (next door to the Shakespeares)
B. The Combe family (The College)
C. Richard Field (28 Bridge Street)
D. William Greenaway (now 46-49 Henley Street)
E. William Walker (29 High Street)
F. Thomas Greene (St Mary's)
G. John and Susanna Hall (Hall's Croft)
H. Alderman John Gibbs (Masons Court)
I. Adrian Quiney (31 High Street)
J. Thomas Rogers (26 High Street, Harvard House, and 27-28 High Street)
K. Hamnet and Judith Sadler (22 High Street)
L. July Shaw (21 Chapel Street)
M. Abraham Sturley (5-6 Wood Street)
N. Richard Tyler (now around 23-26 Sheep Street)
O. William Walford (now The Falcon)
P. Thomas and Judith Quiney (1 High Street)
Q. Alderman William Parsons (26-28 Wood Street)
R. William Reynolds (The Dower House)
S. John Sadler (16 Church Street)

Landmarks

a. The Shakespeares' home on Henley Street
b. High Cross or Market Cross (and from 1614 a whipping post)
c. White Cross
d. Guild Chapel
e. School and Guild Hall
f. Almshouses
g. New Place and grounds
h. The College
i. Holy Trinity Church
j. St Mary's
k. Corn Market
l. Toll Gate
m. The town's first recorded jail (5 High Street)
n. The Swan Inn
o. Muck heaps
p. The Crown Inn
q. The Bear Inn
r. Streams
s. The Walkers' Mill
t. The Angel Inn
u. The King House or Hall (now the White Swan)
v. Rowington Cottage
. . . Borough border

Plate 12 *(cont.)*

Plate 13 A brick floor surface (structure F16) located against the northern foundations of Shakespeare's hall. This may represent a hearth and external chimneystack added to the building by Shakespeare.

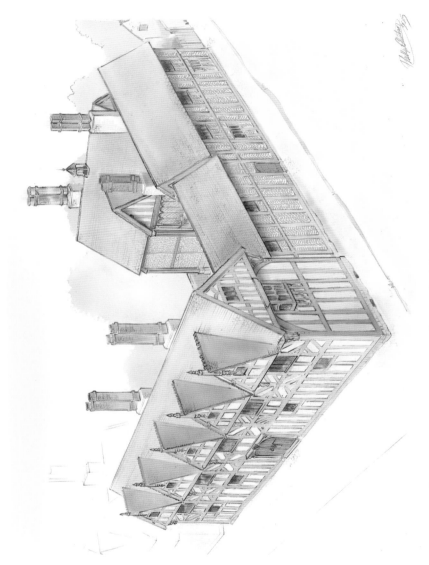

Plate 14 Artistic reconstruction colour-wash of Shakespeare's New Place, northeast view.

Plate 15 An almost complete example of a Midlands purpleware drinking vessel or jug dated to the sixteenth century was recovered during the excavations.

Plate 16 A fragment of sixteenth-century Rhenish stoneware with a legend on it that reads '… TMEIN …'. This probably originally read 'WAN GOT WIL IST MEIN ZIL' (When God wills it, so is my goal) or 'WANN GOTT WILL IST MEIN ZIEL' (When God wills it, my time is up) (Rátkai, 2011).

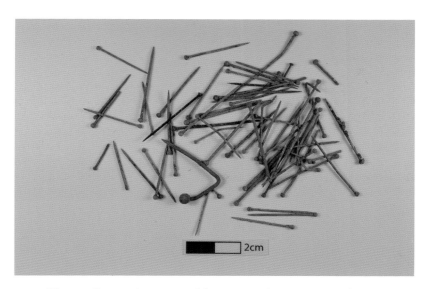

Plate 17 Copper pins recovered from various locations across the site.

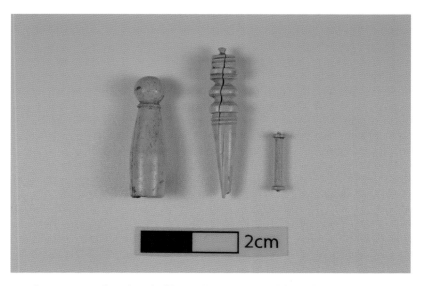

Plate 18 Examples of worked bone objects recovered from the site, including a scoring peg, a possible game piece and objects associated with textile working.

Plate 19 A bone handle from a kitchen utensil that has been carved, over a number of occasions, with motifs. The overall impression of the carvings suggests these were done by a young person in the seventeenth or eighteenth century.

NEW PLACE., STRATFORD.
(SHAKSPEARE'S RESIDENCE.)

Pub.ᵈ by J. Ward. Stratford.

Plate 20 1702 full-colour image of Sir John Clopton's New Place.

Plate 21 Examples of plaster mouldings recovered from the excavations. These would have adorned the ceilings of one or more of the rooms throughout the 1702 New Place.

Plate 22 Large, clay modillion or corbel from the 1702 New Place house. These ornamental brackets would have sat on the exterior of the building, normally just below the cornice. These may have had a structural role or have been simply decorative.

Plate 23 Onion bottle fragments from the oven flue. This short-necked type of bottle was common in the later part of the seventeenth century and into the eighteenth, and would certainly have been familiar to later occupiers of New Place.

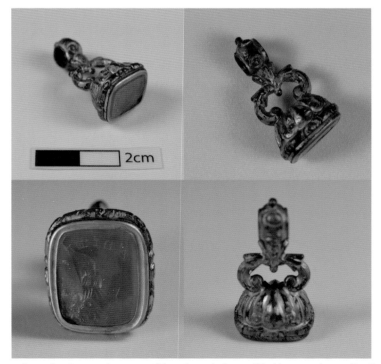

Plate 24 An early-nineteenth century fob seal, made from gilded brass and carnelian/intaglio red glass. The fob seal inset of carnelian/intaglio red glass was engraved with the picture of a sailing ship and the word 'A'DIEU'. This could be a commemorative item of the Henry Grace à Dieu, a sixteenth-century carrack (great ship) contemporary with the *Mary Rose*, the inset having been reused in a later eighteenth–nineteenth-century setting.

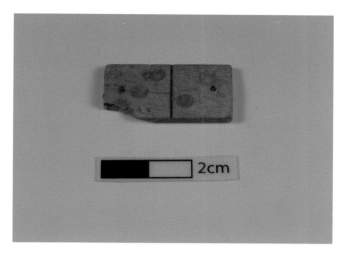

Plate 25 Rectangular bone domino with two and three drilled pips divided by a shallow groove or bar. The remains of pins at each end suggest that the bone was attached to another layer of material, possibly a hardwood such as ebony, which is common in Victorian domino sets.

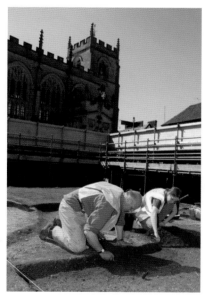

'Having worked on many digs over the years, and currently teaching history and Shakespeare, I found that Dig for Shakespeare brought all these elements together in one extended enjoyable experience. Three years work in sun and dust, rain and mud involved many social interactions. With my fellow diggers I made many friends. With the public and visitors I was able to explain about the site and describe and share our discoveries as they were revealed'.

John Richards—volunteer

Plate 26 The Dig for Shakespeare community archaeology project was completed by volunteers, for example John Richards, and monitored by professional archaeologists, such as Elisabeth Charles (both pictured).

Plate 27 The Shakespeare Birthplace Trust portrait of William Shakespeare, probably 1610–20. Unknown artist. The sitter is depicted finely and exquisitely attired: Shakespeare as the wealthy gentleman of New Place with duties and connections at court.

most prominent men in the town were listed as keeping '1,000 quarters of malt and had in store 525 quarters of barley. They were detailed to send twenty-four quarters of malt a week to Birmingham market and thirteen quarters of malt and five quarters of barley weekly to Stratford market' (Jones, 1996: 33). That is 100 times more malt than the Shakespeares had in February 1598. The importance of the malting industry for Stratford-upon-Avon cannot be overestimated; people came from Birmingham, Banbury and Hampton (near Evesham) to buy it at the town's market (Jones, 1996: 32). The Shakespeares' connections with malt continued and, in 1604, Shakespeare sued the local apothecary, Philip Rogers, who kept a shop on the High Street, for not paying back an outstanding debt on 20 bushels (around half a tonne) of malt. Malt was a valuable commodity and was frequently listed in inventories. Greer notes that, from the Shakespeares' 80 bushels in 1598, Anne could have made 600 gallons of ale and 600 gallons of small beer (Greer, 2007: 229); the former product was lucrative and the latter imperative, since the water itself was not safe to drink.

A commuting brotherhood: Gilbert, Richard and Edmund Shakespeare

Shakespeare's brother Gilbert (only two years younger) provided crucial assistance with Shakespeare's business affairs, and represented his older brother in his purchase of 107 acres of arable land from the Combes in May 1602. The acreage of Stratford-upon-Avon itself was 109 acres, so Shakespeare was buying land that amounted to almost as much as the borough itself. His acreage was distributed among 19 furlongs towards the Welcombe hills to the north of town (for example 'Top of Rowley' and 'Under Rowley' close to the modern-day Rowley Crescent), and 10 acres around the river area off the main road to Warwick (Bearman, 1994: 41). It was a considerable investment: £320 (did Shakespeare inherit money from his father who had died the year before?). Gilbert was highly able, and possibly something of a business partner to Shakespeare. He, too, would have attended the grammar school, and 'wrote a scholar's hand (so we may judge from his signature as witness to the lease of a piece of ground in Bridge Street on 5 March 1610)' (Fripp, 1938: 762). Gilbert, too, may have had significant links with London, if he is the same Gilbert Shakespeare who is listed as a haberdasher in St Bride's Parish in 1597. Although no link has been definitely proven, it is a compelling thought, especially since the London haberdasher with the same name as Shakespeare's brother is recorded as having appeared in court to bail out the Stratford-upon-Avon-born William Sampson, a clock-maker (Eccles, 1961: 108). Greer speculates that Gilbert Shakespeare, along with William Hart the hatter, Shakespeare's brother-in-law (from 1599), may even have supplied the Lord Chamberlain's Men and the King's Men 'with hats and other fripperies' appropriate to their trades (Greer, 2007: 206). If the Gilbert Shakespeare of the St Bride's parish was the poet's brother (and Schoenbaum and Greer are among the Shakespeare scholars who believe he was), that suggests he was apprenticed to a haberdasher in Stratford-upon-Avon, rather than to a glover (his father's trade). There were five haberdashers in the town between 1570 and 1630 (Jones, 1996: 220). Gilbert's apprenticeship as a haberdasher may have been influenced by his father's wool-dealing: haberdashers dealt in gentlemen's clothing and accoutrements, which relied on the woollen industry.

William's brother Edmund, sixteen years his junior, most certainly had ties with London. Like Gilbert and Richard he could have been apprenticed to either his father or another of the town's glovers, or perhaps to a different trade, collaboratively useful to their father's glove-making. Presumably all of their apprenticeships were completed successfully, unlike their elder brother's. Edmund reached his majority in May 1601 (John Shakespeare died in the September), and followed his brother William to become an actor in London, who no doubt introduced him to his most influential contacts and associates. We do not know when Edmund moved to London, and he may have been staying with or living close to William (or Gilbert) from 1601. He was another link between Stratford-upon-Avon, New Place, and Shakespeare's work in London. An illegitimate child named 'Edward, son of Edward Shackspeere, player, base-born' was buried at St Giles, Cripplegate on 12 August 1607. The parish clerk, as Schoenbaum suggests, probably 'showed himself disinclined to make nice distinctions between similar-sounding appellations' (Schoenbaum, 1987: 29). Or, perhaps the clerk was hard of hearing. Edmund had just moved to live in the Vine in Paris Garden Liberty (very close to the Globe) and was listed in the token books for Holy Communion (people had to buy a token in advance and take it with them to the service). But his name is crossed out, suggesting that he died shortly afterwards (Richardson, 2015: 46). He was buried on 31 December 1607 in the church of St Mary Overy in Southwark (now Southwark Cathedral): 'Edmund Shakespeare a player' (Schoenbaum, 1987: 29). Probably William himself paid for the 'forenoon knell of the great bell', and the 20s for interment in the church itself – ten times more expensive than burial in the churchyard (Schoenbaum, 1987: 29). William's brothers Gilbert and Edmund were probably his occasional or regular travelling companions on the London-to-Stratford-upon-Avon road.

Gilbert, Richard and Edmund Shakespeare did not marry, and Richard seems to have been the one who would have been a constant and consistent presence around the family home. He is mentioned in the records of the Bawdy Court on 1 July 1608. The precise nature of the charge is unknown but he was charged a 12d fine 'to the use of the poor of Stratford' (Brinkworth, 1972: 110), so it is likely that he broke the Sabbath.

Shakespeare's cousin and lodger at New Place, Thomas Greene

Then there was Shakespeare's 'cousin', Thomas Greene, the lodger at New Place. No actual, familial bond of cousin (in the way we would understand it) has been established, but it is possible that the Greenes and the Shakespeares (or indeed the Hathaways) were distantly connected. The Greene family was from Warwickshire, and a John Greene of Warwick was probably brother to 'Thomas Green *alias* Shakspere' who was buried in Stratford on 6 March 1590 (Chambers, 1930, Vol. II: 17). Only Greene himself uses the term 'cousin' in relation to Shakespeare, three times between 1614 and 1615 in his personal papers about the disputes over the proposed enclosure of land on the Welcombe hills.

Greene trained as a lawyer in London, first at Staple Inn and then at the Middle Temple. He was called to the bar in October 1602 (Bearman, 2012c: 291). Greene was possibly present at the earliest recorded performance of Shakespeare's *Twelfth Night; or, What You Will* on 2 February 1602, which his fellow law student John Manningham (also a Middle Templar) wrote about (Chambers, 1930, Vol. II: 327–8). Greene became the town clerk of Stratford-upon-Avon from 31 August 1603 (Bearman, 2012c: 295), so living in New Place (next door but one to the Guildhall), was handy for council meetings. Assuming Greene's association with Manningham, it is likely that Greene heard Manningham's gossip about Shakespeare, which was in circulation around the Middle Temple. Manningham's story was not known about in print until 1759 when a version of it appeared in Thomas Wilkes's *A General View of the Stage* (Schoenbaum, 1987: 205–6). Manningham's diary was first published in 1831, and records the following for 13 March 1602:

> Vpon a tyme when Burbidge played Rich. 3. there was a citizen greue soe farr in liking with him, that before shee went from the play shee appointed him to come that night vnto hir by the name of Ri: the 3. Shakespeare overhearing their conclusion went before, was intertained, and at his game ere Burbidge came. Then message being brought that Rich. The 3.ᵈ was at the dore, Shakespeare caused returne to be made that William the Conquerour was before Rich. The 3. Shakespeare's name William. (Chambers, 1930, Vol. II: 212)

How far this gossip about Shakespeare's alleged bout of marital infidelity made it back to Stratford-upon-Avon is not known, but as Greer realistically remarks, 'if Ann had not misdoubted that some fine lady of the capital would throw her modest charms into the shade, she would have been a very unusual woman' (Greer, 2007: 157).

Greene had literary interests, too, and wrote and dedicated a sonnet to his friend Michael Drayton (published in Drayton's 1605 poetry collection). If Greene did not already know Drayton, then he may have met him through their mutual friend Henry Rainsford, from nearby Clifford Chambers (Bearman, 2012: 292). The preface to *The Hystorie of the Seven Wise Maisters of Rome* (1602) and the book *A Poets Vision and a Princes Glorie dedicated to the high and mightie Prince, James King of England and Ireland* (1605) are attributed to Thomas Greene, and there is no reason to suppose that this is not the Thomas Greene who lived in New Place (Bearman, 2012c: 293). He also wrote some verses in Latin (among his papers for 1614), published posthumously.

Greene and Shakespeare's social status bear interesting comparison. Greene was designated an 'Esquire', which means that he 'stood socially higher than Shakespeare' (Fripp, 1938: 763). He was probably a very reliable and steady influence in New Place for the eight years that he lived there. New Place – with its inner courtyard and square of green – had rooms surrounding it on three sides. There was plenty of space for Greene and his family, and it can easily be imagined that they lodged very comfortably in perhaps a set of two or three rooms that formed part of one of the wings. Like Shakespeare, Greene dealt in large sums of money. On 3 September 1612, for example, Greene wrote to Humfrey Collis of Bicknell promising to pay him back £300 (as agreed in March 1609) on 25 March 1613 in the porch of Holy Trinity Church (Fripp, 1938: 764). In 1609 Greene had bought the other half of the share in the tithes that Shakespeare had purchased in 1605 (for £440). Greene paid £60 up front and promised a further £360 in 1613 (Bearman, 2012c: 297). No wonder Greene needed to meet Collis in the church porch on Lady Day. And, like Shakespeare, Greene aspired to a grand house. His lodging all that time in New Place suggests he was saving up for it, or waiting for the right opportunity to make the purchase. In 1610, he nearly moved out of New Place into a house belonging to George Browne. But neither the house nor its garden were ready when they were expected to be. Greene was quite content 'to permytt without contradiccion & the rather because I perceyued I mighte stay another yere at newe place' (Chambers, 1930, Vol. II: 96). Halliwell and Greer are among those who want to believe that Shakespeare did not move back to live in New Place until Greene moved out. But it is surely absurd to suggest that the Greenes, lodging at New Place, would have kept Shakespeare away from his large family home. Greene left New Place in 1611 (after having lived there for eight years), and moved into his own impressive house, St Mary's, which stood next to Holy Trinity's churchyard, with his wife and two children. Their third child, Elizabeth, was born in St Mary's a year later, and was baptised on 28 June. It is possible that she was named after Shakespeare's granddaughter Elizabeth Hall, then aged four years and four months, which would mean that John and Susanna Hall would have attended the christening as sponsors (Fripp, 1938: 763). St Mary's had 90.53m (297 ft) of wall between the house and the churchyard, which Greene was ordered by the corporation (who maintained the churchyard) to repair on 21 June 1611 (Halliwell, 1864: 25). Shakespeare's pattern of social and financial investment in Stratford-upon-Avon was matched – and even bettered – by his cousin Greene not only following suit, but, in fact, rather trumping him.

The close relationship between Greene and Shakespeare is exemplified by their mutual interest and involvement in the enclosures dispute. In what was to be the last year-and-a-half of his life, Shakespeare was involved in local politics that affected 15 acres of the land he owned among the fields on the Welcombe hills and Old Stratford, and the income he and (on his decease) his daughter Susanna derived from it. Enclosure would mean that the fields in which crops were grown would have become no more than pasture for sheep, which is why it could lead to the depopulation of entire villages: people were forced to move on, or face starvation. The threat of enclosure followed quickly after another devastating fire in the town on Saturday 9 July 1614 that, according to a brief printed in December 1614:

> within the space of lesse then two houres consumed and burnt fifty and fower dwelling howses, many of them beeing very faire houses, besides Barnes, stables and other houses of Office, together also with great store of Corne, Hay, Straw, Wood & Timber therin,

amounting in all to the value of Eight Thowsand Pounds & upwards, the force of which fire was so great (the wind sitting full uppon the Towne) that it dispersed into so many places therof whereby the whole Towne was in very great daunger to haue been utterly consumed & burnt: By reason whereof, and of two seuerall fires happening in the said Towne within these Twenty yeares to the losse of Twenty Thousand Pounds more, not onely our said poore subiects who haue now susteyned this great losse, are utterly undone and like to perish, but also the rest of the Towne is in great hazard to be ouerthrowne & undone, the Inhabitants there beeing no waies able to relieue their disressed [*sic*] Neighbours in this their great want and misery. And whereas the said Towne hath been a great Market Towne whereunto great recourse of people was made, by reason of the weekely Market, Faires, and other frequent meetings which were then holden and appointed, and now beeing thus ruinated & decayed, it is in great hazard to bee utterly ouerthrowne, if either the resort thither bee neglected, or course of trauellers diuerted, which for want of speedy repayration may bee accasioned. (Shakespeare Centre Library and Archive, BRU 15/7, no. 106a)

New Place escaped the blaze. The Shakespeares must have felt vulnerable but exceedingly lucky: the Globe Theatre had burnt to the ground on 29 June 1613 (and its replacement had only just opened, a year and a day later – two weeks before the fire in Stratford-upon-Avon). Shakespeare's friend John Combe was buried on 14 July (leaving Shakespeare £5), and his death may have been related to the fire (Fripp, 1938: 815).

The serious proposal to enclose the commonly used arable land almost came to pass. The scheme had been proposed by the steward of the Lord Chancellor, Arthur Mainwaring, who sought support from William Combe: John's uncle and a major landowner. William Replingham, Mainwaring's lawyer cousin in Great Harborough, acted as his agent. Thomas Greene led the opposing faction (both personally and as town clerk) and his diaries for this period give a passing, tantalising glimpse of Shakespeare the commuter: 'At my Cosen Shakespeare commyng yesterday to towne I went to see him howe he did he told me that they assured him they ment to inclose noe further then to gospell bushe' (Chambers, 1930, Vol. II: 142–3). We do not know where Shakespeare was arriving into town from, but Greene talked with him and John Hall (17 November 1614), and kept notes of their conversation, recording that 'they think there will be nothyng done at all' (Chambers, 1930, Vol. II: 143). A few weeks later Greene notes an unsuccessful attempt to meet with Replingham at New Place (Chambers, 1930, Vol. II: 144). Cautiously, though, Shakespeare and Greene entered into a legal agreement for full compensation of their interests should the enclosure be successful. The corporation was against the proposals. Combe and Mainwaring pushed for them too much – even to the point of digging trenches in which to plant the new, enclosing hedges. Greene records that it was the women and children of the town, and nearby Bishopton, who took it upon themselves to fill the ditches up again (Chambers, 1930, Vol. II: 144). And in March 1615 it was decided that the land should remain as pasture.

It may be significant that Greene decided to sell St Mary's and all of his Stratford-upon-Avon investments only a week or two after Shakespeare had died. He sought £870 for them in all: £280 for the house, £550 for the corn tithes and £40 for some other 'privy' tithes (Bearman, 2012c: 301). Francis Collins, the lawyer who had drawn up Shakespeare's will, replaced Greene as town clerk on the same day Greene stepped down from the office. In the end, the corporation could only raise £640 to purchase the property. Greene and his family left Stratford-upon-Avon in May 1617, and moved to Bristol. Greene became a reader at the Middle Temple by 1621, master of the bench in 1623, and treasurer in 1629 (Chambers, 1930, Vol. II: 152).

New Place and Shakespeare's growing reputation

Shakespeare's friends and fellow townsmen Richard Quiney and Abraham Sturley knew how to find their friend and neighbour when he was in London. Quiney visited London at least ten times from autumn 1593 to 1601 and stayed there for anything from a few days up to a few months: 'on two of these visits, it is almost certain that he met up with Shakespeare and it would not be straining the evidence to propose that they met on other occasions as well' (Bearman, 2012b: 475). Their recorded London interactions with the new owner of New Place occurred in 1598, when the town was having to raise as many funds as possible after the fires of a few years earlier, especially in light of the State-imposed curtailing of the malting industry. The earliest mention is dated 24 January 1598. From Stratford-upon-Avon Sturley writes to Quiney in London that:

> our countriman, Mr Shaksper, is willinge to disburse some monei vpon some od yardeland or other att Shottri or neare about vs; he thinketh it verj fitt patterne to move him to deale in the matter of our tithes. Bj the instruccions v [i.e. you] can geve him theareof, and bj the frendes he can make therefore, we thinke it a faire marke for him to shoote att, and not unpossible to hitt. (Chambers, 1930, Vol. II: 101–2)

Later that same year, on 25 October, while in London petitioning the Queen's Council for money on behalf of Stratford-upon-Avon, Richard Quiney wrote to Shakespeare from the Bell Inn on Carter Lane (near St Paul's), asking Shakespeare for a loan of £30. Quiney calls Shakespeare 'Loveing Countreyman', and addresses the letter 'To my Loveinge good ffrend & contreymann, Mr Wm. Shackespere' (Chambers, 1930, Vol. II: 102). Quiney's now famous letter (the only surviving example of any of Shakespeare's correspondence) may not have been sent – perhaps Quiney saw Shakespeare just before he was about to dispatch it – because it was discovered in Quiney's own papers.

A few days later, on 30 October, Richard's father, Adrian, wrote to him in London with an assurance of 10s and mentioning the 'bargen with Mr Sha...' (Chambers, 1930, Vol. II: 103). Then, on 4 November, Sturley wrote to Richard Quiney that:

> Vr letter of 25 October came to mj handes the laste of the same att night per Grenwaj [the carrier], which imported ... that our countriman Mr Wm. Shak. Would procure vs monej, which I will like of as I shall heare when, and wheare, and howe; and I praj let not go that occasion if it may sort to any indifferent condicions. Allso that if monej might be had for 30 or 40l, a lease, &c., might be procured. Oh howe can v make dowbt of monej, who will not beare XXXtie or XLl [30 or 40 pounds] towards sutch a match? (Chambers, 1930, Vol. II: 103)

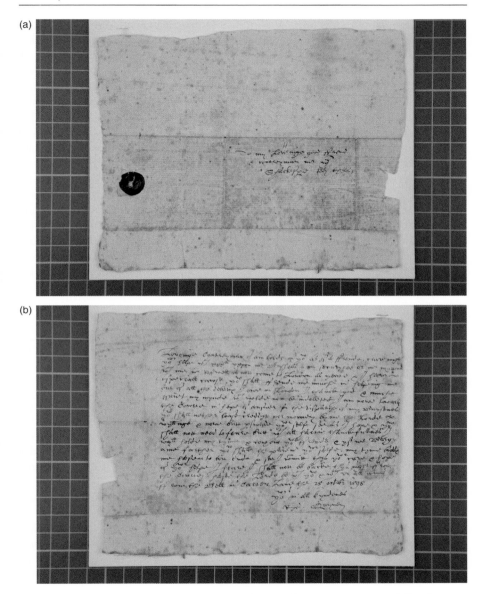

Figure 4.5 (*a*) Richard Quiney's letter as addressed 'To my Loveinge good ffrend & contreymann, Mr Wm. Shackespere'. (*b*) The letter by Richard Quiney to Shakespeare at the Bell Inn on Carter Lane, London, on 25 October 1598 (St Crispin's day).

Sturley's letter supports the interpretation that Quiney happened to see Shakespeare shortly after having written to him. Quiney then wrote a second letter to Sturley and dispatched it to Stratford-upon-Avon on the same day. Greenaway the carrier took it with him, and Sturley's reply (in response to Quiney having said that Shakespeare would lend them the money) was written on 4 November and carried back to Quiney in London. All of these letters confirm that Shakespeare was known to be a man of means, that he could probably provide the money that was needed quickly, and that Sturley and Quiney knew he could almost certainly be relied on to assist them in matters touching Stratford-upon-Avon. They also bear out Shakespeare's social and reputational standing: a man with significant wealth and influence in the capital city, but one who was always rooted in the best interests of his hometown.

New Place reflected Shakespeare's growing reputation back to the town. Between 1594 and 1616, the theatre companies in which he owned shares performed around 170 times before the royal Courts of Queen Elizabeth and King James during the Christmas seasons (Astington, 1999: 234–57). Shakespeare and his fellow company members were probably all there for each of these grand occasions. His rising professional and social status coincided with the shift of theatrical patronage from the aristocracy to the members of the royal household, and the King's Men were no less than the leading theatrical troupe of their day.

Shakespeare and the gardens of New Place

Shakespeare's knowledge of gardening and the natural world is undeniable. My critical assumption here is that he would not have written as extensively about gardening and horticulture as he did if he had not been interested in it, or known a lot about it. Gardening as an activity is comparable to the act of writing. Both activities involve germination, careful preparation, and an audience for the work of art that has been nurtured and (usually gradually) brought into being.

New Place's adjoining land, two barns and two gardens ('de vno mesuagio duobus horreis et duobus gardinis cum pertinenciis' (Chambers, 1930, Vol. II: 95)) meant horticultural opportunities, industry and leisure for the Shakespeares, their lodgers and their servants. There is nothing quaint about the fact that Shakespeare refers to scores of fruits, vegetables and flowers in his work; together they provided food, medicine and pleasure. Fripp is characteristically exuberant when writing about these topics in his magnificent *Shakespeare, Man and Artist*:

> Shakespeare's love of his garden and practical acquaintance with gardening appear in his earlier as in his later work. He must have been his own gardener for years in Henley Street, and have employed one or more gardeners at New Place. In his poems and plays before 1597 he speaks of mint and parsley, fennel, onions, leeks, garlic; of apples, pears, plums –
>
> > The mellow plum doth fall, the green sticks fast,
> > Or, being early plucked, is sour to taste
> > (*Venus and Adonis*, lines 527–8)

Damson, cherries, quinces, figs, 'dangling apricots' (grown as a standard, not against the wall), grapes, strawberries, dewberries, mulberries, medlars, walnuts, chestnuts, hazelnuts and their 'kernels'; of carnations, lilies, roses, 'nodding violets', marigolds, 'pale primroses', oxlips, columbine, woodbine and its 'honey-suckle' flowers, eglantine or sweet-brier, pansies ('love-in-idleness'), myrtle, marjoram, rosemary, and rue. To these he adds in subsequent writings, cabbage and carrot, potato, eringo, lettuce, hyssop, thyme, savoury, radish, gourd ('gross watery pumpion'), turnip; gooseberry and peach; daffodils 'that come before the swallow dares'; lavender, orchids or 'long purples', 'crown imperials', and, noticeable, the box tree. (Fripp, 1938: 465).

So much for the facts. Fripp then goes on to speculate about what the gardens at New Place might have been like:

> The 'great garden' at New Place, no doubt, was typically Elizabethan, consisting of the kitchen-garden, the flower-garden, and the orchard. The flower-garden would be formally, not to say mathematically, laid out, such 'a curious-knotted garden' as we hear of in *Love's Labour's Lost* (1.1.241), with ingeniously designed beds and paths, trellises and an arbour, the whole surrounded by a brick wall or a high hedge carefully cultivated and cut into shapes often fantastic. In the orchard would be grass 'kept finely shorn' [Francis Bacon's essay 'Of Gardens'], and probably a 'thick pleached alley', like Antonio's in *Much Ado About Nothing* (1.2.8), wherein the Prince and Count Claudio walked and were overheard by a servant of the house in secret conversation. In such an alley, between and under the thickly interlacing boughs of two rows of trees – thorn, sweet-brier, privet, or whatnot – the Poet would find welcome retreat with his book or writing. (Fripp, 1938: 467)

Certainly, the Shakespeare Birthplace Trust's presentation of the gardens of New Place has been influenced over the years by this kind of thinking (Edgar Fripp himself was a life trustee), and in 1920 Ernest Law had created an Elizabethan-style knot garden in New Place, partly inspired by Shakespeare's own works.

That New Place had gardens, and, by the time Shakespeare reiterated his ownership of the title in the fine of 1602, two orchards ('duobus pomariis' (Chambers, 1930:, Vol. II: 96) means that gardening was part of what he understood, and that he himself spent time gardening, employed gardeners or talked extensively to people who did. His close knowledge of horticulture means it was part of his world, rooted in Stratford-upon-Avon rather than in London. Lent, the time of lengthening light in the early spring, is traditionally a time of planting, so if Shakespeare was regularly at home during that season then it coincided with an important time for his gardens.

The tradition that Shakespeare planted a mulberry tree starts with the Clopton family, who had built a new house on the site by 1702. A famous actor of the period, Charles Macklin, notes that he was 'entertained under its shade in 1744' (Halliwell, 1864: 231). In the second half of the eighteenth century, the local Stratford-upon-Avon historian and guide John Jordan mentions that the tree 'was grown to a very large size, with wide spreading boughs that shaded many yards of ground, under which were placed benches to sit on in the shade' (Halliwell, 1864: 231). In 1790, the Shakespeare scholar Edmond Malone had an account given to him by the vicar of Stratford-upon-Avon, James Davenport, about one Hugh Taylor (aged eighty-five). Although the story is exaggerated (Taylor claims, for example, that his family lived next door to New Place for three centuries), elements of it ring true. That Shakespeare planted the mulberry tree

> was transmitted from father to son during the last and the present century; that this tree, of the fruit of which he had often eaten in his younger days, some of the branches hanging over his father's garden, was planted by Shakespeare; and that, till this was planted, there was no mulberry tree in that neighbourhood. (Halliwell, 1864: 231)

Halliwell adds a deflationary note that a Taylor family lived in the same ward, but not next door, and that, as far he knows, none of them was named Hugh (Halliwell, 1864: 231). In fact, there was a Hugh in that Taylor family, son of Thomas, who was baptised on 6 September 1761.

But a mulberry tree was felled at New Place by the infamously angry Revd Francis Gastrell and his wife some time between 1756 and 1759 (Halliwell, 1864: 228). Taylor's story corroborates what was commonly believed about the tree. Its particular point of interest is the element of the tree being a status symbol, supporting the image of the Shakespeares proudly planting something new and unusual (and foreign). In Shakespeare's imagination, the new import also evoked one of his favourite writers, and books, Ovid's *Metamorphoses*: Pyramus and Thisbe (whose story Shakespeare bodies forth in *A Midsummer Night's Dream*) are turned into mulberry trees.

James I introduced thousands of mulberry trees into the country in 1609 in order to start a silk industry, which was to remain a localised, cottage concern until the late seventeenth century. And, long before the Shakespeares' mulberry tree became famous, New Place was celebrated for its vines and orchards. In 1631 Sir Thomas Temple of nearby Wolverton – whose sister-in-law lived opposite in what is now the Falcon Hotel – sent Harry Rose over to Stratford-upon-Avon to 'desire Mr Hall Phisic*ion*' to let him take '2 or 3 of the fairest buds on some new shoots of the last year's vines' (Schoenbaum, 1987: 236; Fogg, 2014: 45). New Place occupied verdant and productive ground, and this is reflected in Shakespeare's work and in the accounts of the site itself.

Shakespeare's business investments and money, and New Place

For a summary of Shakespeare's major investments see Table 4.1. The purchase of the land in 1602 was witnessed by Anthony and John Nash, William Sheldon, Humphrey Mainwaring and Richard Mason, and the deed was then 'sealed and delivered to Gilbert Shakespeare to the use of the within named William Shakespeare' (Eccles, 1961: 101). Shakespeare himself seems not to have been present and to have been happy for Gilbert to receive the deed on his behalf. For the tithes indenture (drawn up by his lawyer friend, and corporation member, Francis Collins, who oversaw Shakespeare's will), William

Table 4.1 Shakespeare's major investments

Date	Investment	Cost
1594	Shares in the Lord Chamberlain's Men	Between £50 and £80 (Gurr, 2004: 89 and 108)
Easter and Trinity terms 1597	New Place (reconfirmed in 1602)	At least £120 (not including the cost of any repairs and remodelling the frontage)
1599	Share in the Globe Theatre	£100 (Gurr, 2004: 33)
1 May 1602	107 acres of land (reconfirmed in 1610)	£320
28 September 1602	Copyhold of the cottage, garden and a ¼ acre in Chapel Lane belonging to Rowington Manor	Nominal rent of 2s 6d
24 July 1605	A half share of the tithes for Old Stratford, Welcombe and Bishopton in 'wooll, lambe, and other smalle pryvie thythes' (Eccles, 1961: 104)	£440
1608	Shares in the Blackfriars Theatre	£100 (Gurr, 2004: 34)
10 March 1613	The gatehouse in Blackfriars	£140

Hubaud, Anthony Nash (Shakespeare's granddaughter would later, in 1622, marry Nash's second son, Thomas) and Francis Collins witnessed Ralph Hubaud's (the seller's) signature. Shakespeare himself may or may not have been around, but he did not have to be, since his lawyer, Francis Collins, would have represented him. Fripp notes that the date of the transaction, 24 July 1605, coincided with the baptism of Shakespeare's nephew Thomas Hart in Holy Trinity Church (Fripp, 1938: 634). Shakespeare signed the mortgage deed for the purchase of the gatehouse in London, which was then leased to John Robinson, very probably the same John Robinson of Stratford-upon-Avon who would be one of the witnesses of Shakespeare's will. In the indentures of 1602, 1605 and 1613, Shakespeare is described as 'of Stratford-on-Avon gentleman' (Halliwell, 1864: 24). On 11 September 1611, Shakespeare was listed along with seventy-one leading townsfolk as having contributed towards raising a bill in Parliament 'for the better repair of the highways and amending divers defects in the statutes already made'. Only the amount given by Thomas Greene is listed: 2 s 6d (Schoenbaum, 1987: 279), which could imply that Greene donated the highest amount, or that the collection was abandoned.

There are only two instances of Shakespeare suing his neighbours for debt, a practice that 'was normal in an age without credit cards, overdrafts, or collection agencies' (Schoenbaum, 1987: 241). Usury had been legalised at 10 per cent in 1571 'and any surplus capital could be made to work in this way' (Jones, 1996: 51). In Stratford-upon-Avon, as elsewhere, there were three kinds of loan. Interest was not usually charged on small amounts lent to neighbours, family and friends. Then there were loans for goods and services due 'to a shortage of coin', and then money 'lent upon specialty of bond' when interest was usually charged (Jones, 1996: 51–2). As Bearman observes, 'one could argue that Shakespeare's name [as plaintiff for debt owed to him] might well have been expected to have occurred more often' (Bearman, 1994: 31); his father John was involved in around thirty similar lawsuits (Webster, 2012: 129). Philip Rogers, the apothecary, defaulted on a debt for malt in 1604 and was sued for £6. John Addenbrooke was also sued for £6 and damages on a loan from Shakespeare, a case that lasted from 17 August 1608 to 7 June 1609 (Schoenbaum, 1987: 241). Shakespeare himself may well have been present at some of the various hearings at Stratford-upon-Avon's court of record.

New Place as a writer's house

Shakespeare had different ways of approaching the next play he wanted to write. But even one of the most apparently straightforward of projects – for example, the story of one of the English monarchs that could be found in Ralph Holinshed's *Chronicles of England, Scotland and Ireland* – took him to multiple, printed sources. Deciding what to write next was probably to some extent determined by his co-shareholders of the theatre company and the playhouse; Shakespeare's creative innovations and variety were commercially as well as aesthetically driven. Having decided on the topic of his next play (presumably after consultation with his fellow shareholders), Shakespeare started to read around the story. One access to books for him in London would have been Thomas Vautrollier's print-shop, near the Blackfriars, where Shakespeare's Stratford-upon-Avon friend Richard Field worked. There he could have read, for example, Thomas North's translation of Plutarch's *Lives of the Noble Greeks and Romans* (1579, printed by Vautrollier) and a new edition of Holinshed's *Chronicles* (1587, printed during Field's apprenticeship). After Field had left his apprenticeship with Vautrollier, from 1589 his own list included a second edition of Arthur Golding's English translation of Ovid's *Metamorphoses* (1589), Sir John Harrington's translation of Ariosto's *Orlando Furioso* (1591) and Sir Philip Sidney's *Arcadia* (1598), all of which are among Shakespeare's source works (Rutter, 2015: 167–70). Or, if Shakespeare did not borrow or buy books from Field, he could browse through them and make his purchases from the publishers' stalls close to St Paul's. Each play to Shakespeare represented a research project. Having read and presumably made notes from several sources he was ready to start writing, but still he needed books around him as he did so. Sometimes Shakespeare's retellings are so directly based on his sources that he must have had the books open in front of him as he wrote. The Archbishop of Canterbury's 'salic law' speech (*Henry V*, 1.2.69–77) provides one good example of this, as does the 'England scene' in *Macbeth*. Both read like a 'mechanical adaptation' of Holinshed (Wells, 2002: 147–51).

Shakespeare wrote at different speeds throughout his career, and some plays seem more polished than others. The number of plays he wrote in a year varied.

John Ward (1629–81), the vicar of Stratford-upon-Avon from 1662 to 1681, records that Shakespeare 'supplied ye stage with 2 plays every year' (Chambers, 1930, Vol. II: 249). His observation suggests that Shakespeare was known for having a rhythm as a writer – a steady professional output. New Place, as Shakespeare's domestic and emotional anchor, where he could read, study and reflect, probably helped to form a rhythm in the production of his work. But Ward's record does not say for how many years of Shakespeare's professional career he was supplying two plays a year. It is likely he wrote more than two plays some years and fewer in others.

Playwrights usually only had to be around playhouses when their plays were being rehearsed and mounted for the first time. From 1594 through to around 1612 (when he started to collaborate regularly with John Fletcher) Shakespeare was mainly writing single-authored plays (though there were intermittent collaborations with Thomas Middleton on *Timon of Athens* and George Wilkins on *Pericles*). Shakespeare was the leading dramatist for the company in which he owned shares; his plays, performed by popular actors, were the reasons why people went to the theatres in which he owned those shares. As he became more and more firmly established, his output as a writer became much more of a premium than his availability as a performer (of whom there were plenty). He may have returned to Stratford-upon-Avon for the six weeks when the theatres were closed in Lent, or longer – from the end of the Court Christmas season until Easter – and at other times too; he probably escaped to the town when there were severe outbreaks of plague in London, and during those times when he did not have to join the company on their exhausting regional tours. In short, there were plenty of opportunities within the year to be resident at New Place and to produce the next play. We do not know where on the site he actually wrote, but it is likely it was set back in the courtyard, perhaps one of Hugh Clopton's rooms situated at one end of the hall, south facing, with good sunlight (see Plate 14). We know there was a study, at least by 1635, when it was broken into (see p. 131). If Shakespeare needed a book or two sending up from London, the Stratford-upon-Avon carrier would bring them to him within a week of his request. This effectively means that any or all of the plays from 1597 could have been written, researched or thought about in New Place. One might even go as far as to say that he would not have bought New Place at all if he did not intend it becoming somewhere in which he could base himself as a full-time writer.

As a writer's home, New Place would have contained papers and manuscripts. When his fellow shareholders and actors John Heminges and Henry Condell were compiling the 1623 Folio they almost certainly would have travelled to Stratford-upon-Avon to gather together manuscript sources that contributed to their representing Shakespeare's dramatic authorship and output as fully as possible. The task ostensibly took them seven years, from Shakespeare's death in 1616 until the Folio's appearance in 1623. It is surprising that so immense a labour took Heminges and Condell only that long. In their address 'to the great variety of readers' they express their wish 'that the author himself had lived to have set forth and overseen his own writings', which suggests that Shakespeare had already made a start. Some of the comedies in the Folio were prepared for printing by the scribe Ralph Crane; other plays were set from intricately and heavily annotated copies of the quartos.

Figure 4.6 The Chesterfield portrait, which dates from the mid-seventeenth century, and is the first to depict Shakespeare with a book – a distinctly literary dramatist. Attributed to Pieter Borsseler (*c.* 1660–1728), *c.* 1679, oil on canvas, 1275 × 1200 mm (50.2 × 47.2 in).

But for some of the Folio-only plays, their precise manuscript source is far less easy to identify. *The Comedy of Errors*, *Twelfth Night; or, What You Will* and *Antony and Cleopatra* seem to be based on authorial papers or on scribal copies of them (Wells and Taylor, 1997: 145–7). Records of early performances survive for two of these plays (*The Comedy of Errors* in 1594 and *Twelfth Night* in 1602). Their prompt-books appear to have been lost before the Folio was compiled – perhaps they perished in the fire at the Globe on 29 June 1613. It is possible that, in compiling the Folio, Heminges and Condell made recourse to New Place where they realised that manuscript copies of these plays could be retrieved. Or, perhaps the papers on which the printing of these plays were based were Shakespeare's own fair copies which he had been working on in the early stages of preparing a Folio volume. If the John Heminges listed in the

1620 account book of St Martin's Church, Carfax in Oxford as donating 10s 'toward the Clock and chimes' is the same John Heminges as the co-editor of the folio, then, as Mary Edmond suggests, he was possibly staying with the Davenants in Oxford while journeying to or from Stratford-upon-Avon to collect Shakespeare's papers (Edmond, 2004: 279).

By 1622, the great Folio enterprise, *Master William Shakespeare's Comedies, Histories, and Tragedies*, was being advertised in the catalogue of the twice-yearly book fair at Frankfurt. Shakespeare had most certainly become an international playwright, and the book itself finally appeared at the end of the following year.

New Place: Shakespeare's death and legacies

The precise cause of Shakespeare's death is unknown, but a 1661 account by the vicar John Ward suggests one answer: 'Shakespear, Drayton, and Ben Jhonson, had a merry meeting, and itt seems drank too hard, for Shakespear died of a fever there contracted' (Chambers, 1930, Vol. II: 250). The word 'merry' is in inverted commas in the original manuscript, which might suggest that Ward is recording a phrase used by someone who told the story to him. If Ward did learn this from speaking to Judith Quiney (see p. 84), then this may well be an accurate account of the cause of Shakespeare's death. The three poets and playwrights may have been meeting to celebrate Ben Jonson's having effectively become the Poet Laureate (the role was not formally named as such until 1668). On 1 February 1616, Jonson was awarded 100 marks a year as royal pension and identified himself as 'the King's Poet' (Donaldson, 2011: 322). It was around the same time as Judith Shakespeare's wedding to Thomas Quiney (10 February 1616), so there was plenty to celebrate. Or perhaps the 'merry meeting' took place later in March. In the context of his work on New Place, Halliwell suggested that 'in all human probability' Shakespeare's fatal fever was typhoid (Halliwell, 1864: 28), caused by the stinking and insalubrious ditch that ran along the side of the house. Furthermore, in 1613, some of the neighbours had complained to the corporation about the state and smell of the pigsty belonging to the vicar, John Rogers, just opposite the back of New Place (Halliwell, 1864: 35). This was to remain an ongoing problem. The vicar, Ward, who recorded the story was himself a physician and would have understood how fevers could be 'contracted'. In the nineteenth century, a 'typhoid-carrying brook' was identified that ran into the Avon (Honan, 1998: 406–7). Shakespeare could easily have developed typhoid fever from bacteria in the infected water. Typhoid is highly contagious and death can occur within a few days; a strong person might survive up to a month. So, perhaps the alleged drinking bout took place only a day or two before Shakespeare decided to redraft his will on 25 March (assuming his redrafting of it was spurred on by sudden illness), a month before he died on 23 April. Or perhaps his final illness and the timing of his new will are not connected. Another possible reason for his revising his will when he did is signalled by its date, which Shakespeare may have deliberately chosen: the Feast of the Annunciation, or Lady Day, and, in the old calendar, New Year's Day. He knew his will needed redoing at some point, and it could have been a coincidence that death followed shortly afterwards. Amanda Bevan suggests the surviving will was redrafted from 1613 onwards (Bevan, 2016).

The most personal of all of the documents that survive from Shakespeare's lifetime was, like many wills of its day, hastily composed. It survives only in draft with crossings-out and interlineations. It was, as Susan Brock describes:

> a Warwickshire will. Of the twenty-five legatees, executors, overseers and witnesses named, twenty-one connected him with his life in Stratford. The few exceptions were his theatrical colleagues and the man to whom Shakespeare entrusted the responsibility of ensuring that the instructions in his will were properly carried out, Thomas Russell. (Brock, 2015: 215)

Russell had been born in Bruton, Somerset, and lived at his late father Sir Thomas Russell's manor in Alderminster, four miles from Stratford-upon-Avon, from 1598 to 1611, but his main home was in Rushock, near Droitwich. He connected Shakespeare to the county families of Warwickshire and Worcestershire (Brock, 2015: 215–16). Leslie Hotson suggests that Russell may have dealt in wool with Shakespeare's father, and imagines Russell and William Shakespeare meeting first in Stratford-upon-Avon market whilst representing their fathers' wool dealings (Hotson, 1937: 28) and, through his connections with the Berkeley family, Russell may have been the initial point of contact between Shakespeare and the Earl of Southampton, who became his patron (Brock, 2015: 216). Russell was appointed overseer with Francis Collins, and both men acted as witnesses to the will, along with three others: Shakespeare's neighbour July, Julius or Julyns Shaw, John Robinson (possibly the John Robinson who was the tenant in Shakespeare's gatehouse at the Blackfriars from March 1613) and Robert Whattcott (who had testified on behalf of Susanna Hall when she successfully sued John Lane for defamation of character in July 1613).

Francis Collins, who drew up the will, had acted as Shakespeare's attorney before (for example in his purchase of the tithes in 1605). His 'omissions, interlineations, signs of haste and a surprising level of unconcern with outward forms' were all characteristic of his rushed style, as can be seen from Collins's work on the will of Shakespeare's neighbour and friend John Combe, and in his notes for the corporation when Collins had succeeded Thomas Greene as town clerk from 1617 (Brock, 2015: 214).

Shakespeare died a wealthy man and left bequests amounting to £360 in cash. Widows were often nominated as executrix, but not Shakespeare's: Anne was bequeathed 'my second best bed with the furniture'. This has been variously interpreted as (romantically) referring to the marriage bed, or as a way of maintaining Anne's residential rights in New Place. Lena Orlin suggests that when we read wills we often like to believe that they 'retained their devisers' own vocabulary for characterising possessions', but in fact they usually do not (Orlin, 2010: 299–300). Whilst Shakespeare's interlineated bequest to his widow may remain open to interpretation, it bears useful comparison with the will of his neighbour Thomas Combe made on 22 December 1608, who left his widow 'the use and occupation of all tables, bedsteads and other standards now remaining in and about the said house during her widowhood except the bedstead which I will give and bequeath unto my said son William with the best bed and furniture thereunto belonging to have to his own use' (Wells, 2015: 156–7). In light of this, Shakespeare's bequest to Anne seems like a shorthand version of Combe's.

His daughter Susanna inherited the bulk of his estate (including New Place, the land and the share in the tithes). Perhaps Shakespeare intended to relieve his widow of a legal burden by settling his estate as he did. His daughter Judith was left £100 as a marriage settlement, the interest on £150 while she remained married and a 'broad silver-gilt bowl'. Shakespeare might have had reasons of his own for this significant disparity in his daughters' legacies, or he might have been ensuring a good and reasonable marriage settlement for Judith irrespective of her choice of husband (Bevan, 2016).

On the day after Shakespeare made the latest changes to his will, his son-in-law Thomas Quiney pleaded guilty to fornication at the Bawdy Court. His case

Figure 4.7 A mid-sixteenth-century drinking bowl (*c.* 1540), silver-gilt, of the kind that Shakespeare bequeathed to his daughter Judith.

was notorious and something of a social disgrace. It transpired that Quiney, who had recently married Judith, had (like Shakespeare himself) begotten a child outside wedlock – but with another woman, Margaret Wheeler (who, along with their child, died during the birth; both were buried on 15 March). Shakespeare's granddaughter Elizabeth Hall inherited the rest of his 'plate' (gold- and silverware), which she might choose to have turned into coin at the Royal Mint. His seven-and-a-half-year-old godson William Walker was left 20s in gold. Thomas Combe (John's brother) inherited Shakespeare's sword; interestingly he was only four years younger than Hamnet Shakespeare, 'with whom he may well have played as a boy' (Wells, 2015: 159).

Like Thomas Greene, Combe had trained as a lawyer at the Middle Temple. Shakespeare's fellow actors Richard Burbage, John Heminges and Henry Condell, along with neighbours William Reynolds and Hamnet Sadler (named as 'Hamlet' in the will) were left 26s 8d to buy mourning rings, a common practice. Two local brothers, Anthony and John Nash, also received the same amount, which, although without the stipulation that they purchase mourning rings, was probably intended as the same kind of bequest.

A ring survives that may well have belonged to Shakespeare. It is a seal-ring of the period and was found on 16 March 1810 by a Mrs Martin who was working in a field next to Holy Trinity churchyard. The Stratford-upon-Avon antiquarian Robert Bell Wheler was alerted to the extraordinary find and bought the ring on the same day for its value in gold (22 carats). Wheler's research led him to conclude that Shakespeare was the only person in the town likely to have possessed such an initialled ring, and to make a compelling connection between the ring and Shakespeare's will. The standard legal phrase towards the end of the document, 'whereof I have hereunto put my Seale', shows that the word 'Seale' has been crossed out and substituted by the word 'hand', suggesting that Shakespeare had indeed (and perhaps recently) lost his seal-ring (Wheler, 1814: 159). Wheler adds, 'could, therefore, an impression of this seal-ring be discovered upon any document bearing Shakespeare's signature, its authority, beyond contradiction, would be immediately established' (160).

Figure 4.8 A sword (*c.* 1610) of the kind that Shakespeare might have carried, and bequeathed to Thomas Combe, a near contemporary of Shakespeare's son Hamnet.

Figure 4.9 This seal ring, which bears Shakespeare's initials and a true lover's knot, could, as R. B. Wheler and Edmond Malone supposed on 20 April 1812, have belonged to him (Wheler, 1814: 157–8).

Commemorating Shakespeare in Stratford-upon-Avon and London

Had Shakespeare died in London, he would almost certainly have been buried in Westminster Abbey (as the popular playwright Francis Beaumont had been in March 1616). This claim is easily supported by two early poetic responses to Shakespeare's death, the first of which has been attributed for many years to William Basse (1583?–1653?). But Brandon S. Centerwall makes a compelling case that its author is John Donne because the sonnet was first published in Donne's *Poems* in 1633 (Centerwall, 2006). It is thought to have been composed much earlier though (sometime between 1616 and 1622), and survives in at least thirty-four manuscript versions and seven printed texts of the period. One of those is entitled 'On Willm Shakespear buried att Stratford vpon Avon, his Town of Nativity'

(Wells, 2013: 83). Here is a modernised version of the poem as it appeared in Donne's *Poems*:

> Renownèd Spenser, lie a thought more nigh
> To learnèd Chaucer; and rare Beaumont lie
> A little nearer Spenser, to make room
> For Shakespeare in your threefold fourfold tomb.
> To lodge all four in one bed make a shift
> Until Doomsday, for hardly will a fifth
> Betwixt this day and that by fate be slain
> For whom your curtains need be drawn again.
> But if precedency in death doth bar
> A fourth place in your sacred sepulchre
> Under this curlèd marble of thine own,
> Sleep, rare tragedian Shakespeare, sleep alone,
> That unto us or others it may be
> Honour hereafter to be laid by thee
>   (Centerwall, 2006: 282)

The other early poetic commemoration of Shakespeare was Ben Jonson's 'To the memory of my beloved, the author, Master William Shakespeare and what he hath left us', printed among the commendatory verses in the Folio of 1623. Jonson reiterates the earlier poem's sentiments in alluding to the Abbey but, in contrast, Jonson imagines Shakespeare everywhere:

> My Shakespeare, rise, I will not lodge thee by
> Chaucer or Spenser, or bid Beaumont lie
> A little further to make thee room.
> Thou art a monument without a tomb,
> And art alive still while thy book doth live
> And we have wits to read and praise to give.
>   (quoted in *The Oxford Shakespeare:*
>   *The Complete Works*)

Shakespeare was, by the time Jonson's verse was printed, buried in the crypt of Holy Trinity Church (possibly because of his half share in the tithes (Fripp, 1938, Vol. II: 829), as well as, one suspects, because of his standing in the community as a gentleman and, by 1616, a leading writer of his day). Jonson's words echo those on Shakespeare's memorial bust installed in the church, close to the gravestone, some time before 1623.

Stratford-upon-Avon historian Mairi Macdonald plausibly suggests that the bust was installed by May 1619, when the strongly puritan Thomas Wilson of Evesham took up the post of vicar, because he is unlikely to have allowed the colourful memorial (Macdonald, 2001–02: 207), or, indeed, the classical (pagan), literary sentiments it expresses. The bust was made by the London-based monument-maker Geerhart Janssen the younger (who also produced the effigy of Shakespeare's friend John Combe alongside the high altar in Holy Trinity Church in 1614). Janssen's workshop

Figure 4.10 Shakespeare's memorial bust on the north wall of the chancel in Holy Trinity Church. Installed sometime between 1616 and 1623 (and almost certainly before May 1619, when the puritan Thomas Wilson became the vicar) the effigy is one of two posthumous likenesses of Shakespeare (the other is Martin Droeshout's engraving in the Folio of Shakespeare's plays published in 1623). Pigment of the original paint shows us that Shakespeare had auburn hair, and we can learn from the pose that he was right-handed.

was in Southwark, close to the Globe, so perhaps he knew what Shakespeare looked like. The inscription below the bust reads:

IVDICIO PYLIVM, GENIO SOCRATEM, ARTE MARONEM,
TERRA TEGIT, POPVLVS MÆRET, OLYMPVS HABET

STAY PASSENGER, WHY GOEST THOV BY SO FAST,
READ IF THOV CANST, WHOM ENVIOVS DEATH HATH PLAST

WITH IN THIS MONVMENT SHAKSPEARE: WITH WHOME,
QVICK NATVRE DIDE WHOSE NAME, DOTH DECK Y^S TOMBE,
FAR MORE, THEN COST: SIEH ALL, Y^T HE HATH WRITT,
LEAVES LIVING ART, BVT PAGE, TO SERVE HIS WITT.

Those lines in Latin can be translated as:

> In judgement a Nestor, in intellect a Socrates, in art a Virgil,
> The earth encloses, the populace mourns, Olympus holds.
>   (Centerwall, 2006: 276)

In praising Shakespeare's works, the inscription mentions a 'tomb', though none is visible in Holy Trinity Church – only a gravestone that it is assumed is Shakespeare's, but that bears no name.

Centerwall suggests that the inscription below the bust was written by John Donne (since the words take a similar form to other epitaphs he composed) 'in order to promote the placement of the monument in Westminster Abbey' (Centerwall, 2006: 280). Ben Jonson is another plausible author of the inscription, especially given the classical allusions and use of Latin. Whatever hopes some people at the time may

Figure 4.11 The nameless epitaph (part prayer, part blessing, part curse) on what is assumed to be Shakespeare's gravestone, in the chancel of Holy Trinity Church. It is not known who wrote the words.

have cherished about a reinterment for Shakespeare in Westminster Abbey, by 1623, with the publication of the Folio, Stratford-upon-Avon had become Shakespeare's final resting place. The bust is mentioned in Leonard Digges's commendatory poem ('when that stone is rent / And time dissolves thy Stratford monument'), and Jonson famously refers to Shakespeare as the 'sweet Swan of Avon'. But perhaps it is not surprising that, even in death, there can be perceived something of Shakespeare's restlessness between Stratford-upon-Avon and London.

New Place after Shakespeare: a break-in, a book and a royal visit

The story of Shakespeare's family after his death, his growing reputation in Stratford-upon-Avon, London and further afield, is beyond the scope of this study, but it is worth noting two significant episodes in the life of New Place.

John Hall died in 1635. The bulk of his estate (along with a house in London) was left to his widow, Susanna; his daughter, Elizabeth, was left some meadowland in Stratford-upon-Avon, and a house in Acton, Middlesex; and his son-in-law, Thomas Nash, inherited his books and papers (along with permission to burn his manuscripts). Nash (1593–1647) had married Elizabeth Hall in 1626, and the couple lived in New Place with John and Susanna. In total, Hall left 'goods and cash worth some £2,000' (Lane, 2004: 624). It is not clear whether any of the money, books or papers left by Hall originated from his own inheritance from Shakespeare. But certainly, Susanna was left a very wealthy lady indeed on her husband's decease. Two years after Hall had died, and because a debt of £77 13s 4d had not by then been settled, Baldwin Brooks (who was owed the money and would later become bailiff of the town), did 'breake open the Doores and study of the said howse, and Rashlye [did] seise upon and take Divers bookes, boxes, Deskes, moneyes, bonds, bills, and other goods of greate value', as recorded by Susanna Hall and Thomas Nash when they pleaded their case in Chancery (Honan, 1998: 399–400). Whether or not the diverse papers and books included any of Shakespeare's own will never be known, but Susanna saying that the items were worth 'to the valewe of one Thousand pounds att the least' (Taplin, 2011: 98) might suggest that she was conflating emotional attachment with material worth. Some of her late (and increasingly famous) father's belongings were probably among the items that were taken away by Brookes and his men. The account provides clear evidence for there being a lockable study at New Place by 1637; it was probably there in Shakespeare's time, too.

In the nine or ten days leading up to what would be the first battle of the English Civil War at Edgehill (23 October 1642), about fourteen miles from Stratford-upon-Avon, fourteen leading parliamentarians stayed nine or ten days at New Place. On 24 September 1642, Thomas Nash had been listed first among people from the borough who gave money and plate for 'King and Parliament': 'Parliament was constantly invoking "King and Parliament" in its appeals in order to maximize

support, stressing that the quarrel was not against the king but against his evil coun-
sellers' (Tennant, 1996: 24). Nash's contribution of £100 was (by £95) the largest to
the King's cause (Tennant, 1996: 23). A few days earlier, he had sent 364 oz of plate
'valued at 5s 4d per ounce' (Tennant, 1996: 25), again by far the most significant contribution of plate donated by a townsman to the cause. Since these loans were being
called for at a time of local and national crisis, it is possible that the plate included
some or all of that which Elizabeth had inherited from her grandfather. Nash was
to become a member of the parliamentary subcommittee that convened regularly at
nearby Warwick. He would go on to host other notable parliamentarians during the
Civil War. In February 1644, for example, Nash put in a claim for compensation of
£10 following the six-day visit from Captain Behr and his servants, who stole three
sheep and a calf from New Place, and 'a scarlet Peticoat of my wifes with two faire
laces', two cloaks and a suit of clothes (Tennant, 1996: 84).

In the summer of 1643, Queen Henrietta Maria visited Stratford-upon-Avon and
stayed for two nights, from 11 to 13 July. Lewis Theobald is the first person to write
about her visit, in his 1733 edition of Shakespeare. The understanding that she stayed
at New Place was based on what Sir Hugh Clopton, the then-owner, had told him
(Theobald, 1733: xiv). Like Nicholas Rowe before him, Theobald consulted people in
Stratford-upon-Avon about Shakespeare. The town's archives hold the accounts for
the Queen's visit: 30s to six footmen, and 30s to coachmen and porters; 4s for four
quails; 5s 4d for three hens, one cock and eight chickens; £5 for 'cakes presented to
the Queene'; £3 18s 6d for meat; 15s 18d for beer; £1 2s for beans and oats; 2s for the
bellringers (Halliwell, 1864, 115). It is possible the feasting occurred in New Place
itself and, if so, then the long gallery would be a likely venue.

The Queen herself had recently returned from the Continent, where she had been
raising money and troops in support of her husband, Charles I. On her way to meet
the King in Oxford, she met their nephew Prince Rupert, who had set out to protect
her, in Stratford-upon-Avon. The royal visit would have had a major impact on the
town and the surrounding villages. When she met the King at Edgehill on 13 July,
she had with her 2,000 soldiers, 1,000 horses, and 100 wagons. Stratford-upon-Avon
had never known anything like it before. The understanding that she stayed in New
Place is deduced from the fact that the borough accounts for her visit meant that she
stayed within the legal jurisdiction of the town, and New Place was the largest residence available.

Moreover, the King and Queen were both Shakespeare enthusiasts. In his copy
of the Second Folio of 1632 Charles I wrote 'Malvolio' next to *Twelfth Night; or, What
You Will*, and 'Beatrice and Benedick' next to *Much Ado about Nothing*. He had grown
up watching the King's Men perform at Court. Staying in Stratford-upon-Avon for
two nights provided Queen Henrietta Maria with the happy coincidence of being
able to meet the poet's daughter and to find out more about her father. A book, Henri
Estienne's *Marvellous Discourse upon the Life … of Katherine de Medici* (now in the
Shakespeare Centre Library), is inscribed as having being given to one Colonel
Richard Grace, the Duke of York's chamberlain – 'Liber R: Gracei ex dono amicae
D. Susanne Hall' (Schoenbaum, 1987: 305) – who, it is supposed, was with the royal
party during the visit in July 1643. If so, did he receive the book on the Queen's behalf?

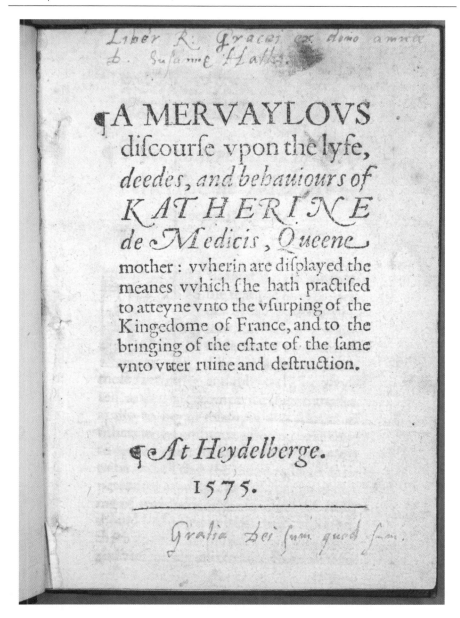

Figure 4.12 From Shakespeare's library? The title-page of a book given by Susanna Hall to the Duke of York's chamberlain, Colonel Richard Grace, possibly during the royal visit of Queen Henrietta Maria in July 1643.

What is strange is that the book is strongly Protestant and presents a diatribe against the Roman Catholic Medici Queen for her involvement in the infamous St Bartholomew's Day massacre, which began in Paris on 23 August 1572, lasted for several weeks, and moved into the surrounding towns and countryside. It is thought that up to 30,000 Protestants perished in the waves of killings. If the book was a gift to Queen Henrietta Maria, then, as Lachlan Mackinnon comments:

> it's an odd gift, a book calumniating a foreign queen accused of meddling, as the Italian Cathérine was in France, to send to another foreign queen accused of meddling, and doubly odd because Cathérine was Henrietta Maria's grandmother. Holding up a cautionary mirror to history like this implies that remarkable trust and intimacy had sprung up between the two women. (Mackinnon, 2015: 82)

If the book were Shakespeare's, Mackinnon speculates, then he may have encountered it through his lodging with the Huguenot Mountjoy family in Silver Street, London; 'equally, he will have known Christopher Marlowe's *The Massacre at Paris* (c. 1593) and may have been interested by the subject or its dramatic possibilities' (Mackinnon, 2015: 81).

Thomas Nash died in early April 1647. In his will he attempted to leave New Place to his cousin Edward Nash. In fact, the house and its grounds still belonged to Susanna, who successfully challenged Nash's will and kept New Place. For two years the home seems to have been an all-female household. Two of the three surviving, direct descendants of Shakespeare were by now widows. Judith and Thomas Quiney had lost the last of their children back in 1638. The prospect of further descendants from Elizabeth was unlikely: she was widowed at thirty-nine. She remarried only a couple of months before Susanna died in June 1649.

Her second husband was Sir John Barnard of Abington (1605–74) of Northamptonshire, a widower with eight children of his own (four sons and four daughters). According to the eighteenth-century scholar Edmond Malone (1741–1812), their wedding took place in All Saints' Church, Billesley. René Weis notes that this was the same church in which she had married Thomas Nash twenty-three years earlier, and on the anniversary of her own parents' wedding (5 June). Given Elizabeth's deliberate coinciding of anniversaries and locations, Weis plausibly suggests that Billesley, which is only about two miles from Wilmcote (and the Arden family's associations), had also been the location for William and Anne Shakespeare's wedding (Weis, 2015: 130).

The Barnards made a legal settlement with regard to New Place in October 1652. Both of them could live there for as long as their natural lives, after which time it would be inherited by Elizabeth's heirs. A few months later Elizabeth settled the future of New Place with two trustees, Henry Smith (a gentleman of Stratford-upon-Avon) and Job Dighton (of the Middle Temple). If she died without an heir, and after the death of Sir John, the trustees would sell New Place and the monies would be given to those whom Elizabeth nominated in her will (Halliwell, 1864: 160–1). Fripp notes that Sir John was 'a reader, and patron of literature, and possessed a library. To him, no doubt, descended books of Shakespeare and Doctor Hall and pictures' (Fripp,

Figure 4.13 A presumed posthumous portrait (*c.* 1690) of Shakespeare's granddaughter Elizabeth, Lady Barnard (1608–70), oil on canvas, 915 × 760 mm (36 × 30 in). This, along with the portrait shown as Figure 4.14, was in the possession of Thomas Hart, fifth in descent from Shakespeare's sister Joan. Both portraits were displayed in Shakespeare's Birthplace from 1793 to 1820, during the time of Mrs Hornby. They were purchased by the Shakespeare Birthplace Trust from the Hornby collection on 4 June 1896.

1938: 905). After the monarchy had been restored, Barnard was made a baronet on 25 November 1661, so Shakespeare's granddaughter became Elizabeth, Lady Barnard. For Stratford-upon-Avon, the Restoration in part meant that 'the long succession of Puritan vicars came to an end' (Fripp, 1938: 907). Judith and Thomas Quiney were still around to have noticed this shift in church culture and spirituality. It is not known how long the Barnards lived there, but they had left and moved to Abington by 1663, and New Place seems to have been occupied by Francis Oldfield (bailiff of the borough from 1665 to 1666): he is listed on the hearth tax returns of 1663 and 1670 as living in a house with ten hearths on Chapel Street/Church Street (Bearman, 2011).

Elizabeth was buried in the Church of St Peter and St Paul in Abington on 17 February 1669 [1670]. Her will, which identifies her as 'Dame Elizabeth Barnard' (Halliwell, 1864: 166), left instructions that New Place, and her land in Stratford-upon-Avon (which had been Shakespeare's), should, on the death of her

Figure 4.14 A presumed posthumous portrait (*c.* 1690) of Sir John Barnard (1605–74), the second husband of Shakespeare's granddaughter Elizabeth, oil on canvas, 740 × 625 mm (29 × 24½ in). See also Figure 4.13.

widower, be sold, and that her first husband's cousin Edward Nash should have first refusal on its purchase. The money from the sale would then form bequests to the value of around £250, including £5 a year (or a lump sum of £40 on her marriage) to Judith Hathaway, daughter of the late Thomas, a cousin of Anne Shakespeare who had lived four doors away from New Place from 1647 to 1655 (Fripp, 1929: 26–7). The other beneficiaries included Thomas's three unmarried daughters; his married daughter, Joan, and her son Edward (for his apprenticeship); and her 'cousin Thomas Welles of Carleton'. Her 'loving kinsman Edward Bagley' was made sole executor and inherited the residue of her estate after the sales. She bequeathed the Henley Street property to Shakespeare's sister's family, the Harts, whose descendants occupied it until 1806 (Halliwell, 1864: 167–9).

Sir John was buried on 5 March 1674. In 1669, he had sold the estate and manor at Abington to William Thursby, a lawyer from the Middle Temple, for £13,750 (Taplin, 2011: 127). Although Barnard left no will, an administration bond was prepared. An accompanying inventory includes '"In the Studdy … all the Bookes" worth £29 11s., "a Rent at Stratford-vpon-Avon" worth £4, and "old goods and lumber at

Stratford-vpon-Avon" worth £4' (Chambers, 1930, Vol. II: 180). Pictures in the parlour, best chamber and little chamber are also listed (Fripp, 1938: 908), presumably including items from New Place that the Barnards took with them when they moved to Abington. René Weis emphatically notes:

> also, it stands to reason that Elizabeth Barnard would have moved important family papers such as copies of deeds and conveyances and the grant of the coat-of-arms to John Shakespeare. While Shakespeare's library probably contained copies of Ovid, Virgil, Plautus, Terence, Plutarch and Holinshed, it is likely that he also owned copies of his plays and poems in quarto. Above all, his family must have numbered among their possessions a 1623 First Folio of the works. All these precious papers would have found their way into a library or 'study' in Abington. (Weis, 2015: 130–1)

Figure 4.15 The herald Sir Edward Walker (1612–77), owner of New Place from 1675 to 1677, by William Dobson (1611–46), *c.* 1645, oil on canvas, 1140 × 890 mm (45 × 35 in).

It has been noted that, on Sir John's decease, his daughters from his first marriage probably removed all of the papers, books, pictures, plate and other valuable objects, including, one supposes, some items of the Shakespeares' from New Place (Higgins, 1903, Vol. I, 69).

After the death of Sir John, the trustees of New Place settled the right to buy the estate and the land 'formerly the inheritance of the said William Shakespeare' (Halliwell, 1864: 171) on the herald Sir Edward Walker (1612–77 (Chambers, 1930, Vol. II: 180). He paid £1,060 for it in May 1675. Walker had served Charles I during the Civil War, and had been with the King in Oxford from 1642 until his surrender there in 1646 (Walker, we can assume, was therefore in Oxford when the Queen arrived there from Stratford-upon-Avon). Charles II chose 23 April 1661 as the day for his coronation (St George's Day and Shakespeare's presumed birthday), about which Walker wrote *A Circumstantial Account of the Preparation for the Coronation* (published in 1820 (Chesshyre, 2004: 824)). He seems not to have spent much time at New Place, and preferred to live in nearby Clopton (in 1662 his daughter Barbara had married John Clopton of Clopton House). Walker leased New Place to Joseph Hunt. But the fact that he bought New Place at all suggests he valued the property for what it represented – its Shakespearian as well as royal connections.

On Walker's decease, which followed shortly in 1677, New Place was passed back to the Clopton family, descendants of the man who had built it almost 200 years earlier. Judith Quiney had died fifteen years earlier, an old lady of seventy-seven, with no surviving issue. Her widower, Thomas, died shortly afterwards. Descendants of Shakespeare's sister Joan lived on Henley Street. William Walker, one of Shakespeare's godchildren, and the only one to be named in his will, was still alive. He was born in 1609, the same year that Shakespeare's Sonnets were published, and he died aged seventy-one in March 1680, the last inhabitant of the town who could claim an intimate connection with the poet of New Place.

References

Arkell, T. with N. Alcock (2010). *Warwickshire Hearth Tax Returns: Michaelmas 1670* (Stratford-upon-Avon: Dugdale Society and the Shakespeare Birthplace Trust).

Astington, J. (1999). *English Court Theatre: 1558–1642* (Cambridge: Cambridge University Press).

Aubrey, John. ([1949] 1958). *Aubrey's Brief Lives*, ed. Oliver Lawson Dick, 3rd edn (London: Secker and Warburg).

Bate, J. (2008). *Soul of the Age: The Life, Mind, and World of William Shakespeare* (London: Viking).

Bearman, R. (1994). *Shakespeare in the Stratford Records* (Stroud: Alan Sutton and the Shakespeare Birthplace Trust).

—— (2011). Unpublished paper on the 1670 Stratford-upon-Avon hearth tax returns presented to the Dig for Shakespeare advisory board.

—— (2012a). 'The Guildhall, Stratford-upon-Avon: The Focus of Civic Governance in the Sixteenth Century', in J. R. Mulryne (ed.), *The Guild and the Guild Buildings of Shakespeare's Stratford: Society, Religion, School and Stage* (Farnham: Ashgate), 97–113.

——(2012b). 'Shakespeare's Purchase of New Place', *Shakespeare Quarterly*, 63.4: 465–86.

——(2012c). 'Thomas Greene: Stratford-upon-Avon's Town Clerk and Shakespeare's Lodger', in P. Holland (ed.), *Shakespeare Survey 65* (Cambridge: Cambridge University Press), 290–305.

Bevan, A. (2016). 'Shakespeare's Will: a new interpretation,' http://blog.nationalarchives.gov.uk/blog/shakespeares-will-new-interpretation (accessed 7 April 2016).

Brinkworth, E. R. C. (1972). *Shakespeare and the Bawdy Court* (London: Phillimore).

Brock, S. (2015). 'Last Things: Shakespeare's Neighbours and Beneficiaries', in P. Edmondson and S. Wells (eds), *The Shakespeare Circle: An Alternative Biography* (Cambridge: Cambridge University Press), 213–29.

Centerwall, B. S. (2006). 'Who Wrote William Basse's "Elegy on Shakespeare"?', in P. Holland (ed.), *Shakespeare Survey 59* (Cambridge: Cambridge University Press), 267–84.

Chambers, E. K. (1930). *William Shakespeare: A Study in Facts and Problems*, 2 vols (Oxford: Clarendon Press).

Chesshyre, H. (2004). 'Sir Edward Walker', in H. C. G. Matthew and B. Harrison (eds), *Dictionary of National Biography*, Vol. LVI (Oxford: Oxford University Press), 822–4.

Colls, K. and W. Mitchell (2012). Dig for Shakespeare Project report for the Shakespeare Birthplace Trust (unpublished).

Donaldson, I. (2011). *Ben Jonson: A Life* (Oxford: Oxford University Press).

Duncan-Jones, K. (2001). *Ungentle Shakespeare: Scenes from His Life* (London: Thomson Learning).

Eccles, M. (1961). *Shakespeare in Warwickshire* (Madison: University of Wisconsin Press).

Edmond, M. (2004). 'John Heminges', in H. C. G. Matthew and B. Harrison (eds), *Dictionary of National Biography*, Vol. XXVI (Oxford: Oxford University Press), 278–9.

Fogg, N. (2012). *Hidden Shakespeare: A Biography* (Stroud: Amberley Publishing).

——(2014). *Stratford-upon-Avon: The Biography* (Stroud: Amberley Publishing).

Fripp, E. I. (1929). *Shakespeare's Haunts near Stratford* (London: Humphrey Milford for Oxford University Press).

——(1938). *Shakespeare, Man and Artist*, 2 vols (London: Humphrey Milford for Oxford University Press).

Greenblatt, S. (2004). *Will in the World: How Shakespeare Became Shakespeare* (New York: W. W. Norton).

Greer, G. (2007). *Shakespeare's Wife* (London: Bloomsbury).

Gurr, A. (1996). *The Shakespearian Playing Companies* (Oxford: Clarendon Press).

——(2004). *The Shakespeare Company 1594–1642* (Cambridge: Cambridge University Press).

Halliwell, J. O. (1864). *An Historical Account of the New Place, Stratford-upon-Avon, the Last Residence of Shakespeare* (London: J. E. Adlard).

Higgins, N. (1903). *The Bernards of Abington and Nether Winchendon: A Family History*, 4 vols (London: Longmans, Green).

Honan, P. (1998). *Shakespeare: A Life* (Oxford: Oxford University Press).

Jones, J. (1996). *Family Life in Shakespeare's England: Stratford-upon-Avon 1570–1630* (Stroud: Sutton Publishing and the Shakespeare Birthplace Trust).

Lane, J. (2004). 'John Hall', in H. C. G. Matthew and B. Harrison (eds), *Dictionary of National Biography*, Vol. XXIV (Oxford: Oxford University Press), 623–4.

Macdonald, M. (2001–02). 'Not a Memorial to Shakespeare, but a Place for Divine Worship': The Vicars of Stratford-upon-Avon and the Shakespeare Phenomenon, 1616–1964', *Warwickshire History*, 11: 207–26.

Mackinnon, L. (2015). 'His Daughter Susanna Hall', in P. Edmondson and S. Wells (eds), *The Shakespeare Circle: An Alternative Biography* (Cambridge: Cambridge University Press), 71–85.

Mulryne, R. (2012). 'Professional Theatre in the Guildhall 1568–1620: Players, Puritanism and Performance', in J. R. Mulryne (ed.), *The Guild and the Guild Buildings of Shakespeare's Stratford: Society, Religion, School and Stage* (Farnham: Ashgate), 171–206.

Orlin, L. C. (2010). 'Empty Vessels', in T. Hamling and C. Richardson (eds), *Everyday Objects: Medieval and Early Modern Culture and Its Meanings* (Farnham: Ashgate), 299–308.

——(2014). 'Anne by Indirection', *Shakespeare Quarterly*, 65.4: 420–54.

Potter, L. (2012). *The Life of William Shakespeare: A Critical Biography* (Oxford: Wiley-Blackwell).

Richardson, C. (2015). 'His Siblings', in P. Edmondson and S. Wells (eds), *The Shakespeare Circle: An Alternative Biography* (Cambridge: Cambridge University Press), 40–8.

Rowe, N. (1709). *Some Account of the Life of Mr. William Shakespeare* (London: Jacob Tonson).

Rutter, C. C. (2015). 'Schoolfriend, Publisher and Printer Richard Field', in P. Edmondson and S. Wells (eds), *The Shakespeare Circle: An Alternative Biography* (Cambridge: Cambridge University Press), 161–73.

Schoenbaum, S. ([1977] 1987). *William Shakespeare: A Documentary Life* (Oxford: Oxford University Press).

Shapiro, J. (2015). *1606: William Shakespeare and the Year of Lear* (London: Faber and Faber).

Taplin, J. (2011). *Shakespeare's Country Families: A Documentary Guide to Shakespeare's Country Society* (Warwick: Claridges for John Taplin).

Tennant, P. (1996). *The Civil War in Stratford-upon-Avon: Conflict and Community in South Warwickshire, 1642–1646* (Stroud: Sutton Publishing and the Shakespeare Birthplace Trust).

Theobald, L. (1733). *The Works of Shakespeare*, 7 vols, Vol. I (London: J. Tonson, F. Clay, W. Feales and R. Wellington).

Webster, M. A. (2012). 'The Stratford Court of Record 1553–1601', in J. R. Mulryne (ed.), *The Guild and the Guild Buildings of Shakespeare's Stratford: Society, Religion, School and Stage* (Farnham: Ashgate), 116–33.

Weis, R. (2007). *Shakespeare Revealed: A Biography* (London: John Murray).

—— (2015). 'His Granddaughter Lady Elizabeth Barnard', in P. Edmondson and S. Wells (eds), *The Shakespeare Circle: An Alternative Biography* (Cambridge: Cambridge University Press), 122–34.

Wells, S. (2002). *Shakespeare for All Time* (London: Macmillan).

—— (2013). 'Allusions to Shakespeare to 1642', in P. Edmondson and S. Wells (eds), *Shakespeare Beyond Doubt: Evidence, Authorship, Controversy* (Cambridge: Cambridge University Press), 73–87.

——(2015). 'A Close Family Connection: The Combes', in P. Edmondson and S. Wells (eds), *The Shakespeare Circle: An Alternative Biography* (Cambridge: Cambridge University Press), 149–60.

Wells, S. and G. Taylor, eds, with J. Jowett and W. Montgomery (1997). *William Shakespeare: A Textual Companion* (New York: Norton).

Wheler, R. B. (1814). *A Guide to Stratford-upon-Avon* (London: J. Ward).

5

A reconstruction of Shakespeare's New Place

Kevin Colls, William Mitchell and Paul Edmondson

The earliest surviving sketch

Paul Edmondson

In 1737, the professional engraver George Vertue (1684–1756) was doing a tour of Oxford with the Earl of Oxford. Before their return to London, they visited Stratford-upon-Avon. Vertue wrote an account of the time he spent there in his notebook. After his description of some of the monuments in Holy Trinity Church he turns his attention to New Place. He sketches it, and above it writes: 'This Something by memory and ye description of Shakespears House which was / in Stratford on avon. where he livd and dyed. and his wife after him 1623' (Simpson, 1952: 56). The authority of Vertue's drawing has often been dismissed: it is only a sketch, and one drawn from memory. But whose memory? On the following page of his notebook Vertue writes:

> in Stratford Shakespeare had several houses. / besides some Land – the Maiden head and Swan an Inn / (now) did belong to him – and a house or two adjoining. / These are actually in the possession of Shakespeare Hart. / a glasier by profession, the remaining Heir of Elisabeth [*recte* Joan] – only / Sister to Wm. Shakespear. she Married to … Hart / whose grandson George Hart. father of this present S. Hart / living, about 70 years of age. (Simpson, 1952: 56)

Vertue also records 'Shakespeare Hart I saw' (Simpson, 1952: 56). Shakespeare Hart (1666–1747), the great-great-nephew of Shakespeare, was indeed seventy-one in 1737, but Vertue is confusing the name of Shakespeare's granddaughter, Elizabeth, who lived in New Place, with the name of Shakespeare's sister, who lived in Henley Street. Frank Simpson suggests that Vertue's drawing is unlikely to have been produced from his own memory (not impossible: Vertue might have known New Place before 1702, when it was replaced by the new Clopton house). Vertue's sketch is far more likely to have been based on someone else's memory: Shakespeare Hart's, the great-great-nephew (Simpson, 1952: 56). During the same visit, Vertue also produced an annotated sketch of Shakespeare's grave and monument in Holy Trinity Church. Two pages after the sketch of New Place, he records having visited Shakespeare's house on Henley Street, and notes that the Harts were proud of their family history and retained the memory that the property had belonged to William Shakespeare (Nicholas Molyneux, personal correspondence; and British Library, Add. MS 70438, p. 19).

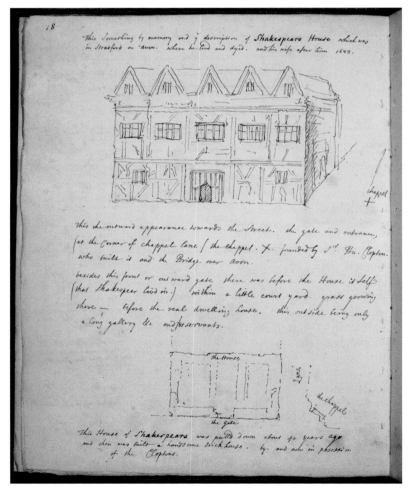

Figure 5.1 The earliest image of Shakespeare's New Place: the engraver George Vertue's sketch from 1737, showing the frontage remodelled in Shakespeare's time and a plan of the site.

The authority and importance of Vertue's drawing, and his accompanying description and plan of New Place, should be emphasised rather than doubted. Vertue had been working as an engraver since 1709. By 1737 he was well accustomed to producing accurate sketches that he would then turn into finely detailed engravings. In 1715, he engraved a large-scale portrait of George I, and, in 1717, was appointed the official engraver of the refounded Society of Antiquaries. He was also a fellow of the society, a privilege usually denied to engravers. His other significant commissions included illustrating Chaucer's works, a history of the Reformation and (also in 1737) James Gibbs's designs for the Radcliffe Camera (Myrone, 2004: 382–3). Vertue was not given to poetic licence as an illustrator. In fact, he was well known for being 'assiduous' and highly detailed in his work, even for the 'dry manner of his reproductions' (Myrone, 2004: 384). He was also a Shakespeare enthusiast. Eighteen years before he drew New Place, Vertue recorded the provenance of what was to become known as the Chandos portrait of Shakespeare, and it is Vertue's evidence, though based on hearsay, that 'indicates that the ownership of the painting could be traced back to a contemporary of Shakespeare' (Cooper, 2006: 54). Vertue also identified another portrait (now apparently lost) within the same collection as the Chandos, a 'lifetime portrait of Shakespeare in oil' (Cooper, 2006: 55). During his visit to Stratford-upon-Avon in 1737, Vertue would have been keen for accurate information about New Place, and to find out as much as possible about it.

If Vertue had asked for a description of Shakespeare's New Place from Hart, then it is probable that Hart was present when Vertue made the sketch to make suggestions and corrections, or at least that Vertue made sure Hart approved of the drawing before he moved on. The five-gabled appearance of New Place in Vertue's sketch makes it look a lot like what is now the Shakespeare Hotel, a little further along on the same side of the street. Hart could easily have pointed out the similarity between the two houses, the surviving property, built around 1600, forming the perfect visual analogy for Shakespeare's lost home.

Underneath his sketch of New Place, Vertue writes:

> This the outward appearance towards the Street. the gate and entrance, / (at the Corner of chapel lane) the chapel X. founded by Sr Hu. Clopton. / who built it and the Bridge over Avon. / besides this front or outward gate there was before the House itself / (that Shakespear livd in.) within a little court yard. Grass growing / there – before the real dwelling house, this outside being only / a long gallery &c for servants. (Figure 5.1)

The frontage that Vertue drew is definitely not the one that Hugh Clopton had originally built in the late fifteenth century. Its style is altogether different. Tara Hamling, an expert in Tudor material culture, comments that the building in Vertue's sketch, with its 'gables and symmetrical placing of windows, is typical of the second half of the sixteenth century, not the 1480s' (Hamling, 2010: 4). This view is supported by Nicholas Molyneux (a timber-framed buildings expert from Historic England), who submitted a report to the Dig for Shakespeare Advisory Board in July 2011 stating 'for me the most significant elements of the (Vertue) elevation are (a) it is symmetrical and (b) it only has two windows on the ground floor … if the main house is of pre-seventeenth-century date then we might expect it to be asymmetrical' (Molyneux, 2011: 1).

Figure 5.2 The Shakespeare Hotel was originally two separate buildings, the first having been constructed in the early sixteenth century, the second around 100 years later. The latter part was built in the early seventeenth century and has similarities to New Place. It had a half-H ground plan, access to which was through an off-centre doorway. Like New Place, there are five gables and three storeys, closely studded throughout. The upper two storeys are jettied, with the eaves facing on to Chapel Street. The building went through much remodelling and originally consisted of a two-storey range before later being given an upper floor. The original windows have moulded mullions and it had stone fireplaces (Bearman, 1988: 20).

Molyneux's observations support the interpretation that Vertue's drawing represents the memory of Shakespeare's great-great-nephew, and that it is likely to be the frontage that Shakespeare had built shortly after having bought the property, or that had been built by a previous owner in the mid-to-late sixteenth century. Vertue's drawing demonstrably does not show a house made of brick and timber of the kind that Leyland wrote about in the first part of the fifteenth century. Although usually dismissed as only a 'sketch', Vertue's work includes details of the kind he would need if he were to do further work on it – a wattle-and-daub frontage, for example, with a distinctive herringbone frame.

Which owner of New Place remodelled its frontage, and when? Bott was not there for very long and seems not to have had enough money, and Underhill had other, larger estates to manage, and was short of capital, so Shakespeare himself is the most likely candidate. For 12 January 1598, the minutes and accounts of the corporation record 10d 'pd to mr Shaxspere for on lod of ston' (Chambers, 1930, Vol. II: 96). This has often been interpreted as a payment to Shakespeare for clearing away the debris caused by his renovation of New Place: 'it is likely enough', comments Chambers, 'but the seller [of the load of stone] might have been his father' (Vol. II: 98). Possible, but the son still seems the more likely recipient of the 10d, given that he had just bought a large house with a courtyard in need of renovation. But a 'load of stone' remains a 'load of stone', and we do not know where it came from.

Where might we find further corroborative evidence for Shakespeare's own remodelling of the frontage? The earliest reference to Shakespeare himself having renovated New Place is by Lewis Theobald in his edition of Shakespeare's works in 1733 (four years before Vertue's sketch), who writes that Shakespeare 'having repaired and modelled it to his own mind, changed the name to New Place, which the mansion house, since erected on the same spot, at this day retains' (Theobald, 1733: xiv). Theobald incorrectly makes the connection between Shakespeare's 'new' remodelling and repairs, and the name of the house; Hugh Clopton had named it New Place more than a century earlier. Shakespeare Hart may or may not have known which owner had built the frontage, but it is perhaps significant that Vertue introduces his sketch with the words 'ye description of Shakespears House' – as though Hart had told Vertue that Shakespeare had built (remodelled) this part of it, the gatehouse – rather than, for example, 'New Place where Shakespeare lived'. By 1737, Shakespeare's posthumous reputation in relation to Stratford-upon-Avon was such that Shakespeare Hart would have been keen to present Vertue with as accurate a memorial reconstruction as possible.

The frontage of New Place: an architectural comparison

William Mitchell

Corroborative evidence, then, supports the likelihood that the frontage as sketched by Vertue represents Shakespeare's own home-improvement. Vertue's use of the phrase 'a long gallery & c [chambers?] for servants' (Figure 5.1) is significant, as long galleries were an architectural feature that became increasingly popular during the mid-to-late sixteenth century in high-status houses, and were becoming more popular in well-to-do, urban houses. Certainly Hugh Clopton would not have known a long gallery at New Place. Figure 5.4 includes details of features that are typical of late-sixteenth-century architecture: for example the gable-ended dormers, which would provide extra light. Situated around nineteen miles from Stratford-upon-Avon, in the village of Long Itchington, the Tudor House is mid-to-late sixteenth-century in origin and comprises only a single long range, which fronts the street (Figure 5.3). The appearance of the external architectural features is thought to be similar to those of New Place. The Tudor House has three storeys with a stone ground floor and a projecting, timber-framed upper storey. At some point in the early seventeenth century, the timber-framed upper floor was added to create a continuous long range with five bays and gables. These additions are similar to the type of alteration that occurred during Shakespeare's occupation of New Place.

Figure 5.3 The Tudor House, Long Itchington, Warwickshire, with a front range evocative of Shakespeare's New Place.

Vertue's sketch portrays a three-storey, half-timbered, square-panel-framed building. Each floor has different architectural features and is separated by a long bressumer beam (Figure 5.4). Between the symmetrically laid-out panels there are angled members and rails between the vertical posts. The panels were presumably infilled by wattle and daub as was the tradition in sixteenth- and seventeenth-century Stratford. It is unclear if the brick-and-timber panel infill described by Leyland as part of Hugh Clopton's New Place was removed entirely or covered over. On the ground floor is a central gateway surrounded by close studding. On each side of the gateway, there is a three-light window, which presumably lit the ground-floor rooms.

The first floor has a five-window range of large, three-light mullioned windows. This floor was the traditional location for a long gallery in Elizabethan and Jacobean house planning. The upper level has five gable-ended dormers, each with three-light windows. There is a suggestion in the drawing that this upper level was jettied (over-hanging), a common feature within urban settings of the time. The upper-level dormer windows may have served as an additional light source to illuminate the long gallery and, if so, would have been part of a high-roofed, grand-looking, first-floor interior. The side of the building that fronted on to Chapel Lane is depicted with a possible doorway. The sketch shows that this building extended to a significant depth along Chapel Lane. No detail is given of the rear of the property. It is not clear if New Place was attached to the adjacent property (Nash's house) through the use of a

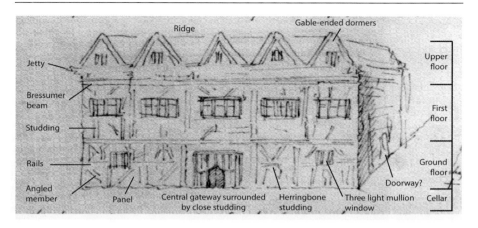

Figure 5.4 Vertue's sketch with architectural annotation.

covered walkway, or whether there was an open passage between them, and there is no detail regarding the buildings behind the gatehouse range. Vertue was most interested in sketching the front of New Place, the range that Shakespeare almost certainly remodelled.

'A long gallery'?

Paul Edmondson

Vertue's mention of a long gallery is imaginatively compelling, as Tara Hamling explains:

> Galleries evolved from covered walkways and the country houses of the greater gentry built from the early sixteenth century onwards, often include a large gallery as an independent, specialized space intended for walking and magnificent display. But it is only in the later part of the sixteenth century that this fashion for dedicated galleries developed to be enthusiastically embraced by members of the lesser gentry. (Hamling, 2010: 5)

More modest, urban galleries often functioned as a corridor (but with the doors on one side only), like the front range on the Long Itchington house (Figure 5.3). Grander examples were to be found in rural mansions. Hamling looks to Little Moreton Hall in Cheshire, whose long gallery dates from the 1580s and seems mainly to have been used as a games room or for exercise during inclement weather (Figure 5.5).

Lena Cowen Orlin, who has made a special study of long galleries, explains that 'in the Renaissance home, they were not given definition by objects' and 'were recognizable solely by their dimensions', and cites the examples of Buckhurst in Essex and Ampthill Park in Bedfordshire as being as long as 77.42 m (254 ft (Orlin, 2007: 229)). But then

Figure 5.5 The long gallery at Little Moreton Hall, Cheshire.

there is the example of Blakesley Hall in nearby Birmingham, built by a merchant, Richard Smalbroke, in 1590, and measuring a more modest 10.67m (35 ft): aspiring gentlemen and the merchant classes wanted to copy this architectural feature of what Orlin calls 'spatial prodigality' in their own, smaller homes (Orlin, 2007: 229).

But Shakespeare's gallery was as long as the width of the burgage (up to 15.85 m (52 ft), only 4.88 m (16 ft) shorter than the one at Little Moreton Hall. His gallery seems to have had a high ceiling, and its dormer windows would have helped to make it a striking, light-filled space on the first floor, overlooking the comings and goings of the street. It, as well as the hall, may have been a place for feasting, too, since it could have accommodated a long table.

But galleries were also places in which to display art collections. Portraits of Tudor monarchs, for example, were easily available through reproductions, and there was a vogue well into the seventeenth century for the merchant classes and the lesser

Figure 5.6 Abraham Sturley's wall-decoration in 5–6 Wood Street, which was probably put up in celebration of James I's coronation in 1603. It was noticed by Tara Hamling when George Pragnell Ltd were renovating their shop's ceiling.

gentry to display pictures in their houses. The art historian Tarnya Cooper notes, for example, that in the early 1600s Richard Mascoll, a butcher in Bristol, displayed a portrait of Elizabeth I in his main room. The monarch's accession portraits were 'owned by merchants ... it is likely that they were available to purchase both ready-made, and to order' (Cooper, 2010: 160). Hamling cites Ben Jonson's dramatic treatment of a domestic gallery in *Poetaster* (first performed in 1601). As Albius and his wife, Chloe, prepare for a visit from the Court, we hear: 'by heaven, wife: hang no pictures in the hall, nor in the dining-chamber, in any case, but in the gallery only, for 'tis not courtly else' (2.1.122–4 (Jonson, 1995: 110; Hamling, 2010: 7)). The actor Edward Alleyn's accounts from 1617 to 1622 reflect his taste for objets d'art, including 'four sets of portraits of English kings and queens, eventually forming a complete set of twenty-six portraits from William the Conqueror to James I' (Hamling, 2010: 8).

If Abraham Sturley's house on Wood Street could proudly display a memorial of James I's coronation as part of an ornate ceiling design, then it is highly probable that a long gallery at Shakespeare's New Place contained images of kings and queens. Tarnya Cooper adds that:

> many of the sets [of paintings] also feature original identifying inscriptions which allowed commentary and prompted dialogue with fellow viewers creating a unique experience

where the visual content served as both an illustration of existing knowledge and as a prompt to imaginative contemplation. It is no surprise then that the popularity of these sets came about at the time Shakespeare and Marlowe were presenting English history before the eyes of thousands of theatregoers both at Bankside in London and around the country when they went on tour. And, one cannot help but wonder, did these images of royal characters reflect their appearance on stage, or vice versa? (Cooper, 2010: 167)

That Shakespeare was acquainted with and inspired by the great art collection displayed in the royal palace of Whitehall, as well as 'the long privy gallery', is compellingly imagined by Shapiro (2005: 28–30). Galleries of the kind Shakespeare had at New Place represent the dissemination of art among the middle classes. Paintings of family members were also understandably popular. His colleague and theatre manager John Heminges left paintings of two of his daughters 'sett vp in a frame in my howse' to his sons-in-law (Honigmann and Brock, 1993: 166).

Perhaps Shakespeare considered his family's gallery a place where he could also display images of the monarchs he depicted on stage (in what, overall, would prove to be about a third of his plays). Such likenesses were readily available through art shops and from those willing to copy them in order to supply a burgeoning industry. And it is in just such a gallery, belonging to Paulina in *The Winter's Tale*, that Shakespeare sets his most moving (and perhaps most memorable) *coup de théâtre*:

> O Paulina,
> We honour you with trouble. But we came
> To see the statue of our queen. Your gallery
> Have we passed through, not without much content
> In many singularities; but we saw not
> That which my daughter came to look upon,
> The statue of her mother.
> *(The Winter's Tale, 5.3.8–14)*

That is the voice of King Leontes who, a few moments later, becomes captivated by the statue of his dead queen, Hermione, which, in the context of the story, turns out to be no less than magically brought to life. Art, as Shakespeare bodies it forth on stage in this scene, can be life-giving, as well as socially impressive.

Representations of classical figures were also popular in long galleries. A picture of Cleopatra hung in the Long Gallery at Ingatestone Hall in Essex (where the King's Men performed), along with 'a picture of Diana, two pictures of a turk (one male and one female), a picture of Henry V, another of Henry VIII and "nine painted shields with poseys upon them"' (Cooper, 2010: 173). The shields may have been representations of the Nine Worthies, a popular Tudor trope of classical mythology that Shakespeare himself adapted and appropriated in *Love's Labour's Lost* (printed the year after he purchased New Place and marking the first appearance of his name on the title-page of a play-text). It becomes highly tempting to imagine all sorts of possible paintings hanging in Shakespeare's long gallery at New Place, perhaps curated with captions and commentaries in his own hand. Such activity would not have been too dissimilar to the way Shakespeare provided a motto for the Earl of

Rutland's jousting tournament impresa (emblematic shield), on which he collaborated with his actor-colleague Richard Burbage in 1613 (and for which both men received 44s in gold). Although the puritan faction of Stratford-upon-Avon seems to have tolerated both religious and secular images appearing in non-church buildings (their main interest being to remove images from church buildings), they probably saw Shakespeare's gallery at New Place as being just the sort of vain enterprise that would interest an actor and theatre-man.

'I know you are now, sir, a gentleman born' (*The Winter's Tale*, 5.2.134)

Paul Edmondson

Shakespeare's gentlemanly status would have been conspicuously displayed on the remodelled frontage. He, and indeed his brothers, had the right to display their father's coat of arms during his lifetime, provided they signalled their filial relationship in how this was done: 'for William, as the first-born son, this would have entailed adding a label – a narrow band with three tags pendant from it – across the top of the shield, to be discarded on the death of his father' (Ailes, 2014: 118). Shakespeare would have known how to display it properly (for example above the main doorway). From time to time, there were visitations from the Heralds to make sure that all those who were entitled to bear their arms in a given area were doing so according to the rules appropriate to their status. In 1599, Shakespeare applied again to the College of Heralds to try to impale the Shakespeare coat of arms with those of the Arden family. This

> would have permitted William and his descendants permanently to *quarter* the two coats in the same way that the Tudor royal arms quartered those of France and England … Shakespeare knew his heraldry and was obviously keen to exploit its potential as a clear visual indicator of his status as a gentleman, successful playwright, and property owner. (Ailes, 2014: 119)

Gentlemen of Shakespeare's status were entitled to wear special mourning garments (hoods and gowns) and were allowed to have painted designs in their houses, on windows, and engravings on their furniture and household objects. Decoration with 'arms, crests and badges' was extremely popular in the period, especially for 'the wealthier among the "middling sort"' (Hamling, 2014: 205). The Revd Joseph Greene, the antiquary headmaster of the Edward VI Grammar School from 1735 to 1772, recorded the following account from Sir Hugh Clopton (born 1672) on the family's purchasing New Place in the late seventeenth century:

> Several little epigrams on familiar subjects were found upon the glass of the House windows, some of which were written by Shakespeare, & many of them the product of his

own children's brain: the tradition being, that he often in his times of pleasantry thus exercis'd his and their talents, and took great pleasure when he could trace in them some petty display of that genius which God & Nature had bless'd himself with. (Fox, 1964: 81)

This extraordinary and compelling account combines the etching of identity into glass with the act of literary composition, at once a familial and intellectual pursuit as the fabric and reputation of New Place had come to be understood and accounted for by a subsequent owner.

Entering the courtyard of New Place

William Mitchell

An eyewitness account is provided by Richard Grimmitt (born 1682/83), who used to play at New Place with Edward Clopton when they were children. When he was an old man, in 1767, Grimmit's recollections were recorded by the vicar Joseph Greene:

> To the best of his rememberance, there was a brick wall next the street, with a kind of Porch at that end of it near the Chapel when they cross'd a small kind of green court before they enter'd the house, which was bearing to the left and fronted with brick, with plain windows, consisting of common panes of glass set in lead, as at this time. (Richard Grimmitt to Joseph Greene, 24 October 1767 (Halliwell-Phillipps, 1883, Vol. II: 134))

Much like Vertue's description, Grimmitt's depicts a residence that consisted of a gatehouse building, fronted on to the street. In the green courtyard stood the hall building, which had a brick façade and leaded windows. Grimmitt does not specify which entrance is used, but the front entrance from Chapel Street or the rear entrance from Chapel Lane work in relationship to his description: the hall would have borne to the left from either of these approaches. The enclosed, grassy courtyard probably looked a little like the quad or court of an Oxbridge college.

Shakespeare's renovation of New Place

William Mitchell and Kevin Colls

Much of our knowledge of Shakespeare's house comes from the analysis and interpretation of the remains of Hugh Clopton's original house, which remained a large part of the house that Shakespeare knew. Shakespeare bought a house that was just over 100 years old and in need of upgrading. He modernised it: his family home, which would express his prestige and wealth. Remodelling the frontage on to Chapel Street was the most definite and striking way of marking this change.

Several structures, which are thought to have originated as a result of Shakespeare's renovations, were identified on the site (Figure 5.7). Their construction technique differed from that of the earlier foundations, as did the construction material, and these are representative of high-status seventeenth-century properties. Stratigraphic relationships were carefully considered, ensuring a definitive dating sequence for these features. Critically, one of the walls (F14; Figure 5.7) had retained its construction cut. Within the backfill of this cut were artefacts dating from the later sixteenth to the early seventeenth century, evidence of its construction date. Close analysis of the brick-and-mortar type of this wall was therefore used to provide comparative dating of the other brick foundations, which did not have such definitive dating.

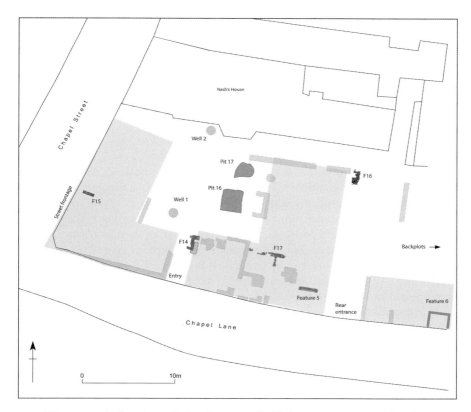

Figure 5.7 Archaeological plan depicting the likely renovations completed by Shakespeare. Fragmentary remains of Shakespeare's renovations were discovered; these predominantly included brick-wall foundations and surfaces (F prefixes). Other late-sixteenth-century pits (pits 16 and 17) are also represented in the location of the courtyard. The large, shaded area represents the New Place building layout as depicted in the schematic plan (Figure 2.1).

The gatehouse range

Shakespeare would have converted the front gatehouse range from Clopton's ground-floor shops with cellaring and chambers above, to a two-and-a-half-storey, five-gabled, 15.85 m (52 ft) gatehouse range with cellaring, domestic living quarters on the ground floor and a long gallery above. Parts of the exterior would have been embellished with the addition of Elizabethan window designs and decorative elements within the timber studding and doorways (probably similar to the front of Thomas Rogers's house in the nearby High Street; see Figure 4.2). Elements of the ground floor of the earlier building may have been retained, attested to by the survival of Clopton's cellar walls. Had these changes occurred, they would have been visibly noticeable within the external timber framing of the building.

Evidence of redevelopment within the cellar

A fragmentary brick wall (F15; Figure 5.7) was located at the southeast corner of the cellar. Similar construction materials were used to those in other seventeenth-century walls. These included red, handmade, unfrogged 20.32 × 9.52 × 5.08 cm (8 × 3¾ × 2 in) bricks laid in a random bond, using lime-mortar. The wall was orientated east to west; this perhaps represented the sole surviving element of the redeveloped stair-wells that led into the original southern cellar.

Shakespeare's adaptation of the hall range

Shakespeare's treatment of the hall remains uncertain. It remained, however, firmly at the heart of the house complex. In keeping with the period, the internal arrangement of the hall space probably underwent a partial or more extensive redesign and modernisation. Specific renovations may have included an extension to the first floor above the service range, to cover the screens-passage or an even larger area, as had happened at other contemporary properties. Hugh Clopton's central, open hearth may have also moved to become set into a wall fireplace, and although the location of the original windows and doorways would have remained, these likely to have been replaced and/or added to by sixteenth-century versions.

During the later sixteenth century there were substantial developments in architecture, brought about by economic prosperity and changes in social conventions. The fate of the open hall within houses of the period differed greatly: it was either replaced, altered or retained, and examples survive of each of these approaches. Nicholas Cooper suggests that:

> while a tall hall might survive in the houses of the great for those whose wealth enabled them to retain a space whose importance was increasingly no more than an evocation of notional relationships – from the mid sixteenth century, it was already becoming the practice for owners of houses with old, open halls to insert a floor into them. (Cooper, 1999: 282)

Within substantial town houses, the open hall was kept as a specific architectural feature well into the seventeenth century, sometimes with a degree of alteration, the extent of which was varied. Often, where usage of the hall was changed, this was due, in part, to the evolution of other rooms in the house, especially the parlour and chamber. The treatment of the hall building depended on whether or not the house was newly conceived or was being developed. As Pantin states, 'after the middle of the sixteenth century, the open hall probably disappeared as an element in the planning of town houses, and, where such a hall survived, it was generally divided into two floors' (Pantin, 1962–64: 206).

New Elizabethan houses were designed differently from the outset, and combined 'elements of traditional English vernacular architecture with the Renaissance concerns for symmetry, increasing decorative complexity, and standards of comfort. The old open hall was replaced by a new hall with first floor above it, and sometimes a third storey' (Price, 1985: 78). The importance of the hall was thus retained, especially within high-status houses where space was not at a premium. Where the open hall was kept, it was done so for a variety of reasons. According to Leech (2000), in his comprehensive study of hall-houses in Bristol, throughout this period 'the hall was no longer the centre of the house in the sense that it was the place for formal meals bringing together the urban household on a daily or regular basis … The principal purpose of the large urban hall was now to symbolise the lineage and honour of wealthy urban families' (Leech, 2000: 6–7).

The likelihood is that upon his purchase of New Place, Shakespeare was acutely aware of the importance of the hall as a symbolic or ceremonial space, and his treatment of it would have reflected this. In all likelihood, Shakespeare's familiarity with and reverence for New Place, and his understanding of the prestige and unique qualities of the property within Stratford-upon-Avon, led him to retain the hall in its original form. It is interesting to compare the area of the floor space with the Shakespeares' Henley Street house. The open hall was 100 m², about 12 m² larger than the ground floor of the Henley Street house. Certainly, the hall, with its high roof and large open space, would have felt much grander by comparison.

The survival of fragmentary brick features within the area of the hall suggests that the fifteenth-century hall saw some redevelopment by Shakespeare. A brick floor surface (F16; Figure 5.7) located on the northeast of the site against the northern foundations of the hall, may have represented a hearth and external chimney-stack attached to the northeastern corner of the building (Plate 13). The surface was 1.7 × 1 m (5½ ft × 3 ft 3 in) and had been broken in several locations. It survived because it had been constructed below the seventeenth-century ground level. It was constructed of red, handmade, unfrogged 20.32 × 11.43 × 5.08 cm (8 × 4½ × 2 in) bricks. Along the south of the surface, randomly laid stones were used as additional surface components. Located on top of the surface was a small section of curving brickwork. The bricks to the north of this were burnt, as was the deposit beneath. This evidence of burning suggests that the structure had been used as a hearth or fireplace, with the curving bricks used to retain the heat of the fire and allow easy collection of the debris. This was the only *in situ* sixteenth-to-seventeenth-century surface surviving in New Place, as it lay beneath the floor levels and was therefore spared from demolition.

The redevelopment of the screens-passage

One truncated and fragmentary brick wall (F17; Figure 5.7) survived towards the south of the hall building (Figure 5.8; Plate 7). This, again, was made up of red, handmade, unfrogged $20.32 \times 9.52 \times 5.08$ cm ($8 \times 3\frac{3}{4} \times 2$ in) bricks. Only one to two courses of the 4×0.4 m (13 ft $\times$ 1 ft 4 in) wall survived. These continued westwards to meet the eastern wall of the kitchen building. This wall appeared to be an alteration or rebuild of the existing structures, perhaps resulting from the upgrading of the hall. Somewhere within this passage, or to the south of it, would have been a stairwell that led to the first-floor chambers, of which this wall may represent a surviving part.

The service rooms

The service rooms probably retained their primary functions as buttery, pantry and kitchens, but seventeenth-century adaptations were introduced, meaning they would

Figure 5.8 Photograph of the screens-passage wall alteration introduced by William Shakespeare. This was presumably built on the location of an earlier temporary or wooden screen at the southern end of Clopton's hall.

have survived in a much altered form. Kitchen rooms in buildings of the time were subject to continuous modernisation and improvement and the functions of these rooms often changed as a result.

Evidence for renovations to the pantry and kitchen buildings.

The archaeological evidence suggests that part-way down the southern range (running along Chapel Lane) on the courtyard side, there was a change in room width. At this location in the early seventeenth century, a brick structure, thought to be the base of a stairwell, was added. This suggests that access into the upper rooms of this range was altered, perhaps as a result of the conversion or alteration to the rooms above. The small section of brick walling (F14; Figure 5.7) was identified towards the west of the service range (Figure 5.9). The structure was constructed of red, handmade, unfrogged 20.32 × 9.52 × 5.08 cm (8 × 3¾ × 2 in) bricks. Patches of plaster survived on the west-facing elevation, suggesting that part of the wall was once visible as an internal structure. The wall survived to a height of eighteen courses and was 'c'-shaped in plan. The construction cut for this wall had survived on its eastern side. This contained pottery from the later sixteenth and early seventeenth centuries, providing definitive evidence of its construction date.

Figure 5.9 Photograph of the kitchen renovation introduced by William Shakespeare. This was constructed part-way along the southern range at the location of a change in room width, and may represent the base of a stairwell. The construction cut is visible in the foreground.

The brick storage tanks

Three large square brick structures were identified on site. One of these was east of the hall building in the area of the garden (Figures 5.7 and 5.10), the second was within the redeveloped kitchen/pantry (F5; Figure 5.7) and the third was recorded further to the east along Chapel Lane. These large brick structures were probably storage pits, located along the periphery of the house within the service range and backplot. The elevations showed evidence of plastering and the bases were once covered by clay. These features suggest the pits had been deliberately waterproofed. They may have been multi-purposed and used as large food- or grain-storage bins, or for rubbish. The example located to the east of the site may have come to be used as a latrine, as it contained greenish, stained deposits on its base: the decayed evidence of waste.

Shakespeare's barns

South of the main buildings and away from the areas of excavation was the location of Shakespeare's barns. Although building regulations introduced in the town

Figure 5.10 Photograph of the brick storage tank located in the area of the garden. There was evidence of plastering on the internal elevations and clay used on the base as a means of waterproofing the tank. This example may have ultimately been used as a latrine.

in response to devastating fires meant that dwellings had be tiled, barns often remained thatched. Shakespeare's barns are mentioned in the deed of purchase of May 1597 and are said to have survived throughout the seventeenth and eighteenth centuries, eventually becoming converted to cottages (Figure 5.11). According to nineteenth- century sources, these barns had been much altered by the time of their demolition:

> Shakespeare's Barn may, in a certain sense, be said to have existed up to 1861. In that year a couple of cottages occupying that portion of New Place garden which adjoins the theatre on the west, were taken down, having in the first instance, been photographed, and then stripped to the framework of which they were constructed. These cottages had been contrived by subdividing the ancient barn belonging to Shakespeare. On removing the thatch, the lath and plaster work from between the beams, and reducing the building to its skeleton structure, it was found that, in the lapse of two centuries and a half, all the timbers of the barn had, from time to time, been replaced, with the exception of some three or four small beams. These were the sole remains of the Poet's Barn. (Bellew, 1863: 14–15)

Figure 5.11 Photograph of the cottages (previously Shakespeare's barns) during removal in 1862. Much of the fabric of the buildings has been removed to reveal the timber-framed structure contained within.

Artistic reconstructions of Shakespeare's New Place

William Mitchell

After comprehensive archival research and archaeological interpretation, new artistic representations of New Place during Shakespeare's ownership have been created by Phillip Watson (Figures 5.12–16, Plate 14). The results represent the most detailed and accurate impressions of New Place to date and illustrate the most likely version of the house as it may have been during Shakespeare's occupancy.

Evidence for the illustrations was gathered from analysis of the archaeological and documentary sources of the structure and layout of Hugh Clopton's New Place. Many of the external features of the house are based on other fifteenth- and seventeenth-century examples. Some of the finer details remain speculative, but Watson's drawings present the most likely scenario. The impressions use the ground plan generated as a result of the archaeological excavations and reproduce this to scale, in the form of detailed sketches from alternative viewpoints. The locations of the courtyard, buildings, rooms, walls, doorways and chimneys are all accurately placed with reference to what was present in the archaeological record, or where they are most likely to have existed.

The ground plans of later medieval houses were analysed with a view to adopting the most common and probable layout. Houses with comparable features such as layout, dimensions, construction, building material and age were used to build a more complete picture of New Place as it is likely to have been. Together these provided the most likely comparisons for the structure of the house and its stylistic embellishments.

The first element of the design to be developed was a plausible version of the house ground plan. Certain landmarks such as the foundations, service range, cellaring and kitchen features were included and used to guide the size and orientation of the main buildings. Some of the wall locations remained conjectural, but were placed in the most likely location through complementary interpretations. The hall depicted has an arch-braced collar roof at the gable ends and, within the centre of the hall, an open hammer-beam truss is speculated (as an explanation as to how the width of the hall was spanned). This type of roof was chosen because of the vernacular nature of the building. The roof angle is both consistent to the period and comparable in stature to the front range.

The reconstructions encompass the complete refurbishment of the frontage range, including the long-gallery storey with gabled dormers, and present the Chapel Lane service and rear entrances, projecting and Elizabethan-style windows, and decorative timberwork. In addition the redesigned internal chambers are represented in the external framework, which would have assimilated the pre-existing architectural elements of Clopton's house. Detailed architectural elements such as the blue Lias stone plinth, the coxcomb crestings, glazed ridge tiles, stone and plain-clay roof tiles, and brick infill of the hall all originate from evidence in the archaeological record.

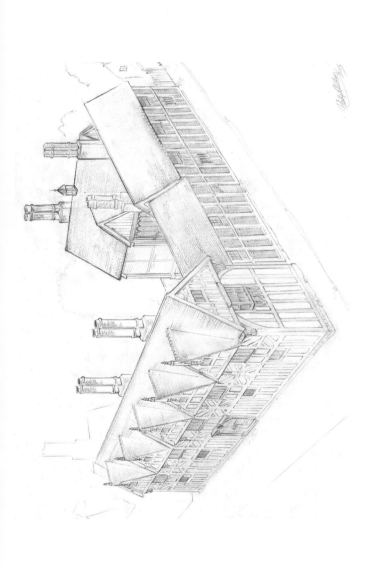

Figure 5.12 Philip Watson's northeasterly reconstruction of Shakespeare's New Place. Running along Chapel Street, the front range, with its large, central gateway, allowed access for a small cart and pedestrians via the smaller wicket gate. Four small, front-facing ground-floor windows illuminate a passage serving four chambers for servant accommodation; a staircase off the central corridor leads up to the first-floor long gallery. Elaborate herringbone first-floor studding, with five roof gables; a decorative, jettied end gable; and a projecting window represent improvements added by Shakespeare. Heavily carved brackets support the jetties, and carved, decorative finials surmount the apex of each of the five gables. Green-glazed ridge tiles adorn the terra-cotta-tiled roofs with decorative coxcomb ridge tiles on the gables. The herringbone-brick-infilled service range on Chapel Lane constitutes the engine room of the house, housing the buttery, scullery, brewery and utility rooms. The large, northeast corner chimneystack was probably added as part of the 1597 improvements. The large gates at the far end provide a true equestrian and service entrance, leading past the separate, single-storey cook-house to the stables beyond.

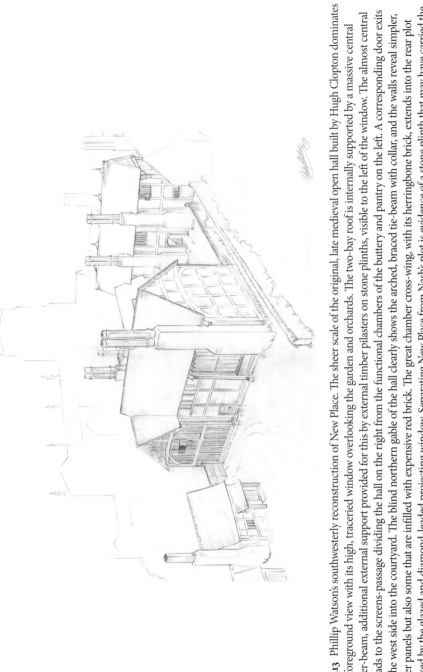

Figure 5.13 Phillip Watson's southwesterly reconstruction of New Place. The sheer scale of the original, late medieval open hall built by Hugh Clopton dominates the foreground view with its high, traceried window overlooking the garden and orchards. The two-bay roof is internally supported by a massive central hammer-beam, additional external support provided for this by external timber pilasters on stone plinths, visible to the left of the window. The almost central door leads to the screens-passage dividing the hall on the right from the functional chambers of the buttery and pantry on the left. A corresponding door exits from the west side into the courtyard. The blind northern gable of the hall clearly shows the arched, braced tie-beam with collar, and the walls reveal simpler, timber panels but also some that are infilled with expensive red brick. The great chamber cross-wing, with its herringbone brick, extends into the rear plot overlooked by the glazed and diamond-leaded projecting window. Separating New Place from Nash's plot is evidence of a stone plinth that may have carried the brick wall which partly enclosed the courtyard. Thatch-topped mud walls were popular ways of marking boundaries. The single-storey building on the left is the cook-house, here depicted with stone roof tiles, accessible to the service functions of the house via the screens-passage door but separated to minimise fire risk.

Figure 5.14 Phillip Watson's northern reconstruction of New Place. The full depth of the structure extends just under 33 m (108 ft) from Chapel Street east along Chapel Lane. The double gates on the right provide equestrian access from muddy Chapel Lane with its small stream, one of two natural waterways within the town's boundaries. The three-bay structure of the hall's cross-wing can be clearly seen with its timbers framing an elaborate herringbone brick infill. Archaeological evidence points to the roof of this portion having expensive stone tiles, a measure against potential fire risk from the ground-floor hearth. It is likely that the main thoroughfare of Chapel Street was paved with a line of blue Lias slabs flanked with rows of cobbles to provide dry access to the businesses and dwellings along the street. It is important to remember that New Place was nestled within a built-up area by 1597. The outline of William Walford's house (later the Falcon) still had two, rather than three, storeys. To the left is what became known as Nash's House with its original, rear range, which preceded the current seventeenth-century structure. Looking down into the New Place courtyard, the two gatehouse chimneystacks can be seen cut into the rear roof overhang.

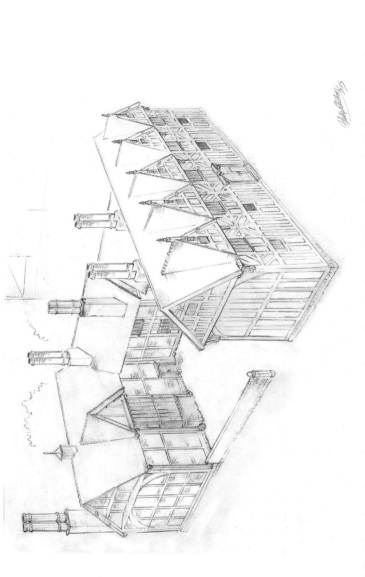

Figure 5.15 Phillip Watson's southeasterly reconstruction of New Place. The close-studded gatehouse end gable lacks a long-gallery projecting window as this overlooks Nash's House, but the visible volume of timber within the structure still conveys wealth. The five roof gables added during Shakespeare's renovation of the frontage are a lavish, decorative feature designed to provide additional light for the long gallery rather than as a third storey. This large, hall window was originally built to illuminate the master's table situated at the northern end of the hall. The step down of the roofline to the service range is partly hidden by one of the gatehouse chimneystacks. As chimney technology developed, large, rectangular, blue Lias stacks became more elaborate, and the twin, octagonal stacks were probably added to the hall during Shakespeare's tenure.

Figure 5.16 Detail of Phillip Watson's reconstruction of the New Place courtyard. Leading off from the courtyard is the rear of the gatehouse range with its two chimneystacks heating the ground-floor servants' quarters and the long gallery on the first floor. For the first time the 'sweep well' is clearly visible, the lifting mechanism of a counterbalanced arm tucked into the southwest corner of the courtyard, enabling even the slightest of servants to raise fresh water for the myriad household requirements. The grassy courtyard is crossed by neat gravel paths, one passing the well to access the screens-passage door to the hall, another heading right towards an opening into the side passage in the northern courtyard wall. The ground-floor doorway on the left, now known to have always been part of Clopton's original build rather than a later addition, accesses the service range and continues through to exit on to Chapel Lane.

George Vertue's sketch has had a significant influence on how the front range has been presented, as have Vertue's and Grimmitt's descriptions of the arrangements of the house. Documentary sources have helped to establish various features such as the use of brick; the number of chimneys; and the presence of the gardens, orchards, barns and outbuildings. Halliwell's account of the 1862 dig proved invaluable for details of the outlying areas of the site that remained unreachable during our excavations. The reconstructions include much of the rear of the property as a result of Halliwell's work.

What was life like in Shakespeare's New Place?

William Mitchell and Kevin Colls

Artefacts that can be attributed to Shakespeare's household did not survive in any great quantity. The paucity of earlier-seventeenth-century material was a surprising element in the excavations. Deposition of waste throughout this period appears to have changed significantly, perhaps as a result of organised waste disposal throughout Stratford-upon-Avon. Areas towards the back of the plot, which were more likely to contain waste pits, remain unexcavated. However, several features and layers did survive across the site that date to around this period, with two large pits in particular being of significance (pits 16 and 17; Figures 5.8 and 5.17). These pits were probably dug towards the end of the sixteenth century in the courtyard and could very well represent episodes of house clearance by Shakespeare after he purchased the property. As such, they represent extremely important finds. The pits contained material that would have originated from both the interior (such as pottery, floor tiles, personal items and food waste) and the exterior (for example roof tiles). The contents of the pits tell us much about the house and the life-style of the previous occupants.

Figure 5.17 Photograph of a large rectangular pit dug and filled in the late sixteenth century. This contained material that originated from the interior and exterior of the house. Analysis of the material has provided a detailed impression of what life was like in the house at the time.

Numerous pottery sherds were recovered that could be dated between the end of the sixteenth century and the middle of the seventeenth century. Sixteenth-century examples included Tudor Green glazed tablewares, Malvern Chase kitchenwares, late medieval oxidised wares, and Midlands purpleware. An almost complete example of the latter in the shape of a drinking vessel was also recovered (Plate 15). Later ceramic examples from the site included slip-decorated wares, slip-coated wares, mottled wares and coarsewares. It is difficult to isolate ceramics in the assemblage that would definitely have been used during Shakespeare's time at New Place. However, he would certainly have been familiar with the later Malvern Chase wares, the late medieval oxidised wares and probably with the blackware and yellowwares (examples of these were also recovered from the site). Also, some tiny fragments of well-decorated, tin-glazed earthenwares hint at the prosperous occupation around the mid- or later seventeenth century.

Shakespeare would have seen Rhenish stoneware, both in Stratford-upon-Avon and certainly in London. Small fragments from around the mid-sixteenth century to the first half of the seventeenth century were recovered. Although Rhenish stoneware is commonplace in coastal regions and ports it is less common in the West Midlands and is generally an indicator of prosperous bourgeois living. An interesting sherd of Rhenish stoneware was recovered that has a legend on it reading '… TMEIN …' (Plate 16). This probably originally read 'WAN GOT WIL IST MEIN ZIL' (When God wills it, so is my goal), or 'WANN GOTT WILL IST MEIN ZIEL' (When God wills it, my time is up). The first saying is known from a Cologne jug made at Komödienstrasse (production date 1549–mid-1570s) but similar texts are known at other production sites, although these are all a feature of the second half of the sixteenth century and linked to the aftermath of the Reformation.

In addition to the ceramics, several objects of personal clothing were recovered, including copper alloy loops, studs, belt buckles, strap loops, pins (Plate 17), and lace chapes or aiglets (used to bind the ends of laces together). These were all traditional forms of clothing accessories for the later medieval period through to the seventeenth century. One example of a copper alloy Nuremberg token of Holy Roman Emperor Frederick III (reigned 1452–93; Figure 5.18) was recovered. Nuremberg tokens are regularly found in London, where they were predominantly used as money substitutes (for example for gaming), and this example was presumably in circulation for some time. It may have even been brought back to New Place by Hugh Clopton from one of his many trips to the capital before being lost or discarded within the house or grounds, eventually ending up in one of the clearance pits mentioned above. Evidence for games and entertainment were also represented, portraying a truly cultured household. A rounded pebble used as a gaming counter and two cylindrical bone tuning pegs for an instrument (such as a lyre) were found (Figure 5.19). A small bone object was recovered that may represent a cribbage scoring peg (Plate 18) as well as a small carved handle belonging to a kitchen utensil, such as a spoon or knife. This latter object had been carved with floral motifs and other lines that appear to be the work of a young person, who may well have tried to write their name on the object (Plate 19). There is also evidence of various crafts being undertaken on site, such as bone-working (offcuts, buttons) and the production and maintenance of textile (thimbles, pins; Plates 17 and 18).

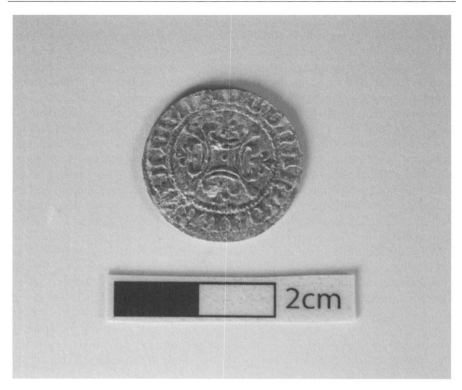

Figure 5.18 Token recovered from the site. This is an example of a Nuremberg token of Holy Roman Emperor Frederick III (reigned 1452–93) and was used as a substitute for regular currency. Other such examples found at sites in London and elsewhere have been shown to have remained in circulation for some time.

A varied array of animal bones were recovered from features dating to this period that can tell us a great deal about dietary habits, food preparation, and the presence of both pests and pets. As on archaeological sites, the majority of the bones were of cattle, sheep and pigs, although unlike the first two examples, the latter showed no signs of butchery marks on the bone. A few goose and chicken bones were recovered. Examples of horse and deer bones were also recovered, including those of roe and fallow deer. Small numbers of bones belonging to rabbits, rats, snipe, pigeons, geese and a thrush species were also recovered, as well as salt- and freshwater-fish remains, including chub and gadid (cod family). Examples of both cats and dogs were present, and there were signs of gnawing on some of the sheep bones (attributed to dogs).

Charcoal fragments were abundant in several features, including the kitchen area, representing the remains from domestic hearths and ovens as well as bonfires at the time of clearance. The charcoal showed the exploitation of several tree species native to Britain, including oak, ash and willow/poplar. Oak has good burning properties and would have made a fire suitable for most purposes (Edlin, 1949; Rossen

Figure 5.19 Bone tuning peg, one of two examples found on the site. This would have been used to peg the strings in place on a small wooden instrument of a type thought to be the predecessor of the modern violin, harp or guitar.

and Olsen, 1985). The archaeobotanical evidence found in samples of a clearance pit shows that cereal grains of barley and wheat were present, although very poorly preserved.

Relics from New Place: real, assumed and wished-for

Paul Edmondson

Monday 21 July 1862 was a big day for James Orchard Halliwell. He had been leading an archaeological dig at New Place – mainly wall-chasing, and eager to find artefacts from Shakespeare's time. On that Monday in July he uncovered 'the only personal relic of any description possessing strong claims to have belonged to the house in the poet's time ... The handle of this knife is made of bone, with an ornamentation upon it of a very antique character' (Halliwell, 1864: 165). A few lines later, his account names the knife as a possible 'veritable personal relic of Shakespeare'. The present whereabouts of the knife is not known. Apart from the bone-handled knife that Shakespeare might have used, Halliwell thought it worth mentioning only 'three ancient mullions' from Shakespeare's New Place: 'a bit of leaden piping apparently of considerable antiquity,

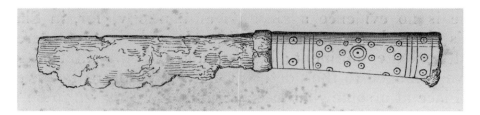

Figure 5.20 A knife with a bone handle attributed to the Shakespearian period, found during Halliwell-Phillipps's excavations of 1862, drawn by him and since lost.

and also a plate lock' (Halliwell, 1864: 164–5). Although there are some examples of masonry from New Place in the collections of the Shakespeare Birthplace Trust, these do not match the illustrations of the ones that Halliwell discovered (Halliwell, 1864: 182). The lead-piping and the plate lock are also apparently lost.

Three other artefacts mentioned by Halliwell are worth acknowledging, none of which was excavated or found by him personally. The first is a glass jug that might have belonged to Shakespeare and that somehow fell into the possession of the town clerk William Hunt around the time of the Garrick Jubilee in 1769. The jug 'undoubtedly belongs to the seventeenth century. That it is of foreign manufacture is no evidence against its authenticity' (Halliwell, 1864: 166). Although Halliwell doubts that the jug is old enough to have been Shakespeare's own, he concedes that it may have been used by some later inhabitants of New Place, hence the Shakespeare connection. It is now in the collections of the Shakespeare Birthplace Trust.

The second object is a medieval key (again no longer traceable) found by a labourer working on an excavation in 1828: 'belonging to Sir [sic.] Hugh Clopton's House in 1490, and which not improbably had continued in use long afterwards, even long enough to have received the distinction of having been handled by the great poet' (Halliwell, 1864: 166). Perhaps – if Shakespeare reused Hugh Clopton's front door in the remodelled front range. Or perhaps it was the key to another part of the house.

Halliwell's third item of note is a piece of coloured glass (lost, but we hope not broken, wherever it is), first mentioned in an early guidebook to Stratford-upon-Avon in 1847. It depicts William and Anne Shakespeare's initials, bound by a lover's knot and bearing the date 1615. The glass was saved by a relative of Mrs Court (whose family used to own Shakespeare's Birthplace before it was auctioned in 1847). An ancestor of Mrs Court 'had been employed to pull down New Place, had saved this square of glass, but attached little value to it' (Halliwell, 1864: 201). Halliwell doubts the story of its discovery, but at the same time attests that it is 'certainly a genuine relic of Shakespeare's time', noting that an ornament of this kind, bearing 'initials and inscriptions of householders, in the windows of halls, was not at all unusual' (Halliwell, 1864: 201). It is not known whether the glass was retrieved during Sir John Clopton's or Francis Gastrell's demolition of New Place. If the former then the lost artefact is evidence for Sir John having recycled materials from Shakespeare's time, which he almost certainly would have done.

Figure 5.21 A seventeenth-century glass jug, 20.3 × 17.8 cm (8 × 7 in), traditionally believed to have belonged to Shakespeare himself. It belonged to the town clerk William Hunt, who bought the site of New Place from Jane Gastrell in 1775. The actor David Garrick is said to have sipped out of it as part of the 1769 Stratford Jubilee. The jug may well have originated from New Place.

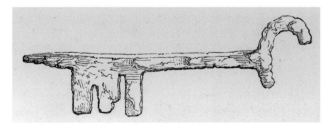

Figure 5.22 A late medieval key, 15.24 cm (6 in) long, from Hugh Clopton's original house, recovered from the garden of New Place in 1828, drawn by Halliwell-Phillipps and since lost.

Figure 5.23 Detail from a lost square glass panel, 22.86 × 17.78 cm (9 × 7 in), depicting William and Anne Shakespeare's initials bound by a lover's knot, and dated the year before Shakespeare died. The figures and the border were yellow with a dark brown outline. It was originally drawn by F. W. Fairholt for a guidebook of 1847.

At least two chairs, both of which may well have been used by the Shakespeare family or other, later residents, are associated with New Place. Both of them claim provenance through the engraver and collector Samuel Ireland (1744–1800). The first chair was purchased by Ireland from Anne Hathaway's Cottage in 1792, and was included in his *Picturesque Views on the Upper, or Warwickshire Avon* three years later. There he refers to an interview with Thomas Hart of Henley Street (1729–93: Shakespeare's great-great-great-great-nephew), who told him that the chair had been given to the Hathaway family by Elizabeth, Lady Barnard, William Shakespeare's granddaughter. It was purportedly William Shakespeare and Anne Hathaway's 'courting chair', which, if true, means that the chair was almost certainly part of the furniture at New Place in order for Elizabeth to have given it to the Hathaway family. Ireland also mentions a 4 × 4 in (10 × 10 cm) purse 'curiously wrought with small black and white bugles and beads,' said to have belonged to Shakespeare (Ireland, 1795: 207–8).

The second chair is made of Tudor oak, made to the ecclesiastical, Glastonbury design, and dates from the early sixteenth century. It apparently belonged to Richard

Figure 5.24 Shakespeare's courting chair? A seventeenth-century oak-and-walnut panel-back armchair, carved with a cabled lozenge centred by a conforming marguerite. Below are two small, sunken rectangles, one containing the Shakespeares' coat of arms, the other the crest of a bird wielding a spear. Although the armorial carvings were almost certainly present when Samuel Ireland purchased the chair, the 'W. A. S.' initials in gothic script were added later (they do not appear in Ireland's engraving of the chair, published in Ireland (1795): 207). However, the initials do evoke the kind of decoration that gentlemen in Shakespeare's time regularly had applied to their furniture.

Whiting, an abbot of Glastonbury, who opposed Henry VIII's dissolution of the monasteries and was executed in 1539. Again, Ireland acquired this chair after visiting Stratford-upon-Avon in 1796, but this time from Thomas Hart himself. Harte said he had obtained it from a Mr Taylor, who used to live next door to New Place, and who had obtained the chair in 1759 when the house was demolished. In order for it to have belonged to Shakespeare, the chair would have needed to survive from the New Place Shakespeare knew (left there by its succession of owners), and incorporated as an item of furniture in the Cloptons' new house from 1702. This is quite possible. Ireland displayed the chair in his shop on the Strand in London where it attracted a lot of attention. From 1795, Ireland's son, William Henry Ireland (1775–1835) started to present what were later discovered to be forgeries of many Shakespearian documents. But the son's unfortunate activities should not reflect badly on what seem like the honest endeavours of his father. The chairs purchased and displayed in good faith by Samuel Ireland in 1792 and 1796 are authentic objects. Both were sold as consecutive lots at auction in 1859 and bought by private collectors. The 'courting chair' came up for sale again in 2002, and was purchased by the Shakespeare Birthplace Trust; the 'Glastonbury chair' was given to the Stratford Festival, Ontario, and is on display in the foyer of their main theatre.

By 1702, the New Place that Shakespeare had known had all but vanished, though some of its foundations remained. These would be reused to build a house of an entirely different style.

Figure 5.25 An early-sixteenth-century ecclesiastical chair in the Glastonbury pattern, assembled without screws, nails, or glue. Now in the collections of the Stratford Festival, Ontario, the chair's provenance has long, if somewhat tenuous, associations with Shakespeare's New Place.

References

Ailes, A. (2014). "'A herald, Kate? O put me in thy books": Shakespeare, the Heralds' Visitations and a New Visitation Address', in N. Ramsey (ed.), *Heralds and Heraldry in Shakespeare's England* (Donington: Shaun Tyas), 105–24.

Bearman, R. (1988). *Stratford-upon-Avon: A History of Its Streets and Buildings* (Nelson: Hendon Mill Publishing).

Bellew, J. (1863). *Shakespeare's Home at New Place, Stratford-upon-Avon* (London: Virtue Brothers).

Chambers, E. K. (1930). *William Shakespeare: A Study of Facts and Problems*, 2 vols (Oxford: Clarendon Press).

Cooper, N. (1999). *Houses of the Gentry 1480–1680* (New Haven: Yale University Press).

Cooper, T. (2006). *Searching for Shakespeare* (London: National Portrait Gallery).

—— (2010). 'The Enchantment of the Familiar Face: Portraits as Domestic Objects in Elizabethan and Jacobean England', in T. Hamling and C. Richardson (eds), *Everyday Objects: Medieval and Early Modern Culture and Its Meanings* (Farnham: Ashgate), 157–77.

Edlin, H. L. (1949). *Woodland Crafts in Britain* (London: B. T. Bashford).

Fox, L., ed. (1964). *Correspondence of the Reverend Joseph Greene: Parson, Schoolmaster and Antiquary 1712–1790* (London: Her Majesty's Stationery Office for the Dugdale Society).

Halliwell, J. O. (1864). *An Historical Account of the New Place, Stratford-upon-Avon, the Last Residence of Shakespeare* (London: J. E. Adlard).

Halliwell-Phillipps, J. O. (1883). *Outlines of the Life of Shakespeare* (London: Longmans, Green).

Hamling, T. (2010). 'New Place' (talk given at the University of Birmingham, the Shakespeare Institute).

—— (2014). "'Wanting Arms": Heraldic Decoration in Lesser Houses', in N. Ramsey (ed.), *Heralds and Heraldry in Shakespeare's England* (Donington: Shaun Tyas), 205–19.

Honigmann, E. A. J. and S. Brock (1993). *Playhouse Wills: 1558–1642* (Manchester: Manchester University Press).

Ireland, S. (1795). *Picturesque Views on the Upper, or Warwickshire Avon, from its source at Naseby to its junction with the Severn at Tewkesbury: With observations on the public buildings and other works of art in its vicinity* (London: R. Faulder).

Jonson, B. ([1601] 1995). *Poetaster*, ed. T. Cain, The Revels Plays (Manchester: Manchester University Press).

Leech, R. (2000). 'The Symbolic Hall: Historical Context and Merchant Culture in the Early Modern City', *Vernacular Architecture*, 31.1: 1–10.

Molyneux, N. (2011). 'New Place and the Vertue Drawing'. Unpublished report for the Dig for Shakespeare Advisory Board, 13 July 2011.

Myrone, M. (2004). 'George Vertue', in H. C. G. Matthew and B. Harrison (eds), *Dictionary of National Biography*, Vol. XII (Oxford: Oxford University Press), 382–4.

Orlin, L. C. (2007). *Locating Privacy in Tudor London* (Oxford: Oxford University Press).

Pantin, W. A. (1962–63). 'Medieval English Town-House Plans', *Medieval Archaeology*, 6–7: 202–39.

Price, J. V. (1985). 'The Development of the Country House', in J. S. F. Walker and A. S. Tindall (eds), *Country Houses of Greater Manchester* (Manchester: Greater Manchester Archaeological Unit).

Rossen, J. and J. Olsen (1985). 'The Controlled Carbonization and Archaeological Analysis of SE US Wood Charcoals', *Journal of Field Archaeology*, 12.4: 445–56.

Shapiro, J. (2005). *1599: A Year in the Life of William Shakespeare* (London: Faber and Faber).

Simpson, F. (1952). 'New Place: The Only Representation of Shakespeare's House from an Unpublished Manuscript', in A. Nicoll (ed.), *Shakespeare Survey 5* (Cambridge: Cambridge University Press), 55–7.

Theobald, L. (1733). *The Works of Shakespeare*, 7 vols, Vol. I (London: J. Tonson, F. Clay, W. Feales and R. Wellington).

6

After Shakespeare: New Place, 1677–1759

Kevin Colls and William Mitchell

After Shakespeare's death in 1616, New Place survived, in the same form, for a further eighty-five years before being destroyed to make way for a new, more fashionable, eighteenth-century house. This building, also called New Place, was the creation of Sir John Clopton. This chapter discusses his motivations for building the property, the architecture and layout of the building, and the archaeological evidence that was left behind.

Who was Sir John Clopton?

When Sir Edward Walker died in 1677, New Place and his other estates were left to his daughter Barbara. Her marriage to Sir John Clopton, in 1662, helped to revive his family's fortunes. The knighthood of Sir John Clopton, which occurred in the same year as his marriage, was probably a result of his new and fortuitous royal connections. Sir John had served regularly as Deputy Lieutenant from 1660 until his death in 1719, and as a Justice of the Peace from 1665. He was returned for Warwick at the first general election of 1679 and was also Recorder of Stratford (1684–1709). Sir John had several children, and upon his death, Edward (1663–1729) inherited Clopton House and Hugh (1672–1751) had already been gifted New Place in 1702 (Styles, 1945: 258–66).

Sir John Clopton and New Place

Sir John was a direct descendant of Hugh Clopton, so, in 1677, the ownership of New Place reverted into the hands of a descendant of the original builder. Sir John, however, proceeded to remove all trace of Shakespeare's house and construct an entirely new, more compact building in its place. By the late seventeenth century, New Place was 200 years old, and in the eyes of the well-to-do Clopton family, it may have appeared as an ageing, old-fashioned, impractical house, ill-suited to modern town life.

Upon its completion, around 1702, he gifted the use of New Place to his younger son, Hugh Clopton (later Sir Hugh; Figure 6.1) and his new wife, Elizabeth Millward. The house, the interior of which remained incomplete, was described by Sir John as:

> one new house standing and being in Stratford-upon-Avon, which house is intended for them the said Hugh Clopton and Elizabeth his intended wife to live in, but the same having been lately built is not finished, or fitted up, and made convenient for them the said Hugh Clopton, his intended wife to inhabit in. (Halliwell, 1864: 186)

Contemporary illustrations and descriptions provide us with excellent insights into the character and finish of the house. The completion of the house in 1702 had required the

> finishing both as to glaseing, wainscoating, painteing, laying of flores, making the staircase, doors, walls, and pertitions in and about the said house, brewhouse, stables, coachhouse and other buildings, and alsoe wallinge the garden, and layeing gravell walkes therein, and doeing all other things proper and reasonable in and about the said house to make the same inhabitable. (Halliwell, 1864: 190)

A testimony of 1785 further describes many of the features of the house and confirms Sir John's involvement, recording that it was he who:

> pulled down the old house to the ground and rebuilt it in a more modern and superb style; the kitchen and the other conveniences were under the ground, which were descended into by stone stairs out of the street defended by iron palisades; the hall door had a flight of steps gradually opening from the street, over which was an iron balcony, which had a fine effect; the top of the roof was flat surrounded with wooden balustrades with seats for company to sit and regale themselves in the summer evenings. (Halliwell, 1864: 191)

A further purchase of land, which was eventually to become the Great Garden at the easternmost extent of the New Place plot, was made in 1728 by the then-owner, Sir Hugh Clopton, from Barbara Ingram, Sir Hugh's sister and wife of the deceased Aston Ingram. This description, quoted by Halliwell from the deed of conveyance, confirms the existence of several other buildings towards the rear of the plot:

Figure 6.1 Portrait of Sir Hugh Clopton (1672–1751), son of Sir John Clopton, who constructed the 1702 New Place and gifted it to Hugh.

all that piece or parcel of ground, lying and being within the borough of Stratford upon Avon, called the Great Garden, and which did formerly belong to New Place, the house wherein he the said Hugh Clopton did then inhabit and dwell, and was near adjoining to the said house and backside thereof, which said garden contained by estimation three quarters of an acre more or less, together also with all barns, stables, outhouses, brick walls edifices, buildings, ways, waters, &c., to the same premises belonging (Halliwell, 1864: 205)

On several occasions Sir Hugh and his treatment of the land immediately surrounding the New Place property are mentioned in the court rolls of the manor and borough. He is presented in 1708, 1712, 1715, 1717, 1728 and 1735 before the court for not doing what was required of a landowner in Stratford-upon-Avon, such as not 'repairing the cross gutter', 'the pitching' and 'the causway or pavement before his doore in Chappell Street'. Later, in 1734 and 1738, Sir Hugh is even presented to the court 'for laying ashes and other rubbish against the Chappell wall' and allowing 'muck and timber at the back-gates of New Place'. (Court rolls of the manor and the borough, Halliwell, 1864: 204–5). The condition of Chapel Lane was very poor, and during this period it remained infrequently used and often avoided.

The internal furnishings of the eighteenth-century house: documentary evidence

A surviving inventory made on 26 September 1753 lists all the fixtures in New Place room by room, from the period of ownership of Henry Talbot, the husband of Katherine Clopton, Sir Hugh's daughter. It details furnishings and fixtures from the basements to the attics, but does not necessarily include every room. The inventory also mentions the hall courtyard and gardens ('wilderness'):

> In kitching, a painted cubord, two dressers one with drawers, the other without, two pewter shelves, an iron stove, a small dresser, an ash grate.– In the scullary, one dresser, one bacon-rack, one hanging shelfe; an old bench; two small shelves.– In the wine sellar, a frame for bottles and a shelfe.– In the larder, two dressers and two shelves.– In the second Do., two dressers and two shelves, an old wooden pot-lid.– In the Servants Hall, two benches and a fier-grate, and some old matting.– In the small beer sellar, a shelfe and a stand to sett liquor upon.– In the Butler's Pantry, a glass cubord and two shelves, and a shooe press.– In the Hall, Shakespears Head.– In the other roomes, six family pictures and three bells with the ropes.– In the House-keeper's roome, a stove grate and one Do. In the garret [One other Do.– These words are erased with the following memorandum – the last grate is put down again by mistake].– In the bed-chamber, one pair of stairs forward lined with paper, one closet hung with scucheons.– In the closet next to the Chapel hung with paper one small grate.– One garret hung with paper.– In the Hall Court, a stone role.– In the Wilderness, a stone dyal. (Halliwell, 1864: 202)

'Shakespeare's head' (most likely a painting) would have been an early example of Shakespeare's rising celebrity status, and a way of the Cloptons signifying that their new house was itself associated with his, at least in name and position. The inventory has enabled a detailed analysis of the archaeological remains to be undertaken, and the identification of specific functions and rooms within the cellars has been possible with a high degree of accuracy.

Why did Sir John Clopton rebuild New Place?

Because of a change in economic fortunes, Stratford-upon-Avon was undergoing a period of significant redevelopment. The house was built in the then-popular Queen Anne style, named after the reigning monarch (1702–14), the term usually used to describe domestic architecture up to the size of a manor house. As such, Sir John was following the changing fashions of the period, an example set by his rebuilding of Clopton House in the later seventeenth century. The newly designed New Place shares many similarities with Clopton House (about a mile away at the edge of the Welcombe Hills), but in a scaled-down form. Sir John's New Place was a modest version of the country house, which was becoming fashionable in urban areas.

The rebuilding of New Place would become the outward expression of the Clopton family's return to influence and wealth, and a symbolic gesture of the re-establishment of their position of authority within Stratford-upon-Avon. The cost of building a new house may well have been significantly less than a complete renovation of the existing property.

Late-seventeenth- and early-eighteenth-century house design

Although the architect of New Place remains unknown, it was probably designed by Sir John himself, following the predominant architectural influences of the period (Laws, 2003: 197). Houses of the Queen Anne style were less overstated than their predecessors, deliberately moderate in proportion and detail, simpler in design and not overly embellished. It was known as 'polite architecture', on account of its simple, regular and symmetrical proportions. The style had risen to prominence partly as a result of the publication in English of Palladio's book on architecture, which was popularised by influential architects of the period including Inigo Jones (1573–1652). Jones had introduced to England the Palladian style, which was taken up later by, for example, Sir Roger Pratt (1620–85), who designed four large, Palladio-influenced houses. Palladio influenced the great artists of the period and was popularised into the eighteenth century by Lord Burlington and William Kent (Cooper, 1999).

What happened to Shakespeare's New Place?

Analysis of the archaeological and historical evidence has confirmed that the entire area of Shakespeare's house, including the hall, service and frontage ranges, was cleared of buildings down to foundation level, prior to the new, smaller building being constructed in its place. All of the floors were taken up and the area was levelled to become gardens. The cellar at the front of the site was all that survived of Shakespeare's earlier (and much grander) building. Those structures that are known to have existed towards the rear of the property, including the barns, appear to have escaped Clopton's renovations. The process of demolition would have involved the stripping of the interior of the property and removal of all the contents before these were ultimately sold on, or reused in the new property. Being valuable assets, the building materials would not have been simply discarded. The roof and wall timbers, bricks and tiles, would have been dismantled and systematically removed so as not to damage them. Tradition records that some of the oak panelling was removed and placed in the Falcon Inn on the opposite side of Chapel Street, and that some of the materials were purchased by John Vendour when he built his house at King's Mead, and by John Hunt, who built a small house for his daughter in Alveston (Halliwell, 1864: 202).

The construction of an entirely new property in place of the old was not a unique occurrence. Examples can be found throughout the period and across the country. The result was the almost complete destruction of Shakespeare's house, leaving only a few fragmentary foundations.

What was Sir John Clopton's New Place like?

An accurate visualisation of the house is possible, as a result of the surviving descriptions, pictorial representations (Figure 6.2, Plate 20) and archaeological evidence (Figure 6.3) noted here. These resources have confirmed both the exact location and the extent of Sir John Clopton's New Place, as well as providing a likely version of the exterior and interior. The results from the nineteenth-century excavations, which identified the house as 'a strong edifice built chiefly of brick' (Halliwell, 1864: 183), were reviewed alongside the modern results to complete a comprehensive understanding of the surviving evidence.

The archaeological evidence: the kitchen basements

The house was constructed on a three-bay plan, a feature typical of the period and one of a number of defining features of high-status houses. Within the basement these three bays were divided further into front and rear rooms (Figure 6.3). The resulting basement rooms were used as underground kitchens and for storage. These basements (and, by association, the house) covered the entire width of the plot (approximately 16 m (52½ ft)) leaving space for the passage at the north, and ran in a southerly direction for 14 m (46 ft).

The kitchen basements were accessed in the northwestern corner by a flight of steps down from the street, traces of which were found in the nineteenth century. Like many basements of the period they were probably vaulted, and part of what appeared to be a surviving groined cellar-arch base was identified when the plot was first excavated (see Chapter 7). This had since been removed and was no longer present. When the foundations were exposed in the nineteenth century, the whitewashings and black streaks representing the washboards were preserved. A well (reused

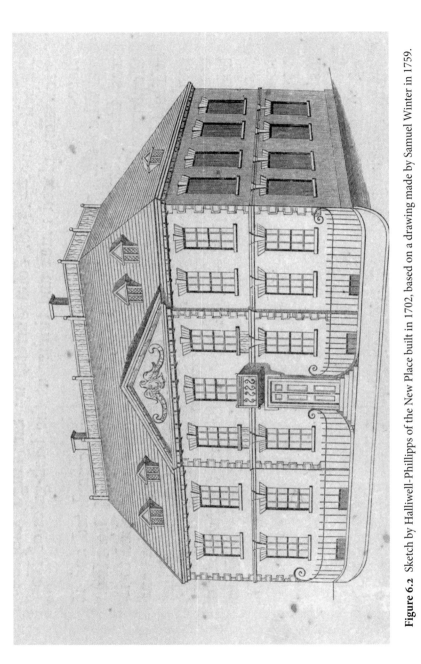

Figure 6.2 Sketch by Halliwell-Phillipps of the New Place built in 1702, based on a drawing made by Samuel Winter in 1759.

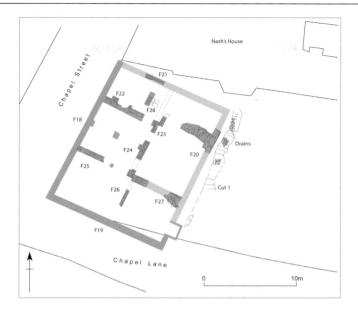

Figure 6.3 Archaeological plan of the 1702 New Place. The top image shows the archaeological features that were identified (dark grey tone), and foundations that are inferred (light grey tone). The bottom image shows the probable function of each of the cellar rooms.

from the courtyard of the first Hugh Clopton's New Place) was found within one of these cellar rooms and was probably used as an indoor pump for the kitchens. There were also indications of former light-openings within the western wall of the basement (Halliwell, 1864: 201–2).

The surviving western and southern boundary walls of the site (F18 and F19 respectively; Figure 6.3) formed part of the original basement walls, and the eastern wall of the basement (F20; Figure 6.3) was exposed during the archaeological excavations. A further basement wall (F21; Figure 6.3) was encountered adjacent to Nash's House, and made up the northernmost wall of the basement. This wall still retained rendering on its internal face and had survived to a significant height (1.3 m (4 ft 3 in); Figure 6.4).

A number of the internal basement dividing walls that were exposed to their base were also identified (F22–7; Figures 6.3 and 6.5). These foundations had previously been correctly identified by Halliwell-Phillipps as eighteenth-century in origin. Most of the foundations that had survived were load-bearing (four courses thick) and were constructed of fairly uniform 21.89 × 10.80 × 5.72 cm (8⅝ × 4¼ × 2¼ in) handmade bricks, bonded with lime-mortar. Two of the walls retained evidence of fireplace recesses. Upon discovery in the nineteenth century, there were deposits of ash still within their ash pits, from the final fires of Francis Gastrell's occupation. The basement foundations included several elements from the fifteenth-century cellar that had been incorporated into the eighteenth-century basement. The basement floor surface was made up of compact, orangey-brown sand, pebble and crushed

Figure 6.4 The 1702 New Place cellar wall as identified in archaeological test pits with intact plaster on the internal face.

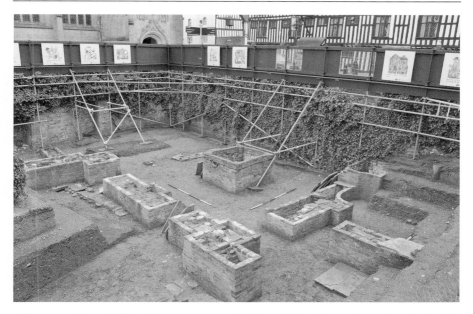

Figure 6.5 The 1702 New Place main internal cellar wall foundations, located within brick boxes that Halliwell-Phillipps built after his excavations in 1862. This may have been partly due to the fact that he left the remains open for the public to visit and he felt the boxes were adequate protection.

brick surface with areas of flagstone flooring (F28; Figure 6.3). Prior to the backfilling of the basement, Halliwell-Phillipps had ensured the survival of the foundations by constructing brick walls around them, and protected them further by placing stone capping on top (Chapter 7).

A large, sweeping, steep cut through the natural ground ran across the site from northeast to southwest (cut 1; Figure 6.3). This represented the foundation cut for Sir John Clopton's New Place. Laid up against the edge of the base of the cut were three small, square, limestone soakaway drains ('French drains'). A downpipe from the roof guttering to the rear of the house would have fed into these to allow water to drain away through the sandy gravels beneath. The drains were filled with demolition debris containing large amounts of glass, metal, brick fragments and tile, present as a direct result of Gastrell's demolition.

The basements contained the larder, the scullery, the small beer cellar, the wine cellar, the butler's pantry, the kitchen and the servants' hall. It is most likely that the kitchen and servants' hall were the rooms towards the rear of the house, as these both contained the necessary fireplaces. This arrangement of kitchen and servants' hall in the basement is mirrored, for example, at Coleshill House in Berkshire (Cooper, 1999: 187), and elsewhere. The basic layout of these rooms would not have changed throughout the entire lifetime of the house.

The ground and first floors

The majority of the ground-floor rooms would have been used for entertaining. The entrance led into the hall, which was very different from the hall that Shakespeare would have known. As Cooper states:

> With the decline of the hall's traditional functions, it could either be used for something else or done away with altogether … in more modest gentry houses the evolving use of the hall is more difficult to trace, but the relocation of the stair and the occurrence of centrally entered halls from the mid seventeenth century onwards can only have been possible with the halls changing functions. (Cooper, 1999: 287)

Other commonly used rooms included the parlour, which was the family's every-day sitting and dining room. The walls of the ground-floor rooms would have been adorned with family portraits and paintings, and finely finished with decorative plaster mouldings, using dentils, ovolos and modillions around the ceiling cornices (Plates 21 and 22). There were bells hung within the rooms to summon the servants. The first floor contained private rooms, including the bedchambers. There would have been a grand chamber for the master of the house and further chambers for family members and visitors. These were hung with decorative wallpapers of the time.

The attics and roof terrace

The servants' bedchambers would have been located in the attics, along with space for storage. It was through these attics that access could be gained on to the roof.

The passage

The passage between what much later became known as Nash's House (immediately next door) and New Place was retained and continued to serve as a shared access to the rear of the properties. This passageway was almost certainly covered at a later date, but no archaeological features survive from that period.

An extension of the southern elevation of Nash's House is present on the historic plans and part of this wall was identified. This extension is likely to be the reason for a gable scar on the adjacent Nash's House, thought for many years to show the roof pitch of Hugh Clopton's original New Place.

The gardens ('wilderness')

Towards the back of the plot, in the area that was formerly the fifteenth-century hall, relatively little evidence from the eighteenth century had survived, confirming that this area was cleared of buildings by Sir John. He converted it to a garden known as 'the wilderness'. A George I coin from 1723 was found at this location.

Further back, towards the rear of the plot, several pits were identified, dating from the tenure of the Cloptons. A possible oven or kiln had survived in the form of a collapsed fired-clay roof and external flue (Figure 6.6). Within and surrounding the flue were large quantities of ash and the finds recovered from the backfill (including pottery, clay pipes and an onion bottle; Plate 23) dated to a single period, *c.* 1650–1720. The structure may perhaps have originally been dome-shaped and made up of clay, with a vent in the roof through which the smoke would have been expelled. The flue would have been the location of the fire opening. It is uncertain what the purpose of the structure was.

Figure 6.6 The collapsed remains of a clay oven and flue located in the backplot area of New Place. It is likely that this feature is associated with the 1702 New Place house.

A large, steep-sided, circular pit, 2 m (6½ ft) in diameter and 1.15 m (3¾ ft) deep, was identified (Figure 6.7). This feature has been interpreted as a temporary pit used to make quicklime for use as garden fertiliser, lime-mortar or plaster (Williams, 2004) and it may date to the reconstruction of New Place during the period of Sir John Clopton.

At the base of the pit was a central, oval-shaped firing pit, filled with layers of slaked limestone and fuel (charcoal). The wood and limestone had been stacked in layers and then fired, resulting in quicklime. The sides of the pit were reddened as a result of the excessive temperatures involved during the processing. An effort had been made to put out the final firing using clean sand, and upon abandonment the pit was filled with demolition deposits and rubbish, dating to the mid-eighteenth century. Several other large pits had also survived.

The outbuildings (dovecote, stables, barns and outhouses?)

Several documentary sources suggest that there were outhouses, stables, barns and a dovecote situated towards the rear of the property. Although the nineteenth-century excavations found several walls and structures dating to Sir John's residency, much work remains to be done in these locations.

Figure 6.7 Lime-burning pit excavated in the backplots of New Place. This pit would have been dug to make quicklime for use as agricultural fertiliser, lime-mortar or plaster.

Building materials

The bricks of Sir John's house differed from those of the earlier periods. They were larger, more sharply edged and more regularly fashioned. Throughout the excavations of the nineteenth century, many tiles, plaster and stone ornaments were found in the back-filled cellars. Stone pilasters, vases and other relics were also found. None of these building materials have survived in any known archive or collection. All that had remained for the modern excavations were small fragments of painted plasterwork from architraves and cornices. These building materials suggested rooms that would have been adorned with stuccoed ornaments, typical of high-status houses of the period.

Artefactual evidence from Sir John's New Place

Several artefacts from the period that can attest to what life was like at the time had survived. These ranged from ceramics to clay pipes. Two finds worthy of specific mention were a fob seal and a domino. The fob seal (formerly attached to a pocket-watch fob; Plate 24) was probably eighteenth-century in origin and was made from gilded brass with intaglio red glass inscribed with the picture of a sailing ship and the letters 'A'DIEU'. This may have commemorated the 'Henry Grace à Dieu', a sixteenth-century carrack: a great, celebrated ship contemporary with, and larger than, the *Mary Rose*. A small, bone domino from around this time was also recovered (Plate 25).

The external appearance of the eighteenth-century house

Several representations of Sir John's New Place survive, though none predate its demolition (Bearman, personal correspondence). These depict a fine, Queen Anne-style residence (Figure 6.8; Plate 20). It was constructed of brick with stone quoin detailing, and had two storeys with attics and basements. The frontage was symmetrical and the house was topped by a hipped dormer roof, containing two large, brick chimneystacks and gable-ended dormer windows, which lit the attic space. The roof had balustrading around a flat platform summit. A central projecting bay incorporated a pediment containing a cartouche: a coat of arms consisting of a bird displayed *affronté*, standing on a scrolling bearing a motto that appears to say 'Loyarte Mon Honneur', the Clopton family motto.

The windows were twelve light sashes and the window heads consisted of gauged brickwork with stone keystones. There appear to have been blind (blocked) windows on the Chapel Street elevation, which probably resulted from the introduction of the

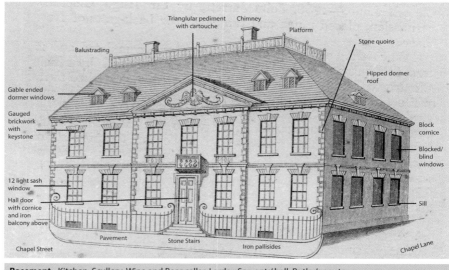

Basement - Kitchen, Scullery, Wine and Beer cellar, Larder, Servants' hall, Butler's pantry

Ground floor - Hall, Hall Court, Parlour, other rooms and 'wilderness' behind

First floor - Bed chambers, Housekeeper's room, closet, other rooms

Attic - Servants' quarters, storage

Figure 6.8 Sketch of the 1702 New Place with the architectural features that are mentioned in the text (Halliwell-Phillipps, 1864), from a drawing made by Samuel Winter in 1759.

window tax in 1696. The house was accessed from Chapel Street via a large, central doorway at the top of some steps. Above the front door was a small, iron balcony, an innovation of the early seventeenth century, which fell out of fashion relatively quickly (Cooper, 1999:188–9). Four window openings from the frontage into the kitchen basement are evident (accessible from stairs that led from the passage alongside Nash's House). The front of the house was flanked by elegant but imposing iron palisades (Lever and Harris, 1993).

Comparative examples of Queen Anne mansion houses

A considerable number of houses survive that have comparable architectural qualities to Sir John Clopton's New Place. This enables us to present New Place firmly in the context of the established tastes and designs of the period, and for our purposes we will look at three examples from Stratford-upon-Avon, and one from nearby Lichfield.

Clopton House

The Clopton family first came into possession of the land at Clopton, about a mile from the centre of Stratford-upon-Avon, in the thirteenth century, and built their house shortly after. Like New Place, this was substantially altered during the seventeenth century and the new Clopton House bears a striking resemblance to the New Place of 1702 (Figure 6.9). Around 1665, Sir John rebuilt the hall range of Clopton House by using his wife's marriage portion (from Sir Edward Walker) together with a loan of £1,095. He also added a new south range to join an earlier, sixteenth-century gatehouse. Sir John created a house that represented the up-to-date style of the post-Restoration period. The new façades were primarily made up of red brick and the roof was of the fashionable, hipped construction, beneath which sat a white-painted cornice. Tall chimneys protruded from the roof. The western elevation contained a doorway that led directly into the hall. This façade was completed by a pediment containing the arms of Sir Edward Walker, who had taken up residence there (Tyack, 1994: 30–1).

Figure 6.9 Clopton House, near Stratford-Upon-Avon. Watercolour by R. B. Wheler, 1825, showing major seventeenth-century renovations completed just before Clopton began work on New Place (of similar architectural design).

Mason Croft, Church Street

Mason Croft (Figure 6.10), named as such because of the Mason family who once lived there, is an early-eighteenth-century town house in Stratford-upon-Avon. It has been suggested that it was designed by the same architect, Francis Smith, who also built the vicarage, now the headmaster's house (Bearman, 1987–88: 85–9). Marie Corelli, the once famous novelist, lived at the house from 1901 until her death in 1924 and was fond of its romantic appeal (Bell, 2011). Architecturally it holds many similarities to Sir John Clopton's New Place. The house has two storeys with an attic and is constructed of brick-and-stone quoins with a wooden block cornice. The frontage is symmetrical and has three hipped dormer windows set into the hipped roof. There are three windows on either side of the oak front door on the ground floor and seven windows on the first floor. The windows are twelve light sashes with chamfered soffits above, and the central doorway has a carved stone architrave around the cornice.

Figure 6.10 Mason Croft, built within a few years of New Place (1710–24).

Stratford Prep School/Old Croft School, Old Town

This building (Figure 6.11) is of early eighteenth-century construction and was at one time home to Captain James Saunders (died 1830), the local antiquary, whose works include a full and important account of David Garrick's 1769 Shakespeare Jubilee. Much like its Stratford neighbours New Place and Mason Croft, this two-storey building is made up of brick with stone quoins and has a wooden block cornice. Its entrance with portico became off-centre during a later extension, which made the frontage appear asymmetrical (Styles, 1945: 221–34).

The Bishop's Palace, Lichfield

The Bishop's Palace was built in 1686–87 in Cathedral Close, Lichfield (Figure 6.12). The architect, Edward Pierce (1635–95), worked with Sir Christopher Wren (1632–1723),

Figure 6.11 Stratford Prep School/Old Croft School, built around 1690. It was extended soon after, ensuring the front was no longer symmetrical.

The Palace at Lichfield.

Figure 6.12 The Bishop's Palace, Lichfield – a popular and influential design that might have influenced Sir John Clopton and his own sense of social status.

the eminent architect, on a number of buildings in London. Architecturally, the house is strikingly similar to New Place, and it is even possible that Pierce had an influence on Sir John Clopton's design. Like New Place, it was built in the Queen Anne style, and comprises two storeys with a seven-window range. The front of the house is deliberately symmetrical and is crowned by a classical pediment, containing a cartouche over the doorway. On the ground floor there were a central hall, parlour, drawing room and chapel. In the grounds were a bake-house, brew-house, pigsty, gardens and orchard (Greenslade, 1990: 57–67).

The occupation of the Revd Francis Gastrell

Sir Hugh Clopton lived at New Place until his death in 1751, when it passed to his two daughters, Katherine and Anne. In 1753, Katherine, who had previously married Henry Talbot, sold New Place to the Revd Francis Gastrell (1701–72; Figure 6.13), a canon residentiary from Lichfield. Perhaps Gastrell was partly attracted by the similarity between New Place and the Bishop's Palace (Figure 6.12). Later, in 1758, in a bid to increase the amount of land already contained within the boundaries of the New Place plot, Gastrell added to the property by purchasing additional land to the rear. Any remaining boundaries between the newly purchased plots are likely to have been removed during this period, thus creating the area now known as the Great Garden. New Place is identified by name on Samuel Winter's plan of 1759 (Figure 6.14), the earliest surviving plan of Stratford-upon-Avon. This shows the main frontage of Chapel Street continuously built up, with a gap along Chapel Lane before a block of buildings towards the rear of the plot.

By the mid-eighteenth century, New Place, like the Shakespeares' former dwelling on Henley Street, was attracting increasing numbers of tourists. Sir Hugh had been

Figure 6.13 Portrait of the Revd Francis Gastrell, who bought New Place from Sir Hugh Clopton in 1756. Dr Johnson told James Boswell that Gastrell's wife, Jane, participated in the felling of the mulberry tree that Shakespeare planted there. In 1759, following a disagreement with the corporation about the payment of rates to assist the poor (Gastrell was living some of the year in Lichfield), he razed the second New Place to the ground.

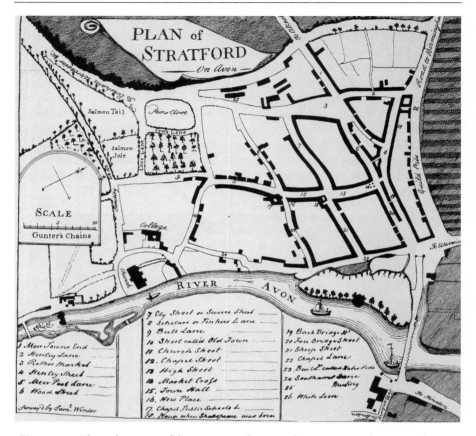

Figure 6.14 The earliest map of the town: 1759 by Samuel Winter. New Place is number 16.

sympathetic towards these Shakespearian pilgrims, but Gastrell was quite unappreciative of the house's association with William Shakespeare. A mulberry tree planted on the site was of specific interest to Shakespearian enthusiasts, since it was popularly thought to have been planted by Shakespeare himself. The influx of visitors wanting to see the tree, as well as its overshadowing the windows of the house, encouraged Gastrell and his wife, Jane, to have it felled in 1758 (Law, 1922: 10).

By 1759, Gastrell was embroiled with the town authorities over the poor-rate contributions he was asked to pay. He refused, because New Place, purchased with his wife's money, was little more than a second home, and the couple did not live permanently in the town. Infamously, Gastrell proceeded to demolish the house in its entirety, leaving only some of the outbuildings and barns (Pringle, 1997: 164). The archaeological evidence has confirmed this account and contributed to the historic narrative. Following this, Gastrell moved away from Stratford, and, in the popular imagination, was effectively banished from the town.

The earliest printed criticism of Gastrell's activities is in a letter published in July 1760 written by an anonymous lady visitor who refers to:

> a mulberry tree of his [Shakespeare's] planting … so large that it would shade the grass plat in your garden which I think is more than 20 yards square [which] this man [Gastrell] on some disgust, has … cut down [and] piled it as a stack of firewood to the great vexation, loss and disappointment of the inhabitants. (Cave, 1760: 308)

Later embellishments of the story have succeeded in securing Gastrell's fate as the villain of the piece. Benjamin Victor, writing in 1771, gives a vivid but exaggerated picture of the townsfolk who:

> gathered together, surrounded the House, reviewed with tears the fallen tree, and vowed to sacrifice the offender to the immortal memory of the planter! In short, such a spirit was on foot that the clergyman, after consulting with his friends, and skulking from place to place, was persuaded to quit the town, where he would never have been permitted to abide in peace and where all the inhabitants have most religiously resolved never to suffer any one of the same name to dwell amongst them. (Victor, 1771: 202)

This view continued throughout the nineteenth century with equally scathing descriptions of Gastrell, such as that in the *West Middlesex Advertiser and Family Journal* of 4 September 1858: Gastrell, 'because he was assessed to the poor rate, cut down a celebrated mulberry tree, venerated by the inhabitants as a memento of their immortal bard, having been planted by his own hand: and this vindictive man, a disgrace to his cloth, also pulled down his house' (British Newspaper Archive, 2013).

In the years since, the blame for the destruction of 'Shakespeare's New Place' has often been attributed to Gastrell. But Sir John had already removed it. Halliwell-Phillipps reminds us that we ought to be glad that the later Clopton structure was removed, because of the opportunity to reveal the remains of Shakespeare's house (Halliwell, 1864: 220).

References

Bearman, R. (1987–88). 'Mason Croft, Stratford-upon-Avon: A Francis Smith House?', *Transactions of the Birmingham and Warwickshire Archaeological Society*, 95: 85–9.

Bell, M. (2011). 'A Brief History of Mason Croft', http://www.birmingham.ac.uk/schools/edacs/departments/shakespeare/about/mason-croft-history.aspx (accessed 23 August 2015).

British Newspaper Archive (2013). 'The Man who Demolished Shakespeare's House: Reverend Francis Gastrell', http://blog.britishnewspaperarchive.co.uk/2013/03/09/the-man-who-demolished-shakespeares-house-reverend-francis-gastrell/ (accessed 24 September 2015).

Cave, R., ed. (1760). 'Extract of a Letter from a Lady on a Journey at Stratford-upon-Avon in Warwickshire to Her Friend in Kent', *The Gentleman's Magazine*, 30 (July): 308.

Cooper, N. (1999). *Houses of the Gentry 1480–1680* (New Haven: Yale University Press).

Greenslade, M. W. (1990). *A History of the County of Stafford* (London: Victoria County History), available at http://www.british-history.ac.uk/vch/staffs/vol14 (accessed 24 November 2015).

Halliwell, J. O. (1864). *An Historical Account of the New Place, Stratford-upon-Avon, the Last Residence of Shakespeare* (London: J. E. Adlard).

Law, E. (1922). *Shakespeare's Garden, Stratford-upon-Avon* (London: Selwyn and Blount).

Laws, A. (2003). *Understanding Small Period Houses* (Marlborough: The Crowood Press).

Lever, J. and J. Harris (1993). *Illustrated Dictionary of Architecture* (London: Faber and Faber).

Pringle, R. (1997). 'The Rise of Stratford as Shakespeare's Town', in R. Bearman (ed.), *The History of an English Borough: Stratford-upon-Avon 1196–1996* (Stroud: Sutton Publishing and the Shakespeare Birthplace Trust).

Styles, P., ed. (1945). *A History of the County of Warwick* (London: *Victoria County History*), available at www.british-history.ac.uk/vch/warks/vol3 (accessed 24 November 2015).

Tyack, G. (1994). *Warwickshire Country Houses* (Chichester: Phillimore).

Victor, B. (1771). *History of the Theatres of London*, 3 vols (1761–71), Vol. III (London: printed for T. Becket).

Williams, R. (2004). *Limekilns and Limeburning* (Princes Risborough: Shire Publications).

7

The archaeologies of New Place

Kevin Colls and William Mitchell

Following the demolition of New Place by Francis Gastrell, the site grew in importance to Shakespearian scholars, enthusiasts and (perhaps more importantly) the local community. Shakespeare's ownership of New Place had irrevocably altered the perception of this plot of land in the hearts and minds of the people of Stratford-upon-Avon, and indeed the world. This chapter presents an overview of the site since the removal of the 1702 house, and particularly focuses upon the archaeological projects that have taken place during the last 150 years – namely that of Halliwell-Phillipps and Dig for Shakespeare. These projects, although separated in time, were conceived with the same intention: to investigate the site of New Place in order to reveal evidence of Shakespeare's residency. The excavations differed in their approach and methodologies, and were both a product of their time. The site of New Place has revealed a very complex archaeological signature that itself helps to write its archaeological biography.

After Gastrell

Gastrell removed Sir John's New Place in its entirety down to its foundations, with much of the rubble being used to fill the cellar and level the site. No further buildings were ever constructed there, and the site remained an undeveloped area of open land. Any building materials and internal fixtures worth reusing would have been sold on to building merchants for use in other properties. In 1775, a few years after the death of Gastrell, his widow Jane sold the remains of his estate, including the site of New Place and the Great Garden, to Mr William Hunt (the town clerk):

> All that large garden or parcel of land near the Chapel upon which a capital mas-suage formerly stood as the same was then walled in together with the barn (later converted to a stable) and dovehouse standing thereupon. And also all that other garden or parcel of land as the same was then also walled in and opposite to the said first mentioned garden. (Receipts from Gastrell's Will, Shakespeare Birthplace Trust Archives: DR 27/187)

The site then passed to William Hunt's son, Charles Henry, who also proceeded to purchase Nash's House in 1785. In 1819, the site of New Place was advertised for sale as part of the estate of the then-owner, William Morris (Bearman, 2011). A series of bankruptcies and conveyance delays followed, with the result that the New Place estate was subdivided and sold off separately.

The site was then purchased by Edward Cooper on behalf of Lucy Smith in 1827 (Shakespeare Birthplace Trust, 464/2/71). This purchase included a stable immedi-ately adjoining the eastern boundary. The stable formed the westernmost bay of the former five-bay barn, thought to have originally belonged to Shakespeare. The other four bays, comprising individual cottages, were sold to other individuals at this time. To the east of the New Place plot, the Great Garden, now documented as a bowling green, was purchased by Edward Leyton, also in 1827. Later that year, a small section of this garden was partitioned off for the creation of the first purpose-built theatre in

Figure 7.1 Image of the Great Garden in 1844, showing the theatre towards the middle of the image and the boundary of New Place to the right. This image clearly shows this area as a community space.

Stratford-upon-Avon. Several images of the Great Garden exist from this period, with perhaps the best thought to be from around 1844 (Figure 7.1). This image depicts the new theatre, the Guild Chapel, and the easternmost boundary of the New Place plot (right-hand side of the image). It is clearly a public space, which groups and families are enjoying. It was most probably still known as Shakespeare's Great Garden, as well as the Bowling Green.

In 1836 New Place and Nash's House were purchased by David Rice, who retained ownership for twenty-six years before he sold New Place to James Halliwell-Phillipps. Throughout this period, the site of New Place was laid out as a formal garden, as illustrated in numerous sources (Figures 7.2 and 7.3). It is unclear if the site was open to the public during this period, but, given the issues faced previously by Gastrell, it seems highly likely that the gardens were open for at least some of the time. Indeed, individuals are depicted in many of the images, and an entrance to the garden existed off Chapel Street (Figure 7.3). The earliest detailed map to feature the site (the 1851 Board of Health map; Figure 7.4) marks it as the 'Site of New Place the Home of William Shakespeare', confirming that there was a developing recognition of its importance. At this time, the New Place plot was laid out as a garden for Nash's House with the entrance off Chapel Lane and an oval carriage drive, framed on the east side by shrubbery. Beyond that lay a back garden with tree-lined walks, formal planting and laid paths.

Figure 7.2 Image of New Place in 1847 by W. J. Linton, showing the site as a well-established garden.

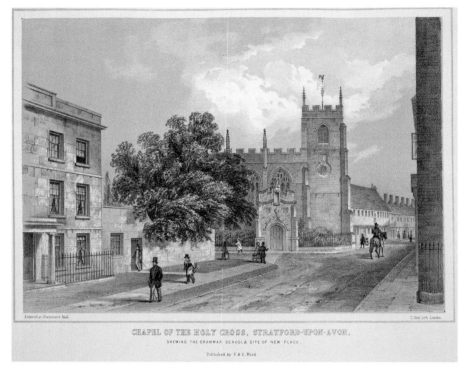

CHAPEL OF THE HOLY CROSS, STRATFORD-UPON-AVON.
SHEWING THE GRAMMAR SCHOOL & SITE OF NEW PLACE.
Published by E. & F. Ward

Figure 7.3 Image of New Place in 1851 by C. Graf, showing the Chapel Street frontage, complete with a large, overhanging tree and a wall with a single entrance.

Halliwell-Phillipps, Shakespeare and New Place

Any historical account of New Place would remain incomplete without mention of the work of James Orchard Halliwell-Phillipps (1820–89). Halliwell-Phillipps was an antiquary, a literary scholar and a principal friend of the Shakespeare Birthplace Trust (Figure 7.5). Throughout his career he wrote on subjects as diverse as science, medieval chronology, literary biography, philology and social history, but his most prolific writings were those on Shakespearian themes. From the 1840s, Halliwell-Phillipps became increasingly interested in Shakespeare, producing substantial works, including the publication of biographical histories, and collected rare works and records. His growing affection was recorded when, in 1842, he wrote of Shakespeare 'I grow fonder everyday' (Halliwell-Phillipps to Joseph Hunter (15 January 1842), British Library, Add. MS 24869). Halliwell-Phillipps's interest in and affinity for Shakespeare remained with him throughout his life. His most comprehensive and accomplished title is probably his *Outlines of the Lives of Shakespeare* (1881), which he revised

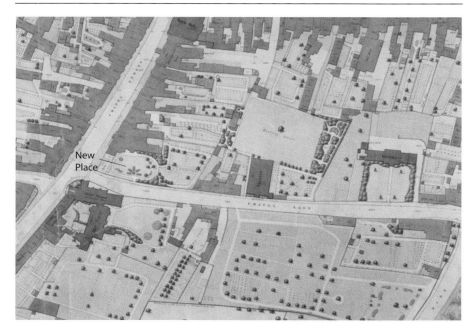

New
Place

Figure 7.4 Stratford-upon-Avon Board of Health map of 1851, showing New Place laid out as a formal garden, the cottages along Chapel Lane, the first theatre in the town and the Great Garden of New Place (the Bowling Green).

and enlarged six times (Halliwell-Phillipps, 1887). This work was a result of his biographical labours and is still recognised as a useful source today (Freeman and Freeman, 2004).

Halliwell-Phillipps spent much of his time scouring the archives of Stratford-upon-Avon and nearby communities for sources of Shakespearian material. Through his detailed research into the historical records, he grew to recognise the importance of the site of New Place and set out to acquire and preserve it, and its associated plots, for future generations. His vision was to reunite once again the land owned and occupied by Shakespeare, and to gather as much information as possible before preserving these in the form of commemorative gardens.

In 1861, Halliwell-Phillipps set about establishing a trust with the aim of raising the funds for the purchase from David Rice of the site of New Place, the plots along Chapel Lane and Shakespeare's Great Garden (Figure 7.6). These purchases were completed by 1862. The buildings included barns, cottages and outbuildings along Chapel Lane, which were subsequently cleared by Halliwell-Phillipps immediately following their purchase (Bellew, 1863: 14–15; Figure 5.12). Although a survey completed at the time suggests that the timbers of these buildings dated from 1700 (Bearman, 2011), dendrochronology did not exist in Halliwell-Phillipps's time, and it is possible that he may have unwittingly removed barns that were in fact earlier in date – even dating back to Shakespeare's time. The final piece of land fronting Chapel Lane,

Figure 7.5 Image of antiquarian and Shakespearian scholar James Orchard
Halliwell-Phillipps around 1863, close to the time of the purchase and excavation
of New Place.

which had been sold to a consortium for the building of the theatre, was acquired by
Halliwell-Phillipps in 1872 (Bearman, 2011). He subsequently demolished the building and 'threw the site into the New Place Gardens' (Styles, 1945: 244–7), finally reu-
niting the ownership of the site of New Place with its original boundaries at the rear.

The archaeological excavations (1862–63)

Halliwell-Phillipps saw himself as a keen antiquarian and amateur archaeologist, and he
set about excavating the site of New Place soon after his purchase, although he was not present all the time during the excavations (Nicholas Molyneux, personal communication,

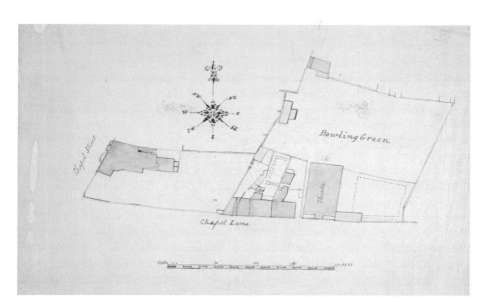

Figure 7.6 Plan of the site purchased by Halliwell-Phillipps in 1861, excluding the theatre plot, which he didn't purchase until 1872.

Figure 7.7 Photograph of the New Place site in 1856, prior to Halliwell-Phillipps's excavations.

2013). A photograph dated 1856 (Figure 7.7) shows the site to be somewhat different from the way it had looked in the 1840s (Figure 7.2). The site that Halliwell-Phillipps excavated was relatively flat, cleared and included newly planted saplings.

His aims for the excavations were similar to those of Dig for Shakespeare: to identify the remains of New Place and recover artefacts that may have belonged to Shakespeare himself. The exact area of Halliwell-Phillipps's excavations was determined during the modern excavations, and it is clear that he completed extensive excavation across the entire frontage of the site. In doing so, he removed much of the material within the backfilled cellars of the 1702 New Place house and exposed the foundations along the frontage (Figure 7.8). He conducted further, more limited investigations to the rear of the plot. The excavations moved in an easterly direction from the plot frontage but stopped short of removing a mulberry tree that grew on the site (Figure 7.9). When foundations that continued outside the front area were identified, these walls were 'chased' by excavating narrow trenches. Several structures were identified using this method, which actually left many of the areas in-between these foundations relatively untouched.

Figure 7.8 Photograph of the Halliwell-Phillipps excavations at New Place, 1864. This image clearly shows the 1702 cellar foundations prior to the construction of the brick boxes.

Figure 7.9 Sketch showing the archaeological excavations at New Place (1864). It certainly appears that the site was open to the public to some extent.

Halliwell-Phillipps suggested there were three phases of construction on the site (Figure 7.10). The primary phase of construction was the house built by Hugh Clopton (*c.* 1483) – the house that Shakespeare would have known. According to Halliwell-Phillipps:

> With the exception of a considerable number of bricks, pieces of brickwork, small portions of the foundations, and the ancient quoining of the well, hardly any relics of the old structure have yet been discovered. Three ancient mullions have been found, and there is a bit of leaden piping apparently of considerable antiquity, as also a plate to a lock. (Halliwell, 1864: 164)

The second phase of building he identified was the construction of Sir John Clopton (*c.* 1702). As we have seen, Sir John pulled down the original buildings and completely built a new residence in their place. Halliwell also notes that some of the earlier building materials were reused in the construction of the new house. However, he also records that Sir John clearly 'rebuilt the house, substituting underground kitchens in the place of the ancient cellars and erecting the new house on a different ground plan' (Halliwell, 1864: 190). Halliwell-Phillipps's deductions have proven to be correct through the modern analysis of the archaeological remains. The third phase he identified he ascribed to 'modern date'. Reinterpretation of these structures during the Dig

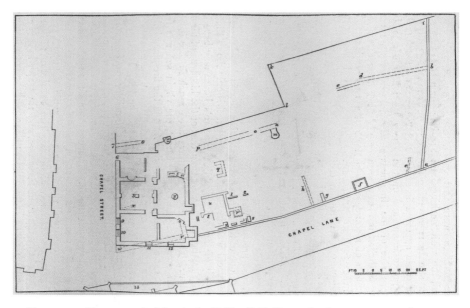

Figure 7.10 Plan created of the site by Halliwell-Phillipps after his excavations, showing his three occupation periods: fifteenth-century New Place, which Shakespeare would have known; eighteenth-century New Place, built by Sir John Clopton; and a third, modern phase (Halliwell-Phillipps).

for Shakespeare excavations has proven, however, that these belonged to a much earlier period (the seventeenth century). Halliwell-Phillipps's nineteenth-century excavations have heavily influenced subsequent interpretations of the site and the modern archaeological investigations. His work on site and his publications (including plans and photographs) have all contributed to the modern analysis.

The site after Halliwell-Phillipps's excavations

The site of New Place appears to have remained open after Halliwell-Phillipps's excavations. For a short period, visitors were able to access the basements and view the surviving remains (Figure 7.9). It is unclear if the site was open and free to all. The documentary sources and the more recent archaeological excavations have confirmed that Halliwell-Phillipps or his team instigated the construction of brick boxes around the delicate remains to protect them. Each box was then sealed by flagstones (Figure 7.11). Upon the removal of these flagstones, as part of Dig for Shakespeare, artefacts were occasionally found sitting on top of the foundations. These objects, including a fragment of a seventeenth-century clay pipe, must have been placed there

Figure 7.11 Photograph of the remains of the 1702 cellar foundations, encased in brick boxes by Halliwell-Phillipps in 1862.

by Halliwell-Phillipps, or more likely one of his team, prior to backfilling the area. They were marking their discoveries for archeologists of the future.

The backfilling appeared to have occurred fairly rapidly using material taken from the excavations. The chosen material had been carefully selected to be free from large blocks of masonry, suggesting that the original cellar backfill had already been sorted. These backfill layers contained large quantities of missed or discarded materials that dated from the medieval through to the Victorian period. In the years following the excavations, the foundations outside the basements were left exposed to be viewed by the public (Figure 7.12) and remained so until the 1960s, when they eventually became covered over.

The well

The well in the centre of the site has received much attention since its discovery by Halliwell-Phillipps in 1862. At this time, it contained the material from the demolition of Sir John Clopton's House by Gastrell in 1759. The well was cleared out and at the bottom was 'discovered an old flat candlestick, which, as it has been carefully

Figure 7.12 Photograph of New Place in 1877 after Halliwell-Phillipps's excavations, showing the site partially backfilled with some of the remains left open. It also shows that the central well has now been built up and covered.

preserved, should be recorded as certainly having no claims beyond the time of Gastrell' (Halliwell, 1864: 197). Halliwell-Phillipps believed this well was eighteenth-century in date. However, Dig for Shakespeare confirmed that it was present in the court-yard of the original New Place and was integrated into the cellar of the much larger front range of Sir John Clopton's 1702 house. When the Halliwell-Phillipps excavation was finally backfilled, the well was raised to ground level and covered to become a focal point (Figure 7.13). Over time, this well became a structure of commemoration. Visitors threw an array of objects, including of course coins, into it. Dig for Shakespeare revealed several thousand coins spanning the entire period of years since the 1860s, and from a variety of countries including South Africa, the United States of America, various South American countries and Japan.

Halliwell-Phillipps's achievements

In recognising the importance of the site of New Place, and through his research and excavations, Halliwell-Phillipps was able to draw attention to a neglected part

Figure 7.13 Sketch of the rebuilt well by W. Hallsworth Waite, 1897. The earliest visitors to the site started to drop coins into one of Shakespeare's wells.

Figure 7.14 Sketch of the excavations published by Halliwell-Phillipps.

of Shakespearian history. In many respects he was a visionary. His campaign to raise money to purchase and preserve the site added to what was an already growing recognition of its significance. He made substantial efforts to protect it for future generations, and demonstrated that the remains of Shakespeare's house had survived in isolated pockets across the front part of the site. He went on to collate and advance knowledge about New Place by producing *An Historical Account of the New Place, Stratford-upon-Avon, the Last Residence of Shakespeare* (1864): a rich, source-based publication based on the documents that were available to him. This was to become the most comprehensive interpretation of the history of New Place, although greater emphasis was placed upon the historical sources than the archaeological results. The exact nature of the excavations was not made entirely explicit. He included various perspective drawings and phased plans of the archaeological areas (Figure 7.14), and other photographs and illustrations exist from this time to complement these.

Despite his admirable intentions and thorough interpretation, though, Halliwell-Phillipps was working at a time in the nineteenth century when archaeology was in its infancy, and many of the more subtle interpretative features that modern archaeologists record today were missed or misunderstood. His efforts were certainly a product of the times he was operating in, and resulted in the destruction and removal of evidence that would have proven useful to modern scientific methods of investigation. Many artefacts not considered to be of importance were neglected, with only the much larger artefacts and wall foundations being deemed worthy of mention. Artefactual evidence such as broken sherds of pottery, bone and building materials was considered of little importance, and these are almost never mentioned in Halliwell-Phillipps's books or articles. Indeed, many objects that Dig for Shakespeare recovered from within the nineteenth-century backfill were reduced in value as finds because there was no stratigraphic information for the artefacts; no one knows where on the site Halliwell-Phillipps and his team had found them. Also, any archive that would nowadays inevitably be one of the results of such an excavation, including the artefacts mentioned in his writings, has since disappeared, which means that no modern analysis of the objects he mentions can be undertaken. Fortunately, Halliwell-Phillipps's excavations did not encompass the whole site or reduce the ground to such an extent as to remove all trace of the archaeological levels. Many areas remained unexcavated.

His single-mindedness in creating an adequate memorial to Shakespeare by resurrecting New Place as a single entity should also be questioned. In removing the theatre and the cottages along Chapel Lane, Halliwell-Phillipps was removing places that were of considerable historical significance in their own right.

The Shakespeare Birthplace Trust

Once New Place had been returned to its former site boundaries, Halliwell-Phillipps could regard the site as a fitting memorial to Shakespeare. He continued to take an active role in the interests of the site through his involvement with the Shakespeare

Birthplace Trust (which had begun to be established in 1847 following the purchase of Shakespeare's Birthplace for the nation). The site of New Place was conveyed to the Stratford-upon-Avon corporation in trust for the Shakespeare Birthplace Trust in 1876 (Shakespeare Birthplace Trust, TR2/1/1, fol. 101d). Around that time, the walls around the site were lowered and an iron palisade was added. In 1877 gravel walkways were laid around New Place and the Great Garden, formalising the arrangement and limiting access (Shakespeare Birthplace Trust, TR2/1/1, fols 109ff.). This new delineation of the site, along with the highlighted remains of New Place, can be seen in the first Ordnance Survey map of Stratford-upon-Avon, drawn in 1886 (Figure 7.15).

The Shakespeare Birthplace Trust formally became custodians of the site (including the site of New Place, Nash's House and the Great Garden) in 1884, by which time it was already open to visitors. The minute books of the Shakespeare Birthplace Trust from that period onwards record a succession of alterations and development, which chart the site's progression from pleasure grounds to a visitor attraction (Shakespeare Birthplace Trust, TR2/1/1–3). Many events and activities were held at New Place. Throughout this period, the Great Garden was freely accessible, but the visitor numbers for the rest of the site, and the revenue these brought, became ever more important for the work of the Shakespeare Birthplace Trust, conserving its Shakespeare houses and adding to its library, archive and museums collection.

By 1910 the Trustees of the Shakespeare Birthplace Trust were concerned that the site of New Place and Nash's House was not attracting visitors, and a restoration scheme for Nash's House was designed and implemented. At the same time, the remodelling of the gardens in a more appropriate 'Tudor' style was considered. This was deferred until after the First World War. Small-scale archaeological excavations were undertaken in the central part of the site in 1900, probably for the purposes of

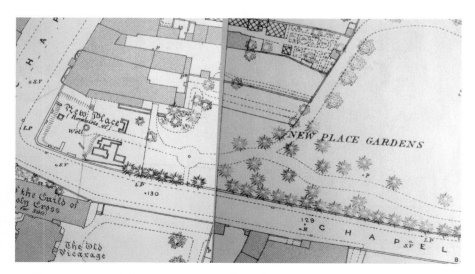

Figure 7.15 1886 Ordnance Survey map of Stratford-upon-Avon, depicting New Place.

laying drainage. A third well was identified and further foundations were exposed. The foundation wall was identified a metre below ground level and was made up of roughly cut limestone blocks. The discovery of the wall was commemorated in a plaque, which was erected nearby: 'Well, and Foundations of the eastern wall of "the Great House" (afterwards called "New Place"). Built by Sir [sic.] Hugh Clopton, Lord Mayor of London, in the reign of King Henry VII. Discovered in November 1900. Shakespeare bought the house in 1597, and died there on the 23rd April 1616.' Brick walls were constructed around these foundations and they were left exposed for the public to view. The identity of the excavators is unknown and there is no further record of their work.

Ernest Law's excavations: 1919–20

Significant excavation was carried out towards the rear of the site during the construction of the Knot Garden in 1919–20 (Figure 7.16), the designer and architect of which was Ernest Law (1854–1930). During this time, the original ground levels were reduced by approximately 1 m (3 ft 3 in) to create the desired level required for the sunken garden. The walls were constructed (using replica Tudor bricks) and clean topsoil was imported. The ground was reduced to the level of where it had probably been in the eighteenth or nineteenth centuries. During Law's excavations, a previously

Figure 7.16 Illustration of a knot garden (from Law, 1922). An example was constructed in 1919–20 at New Place with a view to increasing the visitor numbers.

unknown structure was identified. The 'walls of a chamber or receptacle ten feet long by six feet broad were discovered at about 2½ feet below the present level of the ground'. The lower part of the brickwork was reported to be characteristic of 'Tudor times; that is, bricks of the size, shape, and quality of those days, laid in the old English bond. But dividing the chamber into two is a more modern wall, possibly as recent as the end of the eighteenth century' (Law, 1922: 22). Law suggested that this was 'probably originally connected with the work of the garden – perhaps a garden midden' (22; Figure 7.17). The work itself was not completed by archaeologists; instead, gardeners were instructed carefully to examine all the soil. Although this feature was identified during Dig for Shakespeare, the material within the feature dated to the 1920s.

Dig for Shakespeare: a community experience

The site of New Place remained open to the public throughout the nineteenth and twentieth centuries, so the commemoration of William Shakespeare on the site of New Place, firmly sought after by Halliwell-Phillipps, was definitely achieved. But again, interest in the site began gradually to drop. The Shakespeare Birthplace Trust decided that the story of New Place needed to be retold and brought up to date, with the possibility that the whole of the site would then be re-curated and newly presented. Dig for Shakespeare (Plate 26) was established in 2009 with three aims: to find

Figure 7.17 Stone structure towards the eastern part of the New Place site, identified by Ernest Law during the excavation of the Knot Garden in the 1920s.

out as much as possible about the New Place Shakespeare had known, to present the excavations as part of the general visitors' experience of the site, and to engage with volunteers who would work alongside the archaeologists.

After the completion of a comprehensive desk-based archival report (Mitchell and Kelleher, 2010), the entirety of the excavation was completed by a small team of archaeologists and a large team of volunteers (Figure 7.18 and 7.19). The volunteers ranged from members of the local community of Stratford-upon-Avon and Warwickshire, to volunteers from overseas. The project was led by archaeologists Kevin Colls and William Mitchell (formerly University of Birmingham, subsequently Staffordshire University). Throughout Dig for Shakespeare, the volunteers were encouraged to develop their excavation skills and take ownership of the areas they were working on. Many of the regular volunteers became experienced and confident to undertake all of the general archaeological activities on site, and were able to contribute to the interpretation of the evidence (Colls and Mitchell, 2010: 25).

The digging season ran from March to October, and visitors were able to assist in the archaeological process by washing and cleaning certain finds from the site and sieving all the soils that had been removed. As such, the contributions of all those involved were important to the site narrative. This 'live' aspect of the project did much to encourage support of the community and increase its reputation. Throughout the course of the project, over 200,000 visitors came to see the excavations of New Place, and close to 200 volunteers were involved in the work.

The choice to undertake this work through community and public archaeology was a brave one, but it was a product of its time. As a concept, community archaeology was gaining popularity and is now widely recognised by heritage professionals and archaeologists (Jackson *et al.*, 2014; Smith and Waterton 2013). If undertaken correctly, this approach can increase the engagement of people with their heritage, and foster a sense of ownership, value and community cohesion (Carman, 2005). The feeling of ownership of the site by the volunteers, and the work that they were doing, remained particularly strong throughout the project. Their enthusiasm and dedication, coupled with the intense interest from the visitors, made the project a unique and unforgettable experience for everyone involved. Rarely do archaeologists have the chance to interact with people in the way they did during Dig for Shakespeare.

However, choosing to complete the project using this methodology resulted in a number of significant problems that needed to be overcome. Some of these were successfully negotiated, others not. When considering the importance of the site, perhaps the most difficult decision was whether or not to undertake the excavation work using volunteers, given their highly varied skill levels. Some had basic excavation experience, others were students in the process of learning, but most had never had any archaeological training at all. Help with this issue came from an unexpected source: Halliwell-Phillipps. As a result of his archaeological methods – in particular his seemingly uninterested outlook on the small archaeological objects that we have come to value so highly today – large parts of the site were covered in backfill from his excavations. In archaeological terms, this material is seen as unstratified, or not *in situ* (as it has been removed from its original deposition place), but it nevertheless contained many artefacts that required examination. By participating in that work, volunteers were able to hone their skills before tackling the more complex archaeological

'The prospect of working on a nationally important site and one related to such an important figure in English literary history was too good to miss! The most important contribution I gained was skills and contacts. With all the skills I gained from this dig (such as photography, context sheets, site and section drawings etc.) I was able to successfully apply to University and for other excavations'.

Alistair Galt, former student volunteer

'Working on the site inevitably involved substantial disturbance to the good work done in previous years by the Shakespeare Birthplace Trust professional gardening team. Indeed, sharing the gardener's refuge hut for the source of volunteers' tea and coffee brought the two groups into frequent direct contact'

Nick Lister, volunteer

Figure 7.18 The Dig for Shakespeare volunteers excavating the site of New Place. Testimonials from Alistair Galt and Nick Lister.

features across the site. This is not to say this solution entirely solved the problem. From an archaeological point of view, the most important task was to ensure that the remains were excavated and recorded correctly, and that no damage occurred to the archaeological structures that were being retained on the site. Occasionally the perception arose that only certain volunteers were allowed to work on the important archaeological remains whilst others worked on the less important areas, or were on sieving duty. Other problems arose from the large number of visitors that were present most days (Figure 7.20). Although this was vital in raising the profile of the site, the day-to-day operations of the work were often affected by the steady stream of people, and their accompanying questions. Likewise, issues such as the security of the finds, the well-being of the volunteers and the safety of the visitors had to be more carefully considered because of the nature of the project.

'All of this knowledge that I had taken on had inspired me to dig a trench in my own back garden, within this trench I found a whole range of different finds including a gun handle and some really nice Tudor pottery. When I had these finds, I would take them to the dig and ask Will to help me identify a date of the item and also what it would have been before it was broken up in the ground'

Ellis Powell-Bevan aged 15 - Young Archaeology Club competition winner

'Our Sunday group consisted of a wide range of people, from all walks of life, most of which had never had the opportunity to do anything archaeological before. There was also a wide range of ages amongst the volunteers: we had two 16 year olds through to retirees.'

Lousie Dodd - Volunteer

Figure 7.19 The Dig for Shakespeare volunteers excavating the site of New Place. Testimonials from Ellis Powell-Bevan and Louise Dodd.

The legacy of Dig for Shakespeare

Once the community excavations were completed, the site was again carefully back-filled so that its remains are preserved for future generations. The results of the project can be seen throughout this book, and the book itself would not have been possible in its current form without Dig for Shakespeare. Archaeological reports were produced at the end of each season (Mitchell, 2010, 2011; Mitchell and Colls, 2012, 2013; Charles, 2014; Colls and Mitchell, forthcoming). These were submitted to the Shakespeare Birthplace Trust, along with the finds archive and the Warwickshire

Figure 7.20 Visitors engaging with the 'live' Dig for Shakespeare Project at New Place.

Historic Environment Record. The excavation of the site of New Place has provided the physical evidence to support and re-evaluate the documentary sources. It employed methods, sources and knowledge unavailable in the nineteenth century in order to compile the most accurate resource and narrative for New Place. This has been achieved using the support of members of the academic and local communities. In 2015 and 2016, the construction of a new, modern, landscaped garden and exhibition centre on the site of New Place, and in Nash's House, has utilised the results of Dig for Shakespeare to aid the reinterpretation process, and the preserved features and structures on the site have been carefully designed around.

The project has reached beyond the discipline of archaeology and literature to inspire other creative arts, for example the work of artist Adrian Spaak (Figure 7.21). Adrian writes:

> I became interested in the visual appearance of the revealed underground landscape when Will Mitchell removed the grass surface. It unearthed another unexpected world of texture, objects and layers of charcoal and clay; history was being revealed in sections. I felt compelled to draw from it as source material because it was so unique and it was a once in a lifetime chance to respond to something that was normally hidden beneath the surface and had last been seen properly in 1864. It was very like an ever-changing stage set that demanded a series of responses through drawing, not from a photo in a studio but outside, directly from the dig itself in the sun, wind and rain. The site was a visual motif that

Figure 7.21 Art piece completed by Adrian Spaak, Dig for Shakespeare volunteer and artist.

could be explored over and over again in a sequence of large-scale drawings examining the textures and structures that the team uncovered.

It gave me a stimulus to produce a body of work that I'd never done before in my life. I can relate this to my years in the life drawing classes at the Royal College where I studied the motif repeatedly and saw new things and new ideas were suggested each time I started a new drawing. (Adrian Spaak, volunteer, August 2015)

The result has been an increase in the production of paintings, pictures and scholarly debate on the subject, and we hope the growth of people's interest in both Shakespearian studies and archaeology. On a community level, the project must also be seen as a great success. Many of the volunteers who took part have an increased interest in archaeology and history as a result. Several volunteers are now working in the heritage industry, for example as house guides for the Shakespeare Birthplace Trust. Perhaps more importantly, many of the volunteers have remained friends. For some, the routines and habits they formed during the project – for example, meeting in a café or a pub for lunch, before or after their morning or afternoon excavation slots – still continue even though the dig does not.

The archaeological story of New Place is indeed a complex one, involving as it does the archaeology of communities, the antiquarian buildings and the archaeology of the individual: William Shakespeare. We all co-exist and interact within the same space as he did: the great house of New Place, and the traces it has left behind.

References

Bearman, R. (2011). '*New Place, Stratford-upon-Avon*'. Unpublished report.

Bellew, J. (1863). *Shakespeare's Home at New Place, Stratford-upon-Avon* (London: Virtue Brothers).

Carman, J. (2005). *Against Cultural Property: Archaeology, Heritage and Ownership* (London: Duckworth).

Charles, E. (2014). *Nash House and New Place: Archaeological Test Pit Evaluation and Watching Brief* (Centre of Archaeology, Staffordshire University).

Colls, K. (2013). '*New Place, Stratford upon Avon, Warwickshire, Archaeological Evaluation*' (Stoke-on-Trent: Centre of Archaeology, Staffordshire University).

Colls, K. and W. Mitchell (2010). '*Dig for Shakespeare*', *British Archaeology* (July/August 2010).

—— (forthcoming). 'Nash House and New Place, Stratford upon Avon, Warwickshire: Archaeological Strip Map and Record Evaluation and Excavation' (Stoke-on-Trent: Centre of Archaeology, Staffordshire University).

Freeman. A. and J. I. Freeman (2004). 'James Orchard Halliwell-Phillipps', in H. C. G. Matthew and B. Harrison (eds), *Dictionary of National Biography*, Vol. XLIV (Oxford: Oxford University Press), 86–90, available at http://www.oxforddnb.com/view/article/12020 (accessed 6 August 2015).

Jackson, S., R. Lennox, C. Neal, S. Roskams, J. Hearle and L. Brown (2014). 'Engaging Communities in the "Big Society": What Impact Is the Localism Agenda Having on Community Archaeology?', *The Historic Environment: Policy and Practice*, 5.1: 74–88.

Law, E. (1922). *Shakespeare's Garden, Stratford-upon-Avon* (London: Selwyn and Blount).

Halliwell, J. O. (1864*). An Historical Account of the New Place, Stratford-upon-Avon, the Last Residence of Shakespeare* (London: J. E. Adlard).

Halliwell-Phillipps, J. O. ([1881] 1887). *Outlines of the Life of Shakespeare*, 7th edn (London: Longmans, Green).

Mitchell, W. (2010). '*"Dig for Shakespeare"*: New Place, Stratford-upon-Avon, Archaeological Excavation 2010' (Birmingham Archaeology).

—— (2011). '*"Dig for Shakespeare"*: New Place, Stratford-upon-Avon, Archaeological Excavation 2011. Season 2' (Birmingham Archaeology).

Mitchell, W. and K. Colls (2012). '*"Dig for Shakespeare"*: New Place, Stratford-upon-Avon, Archaeological Excavation 2012. Season 3 (Birmingham Archaeology).

Mitchell, W. and Kelleher, S. (2010). 'New Place, Stratford-upon-Avon, Warwickshire: Archaeological Desk-Based Assessment and Evaluation, 2009' (Birmingham Archaeology).

Smith, L. and Waterton, E. (2013). *Heritage, Communities and Archaeology* (London: A & C Black).

Styles, P. (1945). 'The Borough of Stratford-upon-Avon: Shakespearean Festivals and Theatres', in *A History of the County of Warwick, Vol. III: Barlichway Hundred*, ed. Philip Styles (London: *Victoria County History*), available at http://www.british-history.ac.uk/vch/warks/vol3/ (accessed 10 December 2015).

Closing remarks

Paul Edmondson, Kevin Colls and William Mitchell

The closest Shakespeare comes to depicting an archaeological excavation is the clearing of a space for Ophelia's grave. Hamlet looks on (with Horatio), appalled at the matter-of-factness with which the two clownish gravediggers set about their task: skulls 'knocked about the mazard with a sexton's spade … Did these bones cost no more the breeding but to play at loggats with 'em? Mine ache to think on't' (5.1.87–90). When another skull emerges from the earth a moment later, Hamlet starts to imagine a possible past life for it: 'Why might not that be the skull of a lawyer?', he asks, and then, in lines peculiarly prescient of Shakespeare's own historical record (even perhaps alluding to the transfer of a title to a property by fine), Hamlet continues: 'This fellow might be in's time a great buyer of land, with his statutes, his recognizances, his fines, his double vouchers, his recoveries. Is this the fine of his fines and the recovery of his recoveries, to have his pate full of fine dirt?' (5.1.100–4). Later, as more human remains are unearthed, Hamlet's mind is able to move effortlessly from emperors to beer barrels: 'Alexander died, Alexander was buried, Alexander returneth into dust, the dust is earth, of earth we are loam, and why of that loam whereto he was converted might they not stop a beer-barrel?' (5.1.204–7).

The philosopher, physician and polymath Sir Thomas Browne (1605–82) might have been thinking about *Hamlet* when writing his own meditation on mortality, *Hydriotaphia, Urn Burial, or a discourse on the sepulchral urns latterly found in Norfolk* (1658). Comparing and contrasting cremations to burials, Browne muses: 'to be gnawed out of our graves, to have our skulls made drinking-bowls, and our bones turned into pipes, to delight and sport our enemies, are tragical abominations escaped in burning burials' (Symonds, 1886: 148). Shakespeare and Browne were both reanimators of the past, and looked to it – as biographers do to history and archaeology – as a resource for a performative way of writing: 'what song the Syrens sang, or what name Achilles assumed when he hid himself among women, though puzzling questions, are not beyond all conjecture', Browne suggests (Symonds, 1886: 162). Both writers would clearly have been fascinated by the development and popularisation of archaeology and biography, and it is no coincidence that J. A. Symonds's edition of some of Browne's essays was produced at a time when archaeological investigation, and detective fiction, were becoming highly fashionable.

This book has a wide archaeological perspective (from prehistoric times through to the twenty-first century), and a much narrower biographical one (from around 1564 to 1616, and just after). In trying to understand the past, and the 'puzzling questions' it poses, both discourses must interpret the facts and make reasonable conjecture. As empirical and as uncompromising as they are, earthly remains encourage us to speculate, to take up the position of spectators, to look on what is found, and to think about how others might have lived. Our archaeological task has been to report, accurately and unsentimentally, what we have seen; our Shakespearian task has been to present how our findings, and what we now know about New Place in light of them, have implications for Shakespearian biography.

A thorough understanding of New Place encourages us to think about Shakespeare more as a resident and representative of Stratford-upon-Avon than as a citizen of London (a city that to him represented work, but not family). In relation to Shakespeare's life, New Place represents his social status and aspirations more than any other aspect of it (with the possible exception of his royal court appearances). It localises Shakespeare's life and provides a definite focus for it. He was the only one among his fellow playwrights who made sure he had a fine house, far away from London, to which he could retreat. The house that he bought in 1597 also presents us with a Shakespeare who wanted to take up a late medieval inheritance (in the form of Hugh Clopton's late-fifteenth-century house), rather like someone in the early twenty-first century choosing to buy a Victorian property, in preference to a more modern one.

Shakespeare's taste in a home reflects his literary sensibilities as a writer. When compared to his contemporary playwrights (many of whom wrote city comedies, for example), Shakespeare has a touch of the old-fashioned about him (which some might characterise as Romantic, an adjective that is certainly relevant to his preferred style of comedy). He did, however, as far as we can tell, modernise the frontage of New Place, and install a long gallery, as a well-to-do, fashionable and aspiring gentleman.

How much time Shakespeare actually spent in New Place will, of course, never be known. More work needs to be done in trying to set out a conjectural calendar of Shakespeare's availability: one that factors in when the playhouses were closed, because of plague and at other times; when his company went on tour (assuming that Shakespeare hardly, if at all, toured with them); when he is likely to have been at court; when he is likely to have written the plays, and how quickly he wrote them (for certainly he wrote at different speeds at different times: *Hamlet* and *Troilus and Cressida*, for example, would have required more background reading and research than the more improvisatory *The Merry Wives of Windsor* or *Much Ado about Nothing*); the books he needed around him in order to write; and the likely demands of his familial and financial commitments in Stratford-upon-Avon. We have found it to be compelling that there are very few references to Shakespeare in London between 1604 and 1612, and that the size of New Place, and what it represented culturally, would have been too attractive for him to have spent most of his time away from it.

Archaeological remains will never reveal anything about their effect on Shakespeare's own intellect, imagination and feelings; this is the task of a Sir Thomas Browne, or a sympathetic biographer. But in seeking a context in which to establish corroborative evidence, archaeology has prompted biography to reconsider some of the oral traditions about Shakespeare: for example Davenant's claims, Rowe's and Aubrey's biographical accounts, Ward's notebooks, and Vertue's drawing of New Place. Shakespeare's finances, and where he acquired his money, remain difficult areas of investigation, partly illuminated (and possibly made explicable) by a revisionist reading of his father's financial trajectory, and the rumour of an unusually generous amount of patronage from the Earl of Southampton.

The cultural reputation of New Place after Shakespeare, until the demolition of the second house in 1759, is worthy of more consideration, as, too, are the life and legacy of his granddaughter, Elizabeth, Lady Barnard. In terms of the site, we should like to know more about the connections (documentary and archaeological) between New Place and Nash's House. In later years the relationship between the two properties becomes significant, and the shared ownership and questions about their boundaries are interesting. We should like to know more about the motives and reactions of Halliwell-Phillipps around his own archaeological investigation, and we should like to know what became of the objects he discovered.

Then there are the areas of the site that had to remain unexcavated (the two north-side quadrants of the Knot Garden, areas of the Great Garden that we know were in Shakespeare's ownership, and the parts of the site to the south of the Knot Garden and to the west of the Great Garden occupied by trees and hedges). All of these areas may yet reveal more artefacts from Shakespeare's time, and encourage further conversations between the archaeology of New Place and Shakespearian biography.

References

Symonds, J. A., ed. (1886). *Sir Thomas Browne's Religio Medici, Urn Burial, Christian Morals, and Other Essays* (London: The Walter Scott Publishing Company).

GLOSSARY OF ARCHAEOLOGICAL AND ARCHITECTURAL TERMS

William Mitchell and Kevin Colls

affronté	facing the front
angled bracing	diagonal timber, strengthening a frame
arch-braced collar roof	curved pair of roof braces that form an arch and connect the wall to the beams above
archaeological feature	non-portable element of an archaeological site, for example a pit or a wall
architrave	moulded frame around a doorway or window
backplot	area behind the main house that was often free from substantial structures
balustrading	railing supported by balusters (posts) forming an ornamental parapet
bay	space or compartment between architectural components
bay window	projecting window
block cornice	corbels supporting a *cornice*
bressumer beam	large, horizontal beam used to support the front of a building
burgage	regularly laid-out plot of land
buttery	room used to store and dispense beverages
chamfered soffit	the edge of a corner, on the underside of an overhanging roof, that is cut at an angle

close studding	spaces between studs that are the same width as the studs themselves
construction cut	the excavated trench for a building foundation
context	an individual, unique stratigraphic event
corbel	a project from a wall used for support or as an architectural embellishment
cornice	moulded or decorated projection that runs along the top of a wall or building
cross-passage	see *screens-passage*
dais	raised platform at the upper high end of the hall
dentils	series of small projecting blocks that form a moulding, usually under a cornice
dormer window	a window, set into a structural element of a building, that protrudes from a sloping roof
eaves	overhanging edges of a roof
elevation	external face of a building
flat platform summit	a sloping roof, flattened at its top.
frogged brick	the indentation found in some bricks. Frogged bricks began to appear in the nineteenth century.
frontage	the outward-facing aspect of a building
gable	triangular upper part of a wall at the end of a ridged roof
gauged brickwork	brick moulded, rubbed or cut to an exact size and shape
great chamber (solar)	owner's bed-sitting room, the master bedroom, situated on the upper floor of the medieval house
groined arch	intersection of two vaulted roofs
herringbone brick	decorative, interconnected pattern of brick infill between panelled timber framing
herringbone timber framing	decorative style of timber that uses angled members
hipped roof	roof where all sides are sloping downwards towards the walls
jettied	overhanging upper storey
keystone	large stone positioned at the centre of an arch
larder	room used to store food prior to use
lath	thin, flat strip of wood that, when used with other strips, forms latticework providing a backing for plaster or a support for roof tiles

mercer	dealer in textile fabrics
modillion	projecting bracket underneath a *cornice*
moulding	the ornamental outline of architectural elements such as the *cornice*
mullion	vertical component that divides individual window panes
nogging	brick infill of square-panelled timber framing
nucleated settlement	village or town where buildings are clustered together
open hammer-beam truss	open truss that is decorative in nature, used only in buildings of high status
palisade	fence of upright stakes or iron railings that form a defensive enclosure
Palladian style	Architectural style derived from and inspired by the Venetian architect Andrea Palladio (1508–80)
panel	sunken or raised section of a wall or door
pantry	small room where food and kitchenware are stored
parlour	living room in a private house, most frequently used to receive and entertain guests
pediment	triangular gable inspired by classical architecture found at the top of buildings or above doorways and windows
perch	measure of area, especially for land, equal to 25.29 m^2 (272 ft^2)
pilaster	a rectangular column of timber or masonry that is attached to a wall and that is used for decoration or support
plinth	base course of a building, or projecting part of a wall
portico	covered entrance leading to the main entrance of a building
quoins	dressed masonry blocks that are built into the corner of a wall
rafters	regularly spaced, inclined timbers used to support the roof covering
rail	horizontal member in a timber frame
ridge and furrow	archaeological pattern of ridges and troughs typical of the open field system (created by ploughing during the medieval period)
ridge tile	semi-circular or curved tile used in a roof ridge

roundbarrow	mound of earth over a burial ground, placed in the middle, of prehistoric origin
sash	see *window sash*
screens-passage	cross-passage that bisects the hall. Has hall entrances and doorways to buttery, pantry and kitchen passages. Partitioned by means of a wooden screen, to block from view.
scullery	a small kitchen room used for washing dishes and other household work
servants' hall	the place intended specifically as the servants' eating room and common day room.
spere	short, wooden screen projecting at the side of a doorway, often used to partition the hall and the *screens-passage*
stratigraphy	this involves an examination of archaeological and geological layers to gain an understanding of the chronological age of a feature or site. The oldest layers will usually be found at the bottom of a feature while the youngest layers will be found towards the top.
stuccoed ornament	fine plaster used to finish interior walls
studding	vertical member in a timber frame
truss	triangular framework within a roof, designed to be self-supporting and carry other timbers
vaulted roof	arched roof
vernacular architecture	buildings constructed out of local materials that reflect local needs and traditions
wattle and daub	building material of interwoven laths and twigs (wattle) plastered with a mixture of clay, animal dung and straw (daub)
window sash	window that has two moveable frames. These windows are fixed one above the other and can be moved up and down.

THE DIG FOR SHAKESPEARE ACADEMIC ADVISORY BOARD ARCHAEOLOGISTS AND VOLUNTEERS

Advisory Board

Nat Alcock, University of Warwick
Robert Bearman, Shakespeare Birthplace Trust
(Chair) Paul Edmondson, Shakespeare Birthplace Trust
Ian George, English Heritage
Tara Hamling, University of Birmingham
Kate McLuskie, University of Birmingham
Nicholas Molyneux, English Heritage
Jonathan Parkhouse, archaeologist
Tiffany Stern, University of Oxford
John Taplin, independent scholar
René Weis, University of London
Stanley Wells, Shakespeare Birthplace Trust
Michael Wood, independent scholar and television historian

Archaeologists

William Mitchell (Staffordshire University)
Kevin Colls (Staffordshire University)
Elisabeth Charles
Mark Charles
Shane Kelleher
Samantha Paul
John Halsted
Emma Collins
Paul Collins

Erica Macey-Bracken
Bob Burrows

Volunteers

Thank you to all of the following volunteers who worked on Dig for Shakespeare between 2010 and 2015.

John Adams
Russell Andrews
Shelagh Andrews
Gemma Asbury
Elizabeth Ash
Kirsten Ash
Jess Ashton
Tony Atcheson
Michael Athanson
Anicka Backstrom
Robert Baird
Clive Bardell
Adrian Bates
Evelyn Beal
Kimberly Bellamy
Cyril Bennis
Janet Boneham
Jennie Boneham
Karen Boyles
Alexander Brantingham
Gem Brewer
John Brittain
Heather Britton
Martin Broome
Richard Browne
Lizzie Buck
Sue Buck
Chris Burrows
Ellen Callender
Lucy Callender
Colin Campbell
Joan Campbell
Laura Cannon
Sarah Carrington
Peter Chadwick
Sue Chambers
Ryan Charlton
Peter Cheetham

Gill Chew
Louise Clare
Susan Clark
Michael Clough
Lorraine Coles
Antony Collins
Bernadette Collins
Laura Collins
Malcolm Cook
Bethany Coomber
Cheryl Coomber
Clayre Coopey
Eddie Cousins
Louise Cowdell
Anny Crunelle
Ewa Czumaj
Peter Davis
Linda Digby
Jeanette Dobson
Laura Dobson
Louise Dodd
Allan Duff
Eilidh Duff
Margaret Elsy
Tony Estick
Debbie Ewing
Christine Fell
Claire Forkes
Alistair Galt
Emma Gardner
Heather Garrett
Cameron Grant
Anne Grey
Kerry Grocott
Gido Hakvoort
Janet Hall
John Harris
Jonathan Harvey

John Hawkins
Dominic Heather
Sharland Hewson
James Hicken
Bill Hicks
Alice Hobbs
Matthew Holmes
David Hope
Sara Horaiz
Roger Howells
Trista Huang
Norman Hughes
Karyn Hughes-Jones
Daniel Hume
Alison Hunt
Sarah Jenkins
Ellie Knaggs
Vivienne Lauder
Stephanie Lawrence
Barbara Lister
Nick Lister
Ken Macdonald
Vanessa MacDonald
William Mannin
Joshua Marsh
Linda Martin
Pat Martin
Jane Mason
John May
Fiona McConville
Heather McKechnie
Katie Medlin
Kay Medlin
Brian Miles
Emily Millward
Mary Mills
Anna Moore
Roger Moore
Helen Morgan
Richard Morris
Julie Moss
Nicola Nash
Sally Naylor
Gerald O'Brien
Nina O'Hare
Kelly O'Keefe
Mike Osborne
Sarah Peacop
Driunie Perera

Jennifer Perry
Elizabeth Prater
Louise Ralph
Gemma Reed
Hazel Reed
Tommy Reid
John Richards
Peter Richards
Julia Robins
Rachel Sampson
David Savage
Andrew Scotson
Laura Simcox
Sophie Slater
Jennifer Smith
Lucinda Smyth
Eleanor Stevens
Jeremy Stevens
Gary Stocker
Colin Such
Rita Sweeney
Mark Tanner
Jan Tasker
Eddy Taylor
Jane Taylor
Joyce Taylor
Ken Taylor
Sophie Taylor-Barthorpe
Michelle Thick
Anne Thomas
Rebecca Tillotson
Jann Tracy
Jenny Tyers
Sue Tyler
Kevin Wainwright
Isabel Walker
Maureen Walker
Christine Walsh
Laura Waters
Robin Weaver
Eleanor Webb
Mark Webb
David Westcott
Ken Wheal
Helen Williams
David Wiltshire
Simone Wing
Patricia Wyspianska

INDEX